ESSAYS IN
AFRO-AMERICAN
HISTORY

PHILIP S. FONER

Professor of History
Lincoln University, Pennsylvania

ESSAYS IN AFRO-AMERICAN HISTORY

Temple University Press

Philadelphia

Library of Congress Cataloging in Publication Data

Foner, Philip Sheldon, 1910-
   Essays in Afro-American history.

   Includes bibliographical references and index.
   1. Afro-Americans—History—Adresses, essays,
lectures.   I. Title.
E185.F5913   973'.04'96073   78-16944
ISBN 0-87722-140-5

Temple University Press, Philadelphia 19122
© 1978 by Temple University. All rights reserved
Published 1978
Printed in the United States of America

Contents

Introduction

This volume traces through individual essays several aspects of black life—economic, political, social, and cultural—from the Revolutionary era to the eve of World War I. A few of the essays offer fresh perceptions of familiar subjects, but most deal with hitherto neglected but nevertheless vitally important subjects and personalities.

The first two articles relate to black resistance to reenslavement, and demonstrate the militance and deep craving for freedom that form such a large part of the Negro's past. The next two essays examine one of the major struggles of free blacks in the North—the battle to end discrimination against Negroes on Philadelphia streetcars. The story of this long and bitter struggle, organized and led in the main by blacks, offers rich insight into the nature of white racial attitudes and the contradiction between American ideals of equality and the realities of the black experience. The story also furnishes evidence which helps establish the validity of the view that the black experience has been quite different from that of other ethnic groups in our country.

The fight against job discrimination and exclusion from the trade unions is a theme that runs through several of the essays in this volume. As the number of blacks increased in northern cities, prejudice and discrimination grew, barring blacks from jobs they had traditionally held. The fifth essay surveys the arena of employment and the relationship of blacks to the early labor movement in Pennsylvania. Although blacks had worked at various skilled trades

in Pennsylvania 'cities early in the nineteenth century, they were
driven out by new immigrants from Europe, and found themselves
unable to join the existing trade unions. Such evidence of how black
and white labor were played off against one another is balanced by
the exciting and inspiring story of the *Boston Daily Evening* (a white
labor paper published during the late Civil War and early Reconstruction), which stood up firmly and unequivocally for black political, civil, and economic equality—the sole white labor voice to do
so. Similarly, as the final essay in the volume conclusively demon-
strates, just before World War I the Industrial Workers of the World
(IWW) fought against racism in the labor movement and preached
and practiced labor solidarity regardless of race or color even in the
deep South.

Three outstanding but neglected black personalities appear in the
volume. One is a remarkable black abolitionist who became the
champion of black seamen and, as a one-man lobbyist on their
behalf, fought widespread discrimination and persecution of this
important group of black workers. The other two are pioneer black
Socialists whose careers illustrate the inaccuracy of David Shannon's
observation that Negroes were "not important" in the Socialist
movement.

Thus many threads tie the essays in this volume together. Although they make no pretense of being a systematic history of black
Americans, the essays display the richness and variety of the black
experience. I hope this volume will encourage others to dig deeper in
their studies of blacks in American history.

As much as possible within a descriptive and analytical volume,
my object has been to permit the Negro to speak for himself. How
eloquently and effectively he could do so is illustrated from the very
first essay; indeed, the piece is devoted entirely to an early letter of a
Philadelphia black. The so-called "inarticulate" are quite articulate
in the pages that follow.

Most of these essays first appeared in scholarly journals, and I
gratefully acknowledge the cooperation of the editors of the *Journal
of Ethnic History, Journal of Negro History, Negro History Bulletin,
Pennsylvania Heritage, Pennsylvania History,* and *Science and Society* for their courtesy in permitting me to reprint here the essays
originally published in their journals.

Lincoln University, Pennsylvania   PHILIP S. FONER

ESSAYS IN
AFRO-AMERICAN
HISTORY

1

A Plea
Against Reenslavement*

By a vote of 34 to 21, the Pennsylvania Assembly on March 1, 1780 passed an "Act for the Gradual Abolition of Slavery," thereby giving that state the distinction of being the first in this country to pass a law for the abolition of slavery. The act for gradual abolition provided that children born of slave mothers after the passage of the law were to serve as servants until twenty-eight years of age, after which they were to be free. Blacks already held as slaves could be so retained, but were to be registered within eight months. Registration required the name of the owner, his occupation or profession, and the name of the county and township, district or ward wherein he resided, as well as the name, age, and sex of each slave.

Not satisfied with the Act of 1780, the Pennsylvania abolitionists, led by Anthony Benezet, began a campaign to abolish slavery in the state immediately and completely. But they got nowhere. In fact, the main problem facing blacks was the campaign of owners of slaves, supported by the Scotch-Irish radicals from the backcountry, to require longer terms of service from Negroes whose masters had failed to register them. Responding to this pressure, the Assembly was ready to revise the abolition law, and extend the registration period for the entire state until January, 1782. Under the new bill, Negroes who had been emancipated because of their masters' failure to register them would be reenslaved.

The battle for strict compliance with an unmodified abolition law was led by the abolitionists, mainly the Philadelphia Quakers, but

*Reprinted from *Pennsylvania History,* XXXIX (April, 1972), 239–241.

the most powerful influence in its favor were the pleas of Negroes emancipated because of their masters' failure to register them, urging the Assembly not to reenslave them. One such plea from a black who signed himself "Cato," was published in the *Freeman's Journal* of September 21, 1780 (postscript). Although a brief excerpt appears in Arthur Zilversmit's *The First Emancipation* (Chicago, 1967), p. 136, where the date of the paper is incorrectly given, it has never been reprinted in full.

"Cato's" communication is both a moving document, and one that should add to the material being discovered testifying to the fact that blacks were not as inarticulate in this period as they have been pictured in too many historical accounts. The Assembly responded to such pleas by prohibiting the reenslavement of any Negroes freed by the abolition law.

Mr. Printer

I am a poor negro, who with myself and children have had the good fortune to get my freedom, by means of an act of assembly passed on the first of March 1780, and should now with my family be as happy a set of people as any on the face of the earth, but I am told the assembly are going to pass a law to send us all back to our masters. Why dear Mr. Printer, this would be the cruelest act that ever a set of worthy good gentlemen, could be guilty of. To make a law to hang us all, would be "merciful," when compared with this law; for many of our masters would treat us with unheard barbarity, for daring to take advantage (as we have done) of the law made in our favor. Our lot in "slavery" were hard enough to bear; but having tasted the sweets of "freedom," we should now be miserable indeed. Surely no Christian gentleman can be so cruel! I cannot believe they will pass such a law. I have read the act which made me free, and I always read it with joy—and I always dwell with particular pleasure on the following words, spoken by the assembly on the top of the said law. "We esteem it a particular blessing granted to us, that we are enabled this day to add one more step to universal civilization by removing as much as possible the sorrows of those who haved in 'undeserved' bondage, and from which by the assumed authority of the kings of Great Britain, no effectual legal relief could be ob-

tained." See it was the king of Great Britain that kept us in slavery before. Now surely, after saying so, it cannot be possible for them to make slaves of us again—nobody, but the king of England can do it—and I sincerely pray, that he may never have it in his power. It cannot be, that the assembly will take from us the liberty they have given, because a little further they go on and say, "we conceive ourselves, at this particular period, extraordinarily called upon, by the blessings which 'we' have received, to make manifest the sincerity of our professions, and to give a substantial proof of our gratitude." If after all this, 'we,' who by virtue of this very law (which has those very words in it which I have copied,) are now enjoying the sweets of that "substantial proof of gratitude," I say if we should be plunged back into slavery what must we think of the meaning of all those words in the beginning of the said law, which seem to be a kind of creed respecting slavery, but what is more serious than all, what will our great Father think of such doings. But I pray that he may be pleased to turn the hearts of the honorable assembly from this cruel law; and that he will be pleased to make us poor blacks deserving of his mercies.

Cato

2

The Two Trials of John Read:
A Fugitive Slave
Who Resisted Reenslavement

The bloody battle by thirty-six blacks in September 1851 at Christiana, Pennsylvania, was the first nationally publicized, armed, and fatal resistance to the harsh new law enacted by Congress in 1850 to ensure the return of fugitive slaves. The Christiana story is correctly viewed as "among the major episodes of black resistance in American history."[1] Thirty-one years before and twenty-five miles from Christiana (in what is today Kennett Square, Pennsylvania), a single fugitive slave became involved in armed and fatal resistance to reenslavement. The Christiana resistance was followed by a dramatic treason trial.[2] The Kennett Square resistance led to two trials.

By 1820, escaped black slaves from Maryland and Virginia lived in a number of Pennsylvania communities. These new immigrants— often the targets of harrassment and violence on the streets and in their homes—were objects of ridicule by whites. Their greatest concern, however, was recapture by their former owners. Most of them were in no position to resist recapture and a cry for assistance would have been useless. But one fugitive slave did resist.

On December 20, 1820, the account in the West Chester (Pennsylvania) *Village Record* read:

A dredful [*sic*] Affair happened last Thursday night in Kennet township. A gentleman from the neighborhood of Baltimore, with several assistants in pursuit of a runaway slave, surrounded a house, which the black man had hired, and attempted to force their way into the house. The negro threatened to shoot them if they did not desist; they forced the door and the fellow shot Mr. Griffith through the heart, and he fell

6

dead. His overseer pressed on, and the fellow knocked him down and beat him so that his life is despaired of. The black man then went, told what he had done and gave himself up.

The *American Republican,* also of West Chester, reported:

Murder—On Friday last, a most shocking murder was committed near Kennet Square, in this county, by a runaway negro, from Maryland, upon the person of his master, who had come in pursuit of him. The particulars we have not been able to learn. But we understand he shot his master dead on the spot, and beat a man most unmercifully with the butt of the gun, who had accompanied his master to assist in his apprehension. The black fellow, was, however, arrested and lodged in the jail of this county, to await his trial in February next.[3]

In the following days more facts were disclosed. The runaway (said to be the son of an African queen) had escaped from his master, Samuel Griffith of Baltimore, fled to Pennsylvania, changed his name to John Read, married, settled in Kennet township near West Chester, and supported his wife and child by doing odd jobs. Read claimed to be a free Negro, but always went armed, because, he told neighbors, he feared kidnappers. When Griffith finally learned the whereabouts of his fugitive slave, he set out with his overseer, Peter Shipley, and two other men to recover his property. All were armed and Griffith also carried a pair of handcuffs and a heavy rope.

On the evening of December 14, 1820, Griffith knocked on the locked door of Read's house. When Read asked from the inside who he was, Griffith replied that the group had authority to search for stolen goods. Read, who suspected the men were there to return him to slavery, told them to go away; he had no stolen goods, but if they would wait until morning they could search his house. The four men then began to force the door; Read rolled a cider barrel against it and shouted that if they attempted to come in, he would kill them. The door was torn off the hinges; the click of a pistol was heard, followed by Read's cry, "It is life for life." One of the invaders shouted, "Rush in, Shipley—damn the negro, he won't shoot." But Read did shoot. Griffith was killed, and Shipley was clubbed so severely that he died eight days later of his wounds. The other two, thoroughly frightened, escaped unhurt.[4]

After Read turned himself over to the authorities, he was indicted and tried for murder. The key issues were (1) whether Read, though still a slave, acquired the right of self-defense in Pennsylvania, and (2) whether Griffith was a kidnapper under the Pennsylvania law of 1820.

"No Person held to Service or Labour in one State, under the Laws thereof, escaping into another shall in Consequence of an Law or Regulation therein, be discharged from such Service or Labour, but shall be delivered up on claim of the Party to whom such Service may be due."[5] So read the clause in the Federal Constitution which guaranteed the owner's right to recover his slave. But the Constitution gave no clear answer to such questions as to whether or not Congress alone had the power to legislate on this subject, or whether or not the state legislatures retained a concurrent power. Nor did it provide an answer to the question whether federal officials had the sole responsibility to execute this provision, or if state officials shared this responsibility.

The result was that both federal and state governments assumed the right and the duty to pass laws and provide officials to carry out the fugitive slave clause of the Constitution. An act passed by Congress in 1793 permitted an owner or his agent to seize, or have arrested, his runaway slave and to bring the slave before a federal judge or state judge or magistrate for a hearing. It required the judge or magistrate, after serving satisfactory proof of ownership, to issue a certificate authorizing removal of the slave to the state or territory from which he had fled.[6] However, there was nothing in this act that indicated that the states could not legislate on this subject. Moreover, given the scarcity of federal judges, its enforcement depended almost exclusively on the cooperation of state officials, from the sheriff who usually arrested the fugitive, to the justice of peace who often granted the certificate of removal.

Most of the states also enacted legislation aiding the return of runaway slaves. However, northern states, influenced by black and white anti-slavery groups, also began to modify their laws to prevent the kidnapping of free Negroes under the guise of recovering fugitive slaves. The law passed in Pennsylvania in March 1820 was the first in the United States to prohibit state officials from enforcing the Fugitive Slave Act of 1793. Entitled an act "to prevent kidnapping," it prohibited any justice of the peace from recognizing the national law in a case of kidnapping, and made the kidnapping of a Negro or mulatto a felony punishable by fine of from $500 to $2,000 and by imprisonment of from 7 to 21 years.[7] Although the law did not state clearly that a master had to appear before a justice before taking a black he claimed as his runaway slave out of the state, the fact that such an official was involved was widely viewed as implying that he had so to appear.[8]

In Read's trial, his attorney insisted that Griffith was a kidnapper under the Pennsylvania law of 1820 if he had not planned to take the black before a judge to obtain a certificate of removal before carrying him out of the state. He also argued that a slave had a right of self-defense and, in a moving plea, outlined the difference in the life Read had been forced to live under slavery in Maryland as contrasted with that of his ancestors who "were in their native land, not only free but regal—the rulers over thousands and perhaps tens of thousands of affectionate and happy subjects—dispensing justice, and mercy." It was probably one of the few, if not the only, occasions in American courts up to this time that blacks were not depicted as fortunate to be slaves in America, rather than compelled to live in "barbaric Africa."

In his charge to the jury, the judge ruled that if it should decide that Griffith had really intended to violate the law of 1820, it must find that Read had killed not merely in self-defense to defend his liberty, but also to prevent the commission of a felony. That same afternoon the jury brought in a verdict of "Not guilty."

But Read's troubles with the law were not over. He was remanded for trial for the murder of the overseer, Peter Shipley. Unfortunately for the black, the judge in the second trial was the prosecutor in the first trial, and while he alluded to "the delicacy of his situation," he did not disqualify himself—nor did Read's attorney demand that he do so. In his charge to the jury, the former prosecutor (now judge) insisted that the judge in the first trial was in error in construing the 1820 law as requiring any person claiming a runaway slave to take him before a judge before carrying him out of the state. As he interpreted the law in the second trial a master could take his runaway slave directly out of the state after recapturing him. Hence Read had not acted to prevent a felony. As for his right of self-defense, it did not apply to property, and Read, after all, was his master's property.

On these instructions, the jury this time found Read guilty of manslaughter, and the next day the court sentenced him to nine years in prison.[9] Although it was small comfort to Read, in 1826 Pennsylvania enacted a law "for the protection of free people of colour, and to prevent kidnapping," which provided that the claimant of a runaway slave had to bring him before a judge or court of record before removing him from the state, and furthermore, he had to bring with him impartial witnesses to prove that the black was indeed a fugitive slave. It made it a crime to carry a Negro from the state for the purpose of holding him or her as a slave without a certificate of removal from a state judge.[10]

The trials of John Read aroused wide interest and led the Maryland legislature to ask Congress for additional legislation "to prevent the inconvenience from the ready protection given to escaping slaves in Pennsylvania and the difficulty thrown in the way of the recovery of slaves."[11] In response an effort was made in Congress to amend the Fugitive Slave Act of 1793, but it failed.[12] However, an agreement with Maryland to test the constitutionality of the Pennsylvania law of 1826 led to the 1842 decision by the Supreme Court in *Prigg* v. *Pennsylvania* which decided that the states lacked the power to pass any laws on fugitive slaves, including laws to aid their recovery, and that the Constitution did not obligate state officials to assist owners in regaining their runaway slaves.[13]

A search of the criminal court records in the Archives of the County Court at West Chester, Pennsylvania, the county seat where both trials occurred, reveals no report of the two trials of John Read. However, one paper did carry extended accounts of the trials. This was the *Village Record,* the weekly published in West Chester. While the reports are not complete nor always accurate—even Read's name was spelled differently by the reporter at different times—the columns in the *Village Record* do give us a picture of one of the most important, if neglected, episodes in the history of black resistance to reenslavement.[14]

> The great cause of the Commonwealth against *John Read,* a black man for the murder of *Samuel G. Griffith,* his alleged master, came on for trial on Friday morning the 4th instant, before Judge Ross[15] and his Associates. The counsel for the prosecution were Bernard,[16] Duer,[17] Darlington.[18] For the prisoner, (appointed by the Court.) T. Haines,

Dillingham,[19] Porter, Hemphill.[20] The examination of witnesses on the part of the Commonwealth occupied the time of the court until Wednesday evening. For the defence until Thursday afternoon. It came out on the trial, that the prisoner was the grandson of Muria, an African Queen.

(The State of the facts which appeared in the case, are omitted, on suggestion, as another trial is to take place, where the same facts will be adduced.)[21]

Mr. Barnard opened the cause on the part of the prosecution, and spoke with his accustomed clearness and ability for three fourths of an hour.

Mr. T. Haines opened the cause for the prisoner, & spoke about half an hour, explaining in a lucid manner the facts and grounds on which they should rest his defence.

Mr. Duer for the Commonwealth commenced his argument on Thursday at 4 o'clock and spoke an hour and an half. We had not the pleasure to hear this gentleman & can therefore only speak of his speech from the remarks of others which were that it was an able and sound one.

Mr. Dillingham began to speak in favour of the prisoner at half past 5 and continued something more than an hour when the court adjourned. On Friday morning he resumed his argument and spoke about two hours. His manner was very animated, as one engaged heart and soul for his client:—The matter of his speech was full of the bone and sinew of true eloquence. It was a powerful appeal to the understanding and to the heart.

Mr. Porter rose at half past 11, and spoke more than two hours. I cannot better characterize the speech of this gentleman than by a remark of a by-stander—that it was like a corps of flying artillery—now off and suddenly returning and pouring in a hot and well directed fire. In descanting on the discrepancy of the stories of the witnesses against the prisoner, he happily introduced the scriptural account of the mode in which Daniel depicted the falsehood of the Elders in the case of Susannah.

Mr. Hemphill began his argument at 10 minutes before 3 on Friday, and spoke for three hours and 25 minutes in defence of the prisoner. His address was particularized by that peculiar and attractive simplicity of manner—and familiary of illustration, for which this gentleman is distinguished, and adapts itself so wonderfully to the understanding of the highest and the lowest. He is certainly master of the Socratic and persuasive art of pleading in the greatest perfection of any person we have ever heard. In the course of his argument he feelingly remarked upon the vissitudes [*sic*] of human life. A few years ago and the ancestors of the prisoner, were, in their native land, not only free but regal—the rulers over thousands and perhaps tens of thousands of happy, affectionate and loyal subjects—dispensing justice, and mercy. But now—in a foreign land, he is claimed as a slave, and is a prisoner, standing a trial for his life, as the consequence arising from the defence of his freedom.

Mr. Darlington (Attorney General) followed Mr. Hemphill and spoke from seven until 9, when the Court adjourned. On Saturday morning he resumed his argument and spoke two hours and an half, making in all four and an half hours. The speech of this gentleman exhibited one of the greatest efforts of his powerful mind. The vast mass of facts which had been a whole week in collecting from numerous witnesses—the various points arising out of those facts—appeared to be all embraced and digested by his mind with a facility that marked its force and retentiveness—while the clearness of his argument, the strength of his reasoning and the impressive manner of enforcing his conclusions shewed an acuteness & power of understanding, which leaves him inferior to no gentleman who graces the bar in Pennsylvania.

The most patient attention throughout the whole trial, distinguished the Court and Jury. His Honour Judge Ross, in a charge of an hour and an half, summed up and weighed the testimony, and discussed the great principles of law which the question involved, from which it was apparent, that he had no doubt of the prisoner's guilt.[22]

The Jury on the ringing of the bell in the Afternoon returned a verdict of Not Guilty.

The prisoner was remanded for trial for the murder of Mr. Shipley.

Village Record, West Chester, Pennsylvania, May 16, 1821

The Courts of Oyer and Terminer, &c. Commenced their Sessions in this county on Monday of last week. After the Grand Jury were sworn, Judge DARLINGTON addressed them in a very able charge of about an hour in length. We understand the Grand Jury applied for a copy that it might be published; but the Judge declined to give one, observing that it had been prepared singly with the view to their use as members of the Court. We regret the determination the more as many who heard it expressed their approbation of the charge, and their hopes that it would be published for general gratification. The Court, notwithstanding the extreme heat of the weather, devoted itself with assiduous labor to the business before it, sitting early and late. The principal part of the criminal business being finished, John Read was on Saturday arraigned for trial, for the Murder of Mr. Shipley, but some witnesses being absent it was on motion of Mr. Tilghman[23] postponed until next court.

Village Record, West Chester, Pennsylvania, August 8, 1821

The Jury was qualified on Monday, at 3 o'clock, P.M. in the case of Read, indicted for murder. The trial will occupy the principal part of the week.

Village Record, West Chester, November 7, 1821

The trial of John Read, for the murder of Peter Shipley, came on at the late sessions of the court of Oyer and Terminer, in this County. The case from the particular circumstances attending it, had excited an unusual degree of interest. The prisoner had been tried in May last for the murder of Samuel G. Griffith and acquitted.

On monday the fifth inst. the trial commenced before his Honor, Judge Darlington,[24] President, and Judges Ralston[25] and Davis,[26] Associates. Council for the Commonwealth, Dick,[27] (in the place of Dillingham, prosecuting Attorney, who, having been Read's counsel in the former trial, was of course excluded from taking part against him in this) assisted by Barnard and Duer. For the prisoner Bell[28] and Tilghman.

The following is a brief, and we believe a fair statement of the case.

Read the Prisoner, a Black man, two or three years ago, came into Pennsylvania from Maryland, said he was free, although an attempt was made to hold him in slavery—frequently declared himself afraid of Kidnappers—often went armed.—He married in Pennsylvania and has one child—hired a house in Kennet township, and worked about the neighborhood.

On the night of the 14th of December, 1821 (we now take his own story, as given immediately after the transaction to several) his wife was from home—he was alone—lay down but felt uneasy and could not sleep—got up and made a fire. About midnight thought he heard persons walking about the house—one at length rapped smartly at the door—he asked what they wanted, the person answered they had authority to search, and had come for stolen goods. Read told them to go away—he believed they were kidnappers—if they were not—he had no stolen goods, and if they would wait till morning they might search. Soon after they began to force the door—He rolled a barrel of cider against it—told them if they attempted to come in, he would kill them. They prized the door off the hinges, and it fell over the cider barrel—at the instant he heard the click of a pistol cocking, then said Read, "it is life for life"—one of the persons said "rush on Shipley—damn the negro, he won't shoot." A person attempted to enter—he shot him—another attempted to come in—he struck him with a club the man fell on his knees, as he rose Reed struck him once or twice: then seizing his gun he ran to the neighbours and told them that the kidnappers attacked his house—that he had killed two—asked for more powder, as he was afraid they would pursue him. He made no attempt to escape. After being arrested and in custody—one witness testified that he heard Read say—that after he got out of the house and to the fence, on looking round, he saw one of the men trembling—that he went back and beat him until he thought he was quite dead.

When the neighbours came upon the ground in the morning they found Mr. Griffith lying on the bed, in the black man's house, dead. Mr. Shipley the overseer, for whose murder the prisoner was now on trial, had got up—carried him there, taken his pocket book and watch out of his pocket, and put them in his own, and then went to a neighbouring house about 100 yards off, and prevailed upon Mrs. Harvey, to let him in. There he languished eight days, and died.

The club was found in the house close by the cider barrel—two pistols loaded, one of them cocked, a whip and pair of gloves were found at the door—a pair of handcuffs and rope were found in the pocket of Mr. Shipley. A third pistol in the pocket of Mr. Griffith. There were but two wounds upon Mr. Shipley.

It appeared sufficiently clear that Read was the child of Muria, formerly an African Queen, recently a slave, and no proof of his manumission was shewn. He was claimed by Mr. Griffith, from whose service he had absconded. Having learnt where he was, Mr. Griffith, his overseer Mr. Shipley, and two assistants, Minner and Pearson, came to the house occupied by Read, about midnight; and made the attempt which resulted in the death of both Mr. Griffith & Mr. Shipley, as related.

The principal point disputed were—Whether Mr. Griffith intended to take Read out of the State without taking him before a Judge, in violation of the act of Assembly.

2d, Whether Read knew his Master.

3d, What right could Read, as a slave, acquire of self defence in Pennsylvania.

4th, Whether he returned as stated, that he confessed to one witness, from the fence and beat Shipley.

It is impossible for us, our limits do not admit it—to go into the particular arguments—in relation to the facts and the law, as will be perceived when we state, that the cause began on Monday the 8th, and continued until Tuesday the 14th; occupying the Court and Jury nine and ten hours each day.

It was fully and ably argued. Mr. Dick for the prosecution, took up about one hour and an half, in a sensible and argumentative address. He was followed by Mr. Bell, on behalf of the prisoner in a maiden speech, distinguished for clearness, method and force. Mr. Tilghman for the prisoner, began to speak on Monday afternoon, at 3 o'clock, and spoke until half past seven. The deep and fixed attention of a crowded audience, for four and an half hours, shewed the power of genius, in enchaining in fetters of eloquence, the human mind. The courage and humanity of Mrs. Harvey in rising at the mid-hour of the night, although alone; and taking in a stranger who was moaning at her door for assistance, were adverted to, with much force and beauty, accompanied by the quotation from Walter Scott

Oh woman—&c.

Mr. Duer began his argument in conclusion, on the part of the Commonwealth, on Tuesday morning. He contended that the master had a right under the law of Congress, at any time and place, and at any hour, by himself or his agent, to seize his slave—that the slave had no right to resist his master—that his house was no protection—that therefore, the Master, & the deceased Shipley his overseer, were in the exercise of a legal right—and Read, in resisting, in the perpetration of a wrong—That Read must have known his master, and that therefore, the killing, in resisting the legal attempt to arrest him, was murder in the first degree. Mr. Duer spoke for two and an half hours.

Judge Darlington them summed up the evidence, and laid down the law in a charge of an hour and an half.

He adverted to the delicacy of his situation, having been on the other trial, Attorney for the Commonwealth; but remarked that his regret was considerably diminished, by a consideration that the Jury were the Judges of the law, as well as the fact, in the case before them. He gave a full and lucid exposition of the whole law on the subject. In respect to the construction of the Act of Assembly, of 1820, on which much reliance was placed, he differed from the opinion of Judge Ross, delivered at Norristown. The Counsel for the Prisoner had contended that by this act, the attempt to take any person claimed as a slave out of the State without taking him before a Judge to prove his right, was declared a felony—that from the time and circumstances of the attack, no doubt could exist but that it was the intention of the party to take Read out of the state in violation of that act—that they were therefore in the commission of a felony, and Read was justified in resisting unto death. The Counsel for the Commonwealth maintained that this act was intended to prevent kidnapping, or man-stealing—that it did not apply to a master, who intended to arrest & reclaim his runaway slave, who by the act of Congress, he was authorized to arrest or seize, when and where he could. But Judge Ross had decided that the Act had reference to masters seizing their slaves, and taking them out of the State, without going before a Judge. Judge Darlington was of opinion that such was not the construction, inasmuch as the law so construed inflicted the same penalty (7 years imprisonment in the Penitentiary) upon the acknowledged master, reclaiming his slave, and taking him away, as upon the kidnapper who should attempt to carry off a freeman; and this opinion was confirmed by the construction of the Supreme Court, of the old Act of Assembly in relation to the same subject. He then examined the evidence and weighed it with great perspicuity and impartiality expressing his opinion that there was not conclusive proof, that Read knew his master or overseer; and intimating very clearly, that the witness who testified that the Prisoner confessed he returned and beat the deceased, until he thought him quite dead—was mistaken.

The Jury immediately on the Court opening in the afternoon, returned to the box with a verdict of Manslaughter.

The next day he received his sentence of nine years imprisonment, in the Penitentiary.

Village Record, West Chester, Pennsylvania, November 21, 1821

The only copy of the *Village Record* is in the West Chester Historical Society and I wish to express my gratitude to the staff of the Society for their kind cooperation.

NOTES

1. Jonathan Katz, *Resistance at Christiana: The Fugitive Slave Rebellion, Christiana, Pennsylvania, September 11, 1851: A Documentary Account.* New York, 1974, p. 4.
2. The alleged thirty-six black and five white participants in the Christiana battle, during which Edward Gorsuch, a Maryland slaveowner was killed, were charged with treason against the United States—the largest number ever simultaneously indicted for this high crime. William Parker, black leader of the resistance who killed Gorsuch when he insisted on breaking into Parker's home in Christiana to recapture his alleged slaves, escaped to Canada. The first group of defendants were acquitted by the jury

after only 15 minutes of deliberation, and eventually treason charges against the others were dropped.

3. *American Republican,* Dec. 19, 1820 (copy in West Chester Historical Society, West Chester, Pa.).

4. *Niles' Weekly Register* (Baltimore, 1811–1849), Vol. XXI, Dec. 1, 1821, p. 214; *Pennsylvania Magazine of History and Biography,* Vol. XIII, 1889, pp. 106–9.

5. Article IV, sec. 3, par. 3.

6. 1 *Stat.,* 302–5. For the background leading to the enactment of the law *see* Philip S. Foner, *History of Black Americans: From Africa to the Emergence of the Cotton Kingdom* (Westport, Conn., 1975), pp. 413–14.

7. John Purdon, ed., *Digest of the Laws of Pennsylvania* (Philadelphia, 1824), pp. 576, 621.

8. George M. Stroud, *A Sketch of the Laws Relating to Slavery* (Philadelphia, 1827), pp. 168–69.

9. *Niles' Weekly Register,* Vol. XXI, Dec. 1, 1821, p. 214; *Pennsylvania Magazine of History and Biography,* Vol. XIII, 1889, pp. 106–9.

10. William R. Leslie, "The Pennsylvania Fugitive Slave Act of 1826," *Journal of Southern History,* Vol. XVIII, Nov. 1952, pp. 429–45. For the text of the law, *see Acts of the General Assembly of the Commonwealth of Pennsylvania* (Harrisburg, 1826), pp. 150–55.

11. *American State Papers,* (38 vols., Washington, D.C., 1832–1861): *Miscellaneous,* Vol. II, p. 752.

12. *Annals of Congress,* 17th Cong., 1st Sess., pp. 557, 710, 1379–80, 1415, 1444.

13. *Prigg v. Pennsylvania,* 16 Peters 539 (1842). For a challenge to the traditional interpretation of the decision in *Prigg v. Pennsylvania, see* Joseph C. Burke, "What Did the Prigg Decision Really Decide?" *Pennsylvania Magazine of History and Biography,* Vol. XCIII, Jan. 1969, pp. 73–85.

14. Only one previous account of the case of John Read has been published. The *Pennsylvania Magazine of History and Biography* Vol. XIII, 1889, pp. 106–9, carried an article under the title, "What Right Had a Fugitive Slave of Self-Defense Against His Master?" The article contains a brief summary of the two trials of John Read. Part of the article is reprinted in Herbert Aptheker, editor, *A Documentary History of the Negro People in the United States* (New York, 1951), pp. 73–74. Here it is entitled, "A Negro Resists the Kidnappers, 1820." Strangely, there is no mention of the case of John Read in Thomas D. Morris, *Free Men All: The Personal Liberty Laws of the North, 1780–1861* (Baltimore, 1975), even though the work devotes many pages to fugitive slaves in Pennsylvania.

15. Judge John Ross was appointed presiding judge in 1818.

16. Isaac D. Barnard was appointed district attorney in 1817.

17. John Duer, Jr., was appointed district attorney in 1809.

18. Isaac Darlington was appointed district attorney in 1821.

19. William H. Dillingham was elected to the Pennsylvania Assembly in 1837.

20. William Hemphill was rated "among the ablest" lawyers in Pennsylvania (Wilmer W. MacElree, *Sidelights on the Bench and Bar of Chester County* [West Chester, Pa., 1918], p. 188).

21. The facts were presented in the *Village Record* of Nov. 21, 1821. *See pp. 13–15.*

22. As is indicated in the report in the *Village Record* of Nov. 21, 1821, this is not an accurate statement.

23. Benjamin Tilghman had been a deputy attorney-general and was considered a leading lawyer. "Students sought his office eagerly." (MacElree, *op. cit.,* pp. 213–14.)

24. Isaac Darlington had been appointed presiding judge in August 1821.

25. Judge John Ralston was appointed an associate judge in 1802.

26. Judge John Davis was appointed an associate judge in 1803.

27. Thomas B. Dick was admitted to the bar in 1790.

28. Thomas S. Bell was appointed district attorney in 1824.

3

The Battle to End Discrimination
Against Negroes
on Philadelphia Streetcars:
(Part I) Background
and Beginning of the Battle*

Ante-Bellum Philadelphia presented an interesting contradiction so far as black Americans were concerned. The city had always been in the forefront of the antislavery movement and had given birth to the oldest abolitionist society in the country, the Pennsylvania Society for Promoting the Abolition of Slavery, the Relief of Free Negroes Unlawfully Held in Bondage, and for Improving the Condition of the African Race. As the number of slaves in Pennsylvania declined through the operation of the gradual abolition law, the society suffered from a "decline of energy, and [a] gradual tendency to a state of apathy." But abolitionism continued to grow steadily in Philadelphia and the Garrisonian wing of antislavery was stronger in that city than anywhere outside of New England.[1] Philadelphia was also the leading center of the free produce movement in the North which had as one of its aims the elimination of slavery by boycotting goods made by slave labor.[2]

But Philadelphia was also the most anti-Negro city of the North and the most rigidly segregated metropolis above the Mason-Dixon line. This seeming contradiction is actually not too difficult to explain. Philadelphia in 1860, with its 22,185 Negroes, had a larger black population than any other northern city. The national census of that year revealed that Boston's 2,261 Negroes made up one seventy-seventh of the population, and New York's 12,472, one sixty-third of the population. Negroes comprised one twenty-fourth of the population of Philadelphia.[3] It is a well established fact of American

*Reprinted from *Pennsylvania History,* XL (July, 1973), 261–290.

history that the degree of hostility to blacks varied with the size of the Negro community.

In the years before the Civil War it was customary for anti-slavery writers and speakers to refer to New York City as "the prolongation of the South" where "ten thousand cords of interests are lined with the Southern slaveholder." But Philadelphia outdid even the Empire City in its hostility to antislavery agitation and the demand for equal rights for Negroes.[4] When John Brown's remains were brought to Philadelphia after his execution in Virginia, James Miller McKim, the Philadelphia abolitionist, planned to secure the services of an undertaker and allow Mrs. Brown a day's rest before proceeding on to North Elba where the burial was to take place. The mayor of Philadelphia met them at the railroad station and insisted that Brown's remains be sent out of the city aboard the next train, as he feared that otherwise he would be unable to maintain order in the face of the rising tide of anti-Negro feeling in the city. The mayor threatened to use the police and even the military, if necessary, to get the remains of the great champion of black people out of the city. Brown's remains had to be taken to New York City where no objection was raised to their being turned over to an undertaker for two days.[5]

Instead of enforcing the law, Philadelphia mayors were repeatedly advising Negroes and their abolitionist friends not to provoke white mobs. In 1839 the mayor warned Lucretia Mott, one of the "noble few [Quakers] who have cleansed their garments from the foul stain of prejudice," not to offend white Philadelphians by walking in the streets with colored people. She replied that she had been in the habit of walking with Negroes as the occasion offered, and, as it was a matter of principle with her to make no distinctions on account of color, she expected to continue to walk with them, and she did. But the *Friend,* a conservative Quaker antislavery journal published in Philadelphia, cautioned abolitionists to heed the mayor's warning, since in the City of Brotherly Love, it was dangerous to mix up with the abolition question, "the warfare against what they are pleased to call prejudices in regard to the colored race."[6] There was solid reason for this advice. Philadelphia was the scene of increasing hostility and violence directed against Negroes before and after 1834 when for the first time the city had "a full-scale race riot." In the course of three nights of rioting, one Negro was killed, many were severely injured, two churches and many private dwellings were attacked and damaged.[7]

As the Negro population of Philadelphia increased with the flow of fugitive slaves, the rights of black people were drastically reduced. In 1813 the mayor, aldermen, and a large body of distinguished citizens of Philadelphia sent a memorial to the legislature complaining that the great number of Negroes in the city were "becoming nuisances." The memorial pleaded for legislation to require all blacks to register, to provide for binding out to service convicted Negroes "for the purpose of compensating the persons they may have plundered," and for a special tax on free Negroes to provide for impoverished Negroes. They even proposed "preventive detention," urging that the police be authorized to apprehend any black, whether a vagrant or a man of reputable character, who could not produce a certificate that he had been registered, and that a justice be empowered to commit him to prison for six months. Fortunately, the free Negroes of Philadelphia, led by James Forten, and their abolitionist allies, were barely able to defeat the discriminatory legislation. But in 1838, despite the vigorous protest of 40,000 Negroes, written by the distinguished black Philadelphia abolitionist Robert Purvis, the state legislature adopted a new constitution which included a provision limiting the franchise to adult *white men.*[8] The legislature acted later to deprive Negroes of equality of educational opportunity. For a long time it had simply ignored blacks in establishing public educational facilities, but in 1854 it required school directors to establish separate schools in districts where there were twenty or more colored pupils. Where such separate schools were established, officials were not to be compelled to admit colored children to the white schools. Negro children attended segregated schools or no schools at all, and this applied to the private schools of the Quakers as well as the public schools.[9] "They will give us good advice," wrote Samuel Ringgold Ward, the black abolitionist. "They will aid us in giving us a partial education—but never in a Quaker school, beside their own children. Whatever they do for us savors of pity, and is done at arm's length."[10]

The place of Negroes in Philadelphia was as God ordained it should be, said a best-selling book published in the city in 1851. It bore the flaming title, *Negro-Mania,* and its author, John Campbell, was a member of the Social Improvement Society of Philadelphia. The book had been written after eight weeks of discussion in the society on the question, "Can the Colored Races of men be made mentally, politically and socially equal with the white?" It summarized the views of the leading white Philadelphians who had participated. After a lengthy discussion designed to combat the "sickly sentimentalism . . . maudlin philosophy and pseudo philanthropy" of Philadelphians who advocated equal rights for blacks, Campbell asked his fellow Philadelphians if they would "ever agree that blacks shall stand beside us on election day, upon the rostrum, in the ranks of the army, in our places of amusement, in places of public worship, ride in the same coaches, railway cars, or steamships?" His answer, widely approved by white Philadelphia, was specific: "Never! never! never! nor is it natural or just that this kind of equality should exist. God never intended it. . . ."[11]

Little wonder black Americans hated Philadelphia. "There is no more regard shown by the whites for the common and natural rights of the colored people here, than there is at Richmond," wrote John Oliver in 1863.[12] "The city of Philadelphia generally has no sense of justice, where colored peoples rights are concerned, or no disposition to do justice to that despised race," the Reverend B. F. Barrett declared in a fiery sermon delivered at his church at the corner of Broad and Brandywine Streets on September 23, 1866.[13] But it was Frederick Douglass who most frequently and bitterly heaped scorn upon the city "for the insult and degradation offered to the colored citizens of Philadelphia."[14] In 1849 he pointed out that Philadelphia had long been "the scene of a series of most foul and cruel mobs, waged against the people of color," and noted that for the colored man and woman it was "one of the most disorderly and insecure cities in the Union." "Shame upon the guilty city!" Douglass cried. "Shame upon its law-makers and law-administrators!"[15] Knowing the city, Douglass predicted that once the Fugitive Slave Bill of 1850 became law, "a vigorous slave-catching business will be driven in Philadelphia."[16] Following a visit to the city at the beginning of 1862, Douglass wrote indignantly:

> There is not perhaps anywhere to be found a city in which prejudice against color is more rampant than in Philadelphia. Hence all the

incidents of caste are to be seen there in perfection. It has its white schools and colored schools, its white churches and its colored churches, its white Christianity and the colored Christianity, its white concerts and its colored concerts, its white literary institutions and its colored literary institutions . . . and the line is everywhere tightly drawn between them. Colored persons, no matter how well dressed or how well behaved, ladies or gentlemen, rich or poor, are not even permitted to ride on any of the many railways through that Christian city. Halls are rented with the express understanding that no person of color shall be allowed to enter, either to attend a concert or listen to a lecture. The whole aspect of city usage at this point is mean, contemptible and barbarous . . .[17]

It was the street railway situation which aroused the widest indignation among Philadelphia's Negroes. One could choose not to attend a concert or a public lecture and avoid being humiliated. Sarah Forten, daughter of James Forten, Philadelphia's black sail manufacturer and pioneer advocate of Negro equality, advised Negroes to avoid facing discrimination rather than suffer humiliation. Her family, she wrote her friend Angelina Grimké, seldom went to public places unless they were open to all and therefore did not have to suffer the mortification that usually followed.[18] It was possible for blacks to send their children to separate schools, even though they were inferior, and hope they would obtain the rudiments of an education. But how could they get from one place to another in the city, how visit friends and relatives, how even get to work to the servile jobs open to blacks without using the public transportation facilities?

On June 9, 1857, the Philadelphia and Delaware River R.R. Company, operating a steam road, secured from the General Assembly of Pennsylvania, a supplement to its charter, authorizing the construction of a street railway on Fifth and Sixth Streets to be operated by horses. On January 20, 1858, the first streetcar line in Philadelphia was open to the public. Within the next two years eighteen more street railway companies were in operation, and in January, 1859, Mayor Alexander Henry proudly announced that no "public improvement . . . has ever promised more general benefit to the community."[19]

But black Philadelphians could not share the mayor's joy. The improvements in Philadelphia's transportation system were not for the black citizens. Negroes had been able to travel with some difficulty on the steam road, but the city omnibuses which preceded the streetcars drawn by horse had already set the policy for the companies which took over their routes. In 1854, on his return from Europe, William Wells Brown visited Philadelphia. He and two British friends hailed an omnibus on Chestnut Street. The white men were furnished with seats, but Brown was told that "We don't allow niggers in here." "The omnibuses of Paris, Edinburgh, Glasgow, and Liverpool had stopped to take me up, . . ." he wrote angrily, "but what mattered that? My face was not white, my hair was not straight; and therefore, I must be excluded from a seat in a third-rate American omnibus."[20]

Brown's experience forecast what was to follow on the horsecars. Of the city's nineteen streetcar and suburban railroad companies, eleven refused to admit Negroes to their cars. The other eight reluctantly allowed them to ride but forced them to stand on the front platform with the driver, even when the cars were half empty, and though it was raining or snowing. In many parts of Philadelphia, Negroes seeking transportation had to walk or hire an expensive carriage.

"While all colored men, women, and children are refused admittance to the cars or expelled from the very platform at the pleasure of the conductors," wrote an observer after a study of the streetcar situation, "the worst classes of the whites may ride. It is a common thing in the cars to see the rules which forbid smoking violated; to hear men swearing and using improper language in the presence of ladies; to be annoyed by the disgusting behavior of intoxicated persons; to have women of the town take places by respectable ladies. These annoyances are common in the street cars as in the streets; yet the rules which exclude all colored passengers are justified on the pretext that they would protect the comfort of passengers."[21]

At the outbreak of the Civil War, thinking that the nation's struggle for survival might induce a change in policy, a Negro passenger brought an action for damages against a conductor who ejected him from a car. The court rejected the action and upheld the right of companies to exclude Negroes. Judge Hare pointed to the fact that Negroes were excluded "in our theatres, our schools, our lecture-rooms, our churches, and in fine, in all places where men congregate in public or private, for the transaction of business in common, or for enjoyment." It was too much to expect that a race "long civilized" would desire to travel in the company of those "emerging from the shades of barbarism." He concluded: "In the belief then, that the regulation [excluding Negroes] now before us is a wise one, or if not wise, will work its own cure best when least molested, we enter judgment for the defendant." The Philadelphia Female Anti-Slavery Society branded the decision "an illustration of the hypocrisy of a people calling themselves democratic and christian," but the companies, now reinforced by the court, continued their practices unchanged.[22] Even black soldiers returning to their camps to fight for the Union were rejected from the horsecars. The Reverend Robert J. Parvin, of Chestnut Hill, described the following incident:

A few minutes before six o'clock on Monday evening two non-commissioned officers of the United States army, belonging to a regiment now forming at Camp William Penn, stepped on the front platform of a Fifth street car . . . on their way to the Berks-street depot of the North Pennsylvania Railroad. It was the last car by which they could reach the train to convey them out to their camp that night. When these well-dressed and well-behaved colored soldiers stepped on the platform there was no one else on it except the driver. They were almost immediately seen by the conductor, who rushed through the car and ordered the men to "get off." One of the soldiers replied, "We want to reach the train to get out to camp tonight." "I can't help that, you can't ride on this car," was the answer. As the men did not move at once, the conductor put him off. The men, without resistance, but with an indignation they could not express, *were forced from the platform.* . . .

The men were then on the sidewalk, within a short distance of us, but the conductor would not listen to their being allowed to stand on the vacant platform. . . . We reached the Berks-street station just in time to take the train on the North Pennsylvania Railroad, and the two soldiers were left behind. . . .

I have seen colored soldiers on the battlefield. I have seen them defending fortifications, which a few hours before, they had taken from the Southern rebels, at the point of a bayonet. I have seen them suffering in their wounds received in our defence, but I never before saw them forcibly driven from the privilege of standing on the platform of a railway car.[23]

Negro regiments were organized and trained at Camp William Penn, a few miles from the city. It was a common sight to see on the road leading to the camp hundreds of Negro men and women walking to visit their husbands and sons to say a last farewell before they left to fight for the Union. "These are the people whom our City Railway Companies exclude from their cars," the Female Anti-Slavery Society declared bitterly. "Our colored population promptly responded to the call for men to drive back the rebel invaders of Pennsylvania; they go willingly in the face of death, and worse than death, to bear their part in the fierce struggle for the Nation's life. Is it *thus* that Philadelphia should requite them?"[24]

But Philadelphia was unmoved. Nor was it influenced by the fact that mothers and wives of wounded black soldiers found it impossible to visit their kinsmen in local hospitals, either because they could not ride on any of the cars in the direction or because they were compelled to stand on the front platform in the most miserable weather. One black woman wrote indignantly in 1864:

> We have in this city three societies of ladies for the relief of the sick and wounded soldiers. . . . These ladies, whenever they desire to visit their brethren at the hospitals, either to minister to their wants or attending them when dying, are constrained to pay for carriage hire, at an expense of six or seven dollars, thus expending money that would be otherwise appropriated to the soldiers were they permitted to ride in the cars. . . . Now, we do think this is a great outrage, not only upon us but upon the men who, regardless of the prejudice they have always encountered in this land of their birth, have at the call of their country rushed forth to aid in putting down the rebellion, and now they are wounded, many disabled for life, are deprived of seeing those dear to them, because the directors of the city passenger cars refuse to let colored people ride, which, to say the least, is a stigma upon the city of Philadelphia.[25]

Here is what happened to the wives of two wounded soldiers when they attempted to visit them at the hospital. The description is by a white Philadelphian who witnessed the brutal incident which occurred in the summer of 1865:

> On Thursday evening last, accompanied by a lady, I took a seat in a Spruce and Pine street car, going west. When the car arrived within a few feet of Eighth street it was hailed by two colored women. The car was stopped, and the women got in. All passed quietly for some time.

William Still, *The Underground Railroad* (Philadelphia, 1872), 215

The conductor received the fare from the women, and no objection was made to their presence until nearing Eleventh street, when the car was stopped and the women ordered to leave. This they declined doing in a mild and peaceable manner, pointing out that they were going to visit their wounded soldier husbands. Several minutes were spent in endeavoring to persuade the women to leave, but to no purpose. The car was then driven at a furious rate as far as Broad street, when it stopped to admit a passenger. The colored women attempted to get out, but were prevented, the conductor informing them that they would be taken to the depot and whitewashed. At Seventeenth street a lady wished to get out. The conductor would not stop for fear of losing his prisoners. At Nineteenth street I pulled the strap. The car stopped and I got out. The colored women rushed to the door to make their escape. One succeeded in reaching the platform, where she was seized by some ruffians. She cried frantically for help; and fear, I suppose, induced the outlaws to release her. The car had started when she sprang from the platform, she barely escaping injury. The other woman did not succeed in making her escape. During the trip the women were incessantly assailed with oaths, threats, and most disgusting language from the driver, conductor and the passengers, including a white woman, whose language was positvely loathsome.

This Philadelphian added that he wrote the account "to learn if, when respectable white ladies enter a streetcar, they can have some surety that they will not be insulted and their feelings outraged by such disgusting behavior, perpetrated by men who pride themselves on being white men."[26] Evidently the bodily injuries, to say nothing of the humiliation of the Negro women, were not as important as the fact that white women might be forced to witness these disgraceful events.

Mrs. Frances E. W. Harper, the most popular Negro poet of the era, travelled widely during the Civil War as a lecturer. Only in Philadelphia did she come up against the tyranny of the streetcar companies. Attempting during a downpour in March, 1866, to obtain passage in a car, she was sent to the platform to ride with the driver. She replied that she had just ridden in the cars in Southern cities and asked, "Are you more heathenish here than there?" The conductor did not bother to answer but pushed her to the platform, remarking finally that it was "against company rules to let colored persons ride in the cars." Mrs. Harper refused to accept the discriminatory practice, walked several miles in the rain, and the following day, shot off a letter to the Philadelphia *Evening Telegraph,* asking:

> Can it be possible that Philadelphia virtually says to the wives, widows, daughters, mothers and sisters of those men who helped turn the tide of battle in our favor, that they must either stand upon the platform, or plod their way through all weather rather than have the privilege of entering the cars?—a privilege freely accorded to us in other cities. My business calls me from city to city, and from Louisville to Philadelphia: no conductor asks me either to ride on the platform or wend my way through the rain, as I did yesterday.[27]

Robert Smalls, born a slave in Beaufort, South Carolina in 1839, catapulted to national fame in May, 1862, when he led fifteen other slaves in delivering the *Planter,* a Confederate gunboat, to the Union navy outside Charleston harbor. He won commendation from Congress and President Lincoln and served throughout the war as a Union pilot. But none of this cut any ice on Philadelphia's streetcars. The *Planter* was at the navy yard in Philadelphia undergoing repairs. When Smalls and a white sailor attempted to board a car to visit the famous vessel, the conductor would not allow the Negro to ride. The sailor pointed out who his companion was, but the conductor stuck to his statement, "Company regulations. We don't allow niggers to ride!" Smalls and his sailor friend had to walk several miles to the navy yard.[28]

Of the scores of humiliating and brutal incidents arising from the policies of the Philadelphia streetcars, perhaps the following is the most shocking. It involved the Reverend William J. Alston, rector of St. Thomas's Colored Episcopal Church. Here is an excerpt from the letter he addressed in July 1864, "To the Christian Public of Philadelphia":

> Within the past week, my only living child having been at death's door, by our physician we were directed to take him over the Delaware river as often as convenient. On our return to the Philadelphia side, on one occasion, the child became completely prostrated. I held my ear to his mouth three several times to ascertain whether he was still alive. Such a death-like appearance came over him. I felt the necessity of reaching home as soon as possible, and to my satisfaction (for the time being), I saw one of the Lombard and South street cars approaching,

which I hailed, was on the act of entering, when the conductor arrested my progress by informing me that I could not enter—*being colored.* I referred him to the condition of my child, but all to no purpose; he ordered the driver to go on, regardless of our humble plea. . . . Had the cars been overloaded, that would have been excuse sufficient; but the fact of the case is, that the only persons on the cars referred to were the conductor and the driver.

In the face of these facts, we ask the Christian public of Philadelphia, can you look on in silence, and see respectable colored citizens excluded from the privilege of availing themselves of the *public* facilities for going from one extreme of the city to the other? . . .

Is it humane to exclude respectable colored citizens from your street cars, when so many of our brave and vigorous young men have been and are enlisting, to take part in this heaven-ordained *slavery extermination,* many of whom have performed commendable service in our army and navy—in the former of which your humble subscriber has two-brawny-armed and battle-tired brothers? Finally, we ask, is it in accordance with Christian civilization to thrust out of your street car the dying child of an humble servant of Christ, in whose congregation there exists an active auxiliary to the Pennsylvania branch of the Women's Sanitary Committee of the United States?

We beg you to remember the words of Him by whom soon you and I are to be judged . . . ; "Verily, I say unto you, inasmuch as ye have done it unto one of the least of these, my brethren, ye have done it unto me."[29]

Not a single white clergyman in Philadelphia responded to this plea. To be sure, the theme of many sermons in the churches the Sunday following the publication of the Reverend Alston's appeal did deal with the streetcars, but they concerned the only problem that bothered Philadelphia's white religious community—the operation of cars on Sunday. "The sanctimonious city of Philadelphia has such a high regard for the holy Sabbath," observed a contemporary journal, "that it will not allow the cars to run on that day, and yet on Monday morning it so far forgets the law of doing unto others, etc., that it will not allow a wounded negro soldier to ride in its cars." Of such Christians Frederick Douglass said, in a letter to the students of Lincoln University, "They would have us among the angels in heaven, but do not want to touch elbows with us on earth."[30]

James M. McPherson has characterized the battle against streetcar segregation in Philadelphia as "a microcosm of the Negro's battle for equal rights and human dignity."[31] The opening gun in this long struggle was fired by William Still. The son of slaves, Still rose to prominence in the Society for Promoting the Abolition of Slavery, became an active agent of the Underground Railroad, and a prosperous coal merchant.[32] Still published a letter in the Philadelphia *North American and United States Gazette* on August 31, 1859, under the heading "Colored People and the Cars." This was nineteen months after the first streetcar line opened in Philadelphia. Writing "as a colored man," Still voiced "the sore grievance of genteel colored people in being excluded from the city passenger railroad cars, except they choose to 'stand on the front platform with the driver.'" He observed that "however long the distance they may have to go, or great the hurry—however well or aged, genteel or neatly attired—however hot, cold or stormy the weather—however few in the cars, as the masses of colored people now understand it, they are unceremoniously excluded." Surveying the national scene, Still pointed out that in Philadelphia the proscription against Negroes on the streetcars was more severe than "in any of the leading cities of the Union." Yet this was the City of Brotherly Love, the city of the Quakers, and one of the cities most famous for "great religious and benevolent enterprises, so pre-eminently favorable to elevating the heathen in Africa, while forgetful of those in their very precincts—those who are taxed to support the very highways that they are rejected from."

Still conceded that the proscription might be based upon the "erroneous impression" that the colored people of Philadelphia were made up only of those who lived in poverty and squalor in the city's slums. Not so, he argued. This "degraded class" was by no means a "fair sample of the twenty thousand colored people of Philadelphia." He pointed to the parts of the city "where the decent portions of colored people reside," the eighteen or twenty colored churches with their Sabbath schools, the twenty or so day schools, the dozens of beneficial societies for the support of sick and disabled members, the comfortable, even luxurious homes and valuable businesses owned by "industrious sober and decent" colored people—all proof that the Philadelphia Negro was "by no means so sadly degraded and miserably poor as the public have generally been led to believe." Yet all this was beside the point. For even if Stephen Smith, one of Philadelphia's Negroes who had amassed considerable wealth in the lumber and coal business, should enter a car, he, too, would be forced to stand on the front platform. Indeed, should Elizabeth Greenfield, the internationally famous "Black Swan," wish to enjoy a ride to Fairmount Park, she, too, "must stand on the 'front platform by the driver.' " "The fact that her extraordinary acquirement as a vocalist have won for her the very highest distinction both in this country and Europe, does actually weigh nothing when entering a City passenger Railroad car—the front platform is the place for all the Creator chose to make with a dark skin." Still closed his communication with the expression of hope that "ere long, decent colored men and women will find the same privilege in the City Passenger Railroad cars of Philadelphia that are extended to colored men and women in other cities."

Still's letter was widely reprinted in the antislavery press,[33] but in Philadelphia it aroused no interest. Philadelphians did not even bother to defend their prejudices by pointing out that Still was not quite accurate in his comparison between their city and other metropolitan centers on the question of streetcar segregration. As proof of his assertion that the Quaker city was the worst in the nation in this respect, Still cited the fact that in New Orleans Negroes— slaves as well as free—rode without discrimination in all the city cars and omnibuses. Actually, while streetcar segregation in New Orleans was not required by law, it was practiced as company policy from the time the cars were placed in service in the 1820s. Several lines excluded Negroes altogether, but others operated special cars for blacks, identified by large stars painted on the front, rear, and both sides. Still also claimed that Negro women could ride freely in the city omnibuses of Cincinnati while colored men did face some discrimination. In actual fact, complete segregation existed on streetcars in Cincinnati until after the Civil War.[34]

Since Philadelphia, to paraphrase Lincoln Steffens, was Jim Crow and content, Still's letter did not disturb the citizens' equanimity. Only one Philadelphian took the trouble to comment on Still's letter. A citizen who described himself as belonging to the class which had the "right to use freely the passenger railway cars in our city," sent a communication to the *North American and United States Review.* He commended Still for having stood up for the rights of people, adding: "If a similar intelligent and firm support of all their rights were characteristic of the colored race, it can hardly be doubted that their condition in our community and in our country would be vastly improved."[35] It is doubtful, however, that the entire black population of Philadelphia viewed Still's communication in the same light. His effort to convince the bigots that prejudice against colored people was due to their mistaken conception that the Negro who lived in the city's slums was representative of the black population seemed to quite a few blacks as advancing the elitist proposition that it was legitimate to Jimcrow poor Negroes. In later years Still was accused of seeking to open the streetcars without discrimination to the wealthy, so-called respectable blacks, a charge he heatedly denied.[36]

Be that as it may, Still's letter opened the cars neither to the wealthy Stephen Smiths nor the colored residents of the slums. Meanwhile, the outrages daily committed on Negroes seeking public transportation multiplied. In 1861 the next move was made to end these practices. This time it came from the Social, Cultural and Statistical Association of the Colored People of Pennsylvania. Organized in September, 1860, as a body "embracing the public interests of the colored citizens of Philadelphia," the association announced its plans to call meetings and engage in other activities "to diffuse a knowledge of the condition & wants of the colored people, and to remove prejudice in any directions where their civil rights are discriminated thereby."[37] Late in 1861 William Still, the association's corresponding secretary, proposed to the executive committee that a petition be circulated among white Philadelphians requesting the Board of Presidents of the City Railways to end segregation on their lines. A car committee was appointed, and the work of collecting signatures to a petition got underway. For four months the committee, made up of Still, Isaiah C. Wears, Samuel S. Smith, and the Reverend J. C. Gibbs of the First Presbyterian Colored Church, visited various groups in Philadelphia, including the prestigious Merchants' Exchange, with their petition. They requested the privilege of gaining the floor to present arguments in favor of the appeal and solicit signatures. By June, 1862, 369 prominent white Philadelphians had signed the following petition:

> The colored citizens of Philadelphia suffer very serious inconvenience and hardship daily, by being excluded from riding in the city passenger cars. In New York city, and in all the principal Northern cities, they ride; even in New Orleans (although subject to some

proscription,) they ride in the cars; why, then, should they be excluded in Philadelphia, a city standing so preeminently high for its benevolence, liberality, love of freedom and Christianity, as the City of Brotherly Love?

Colored people pay more taxes here than is paid by the same class in any other Nothern city. The members of the "Social and Statistical Association," although numbering less than fifty members, pay annually about five thousand dollars into the Tax Collector's Office.

Therefore, the undersigned respectfully petition that the various Boards of the City Passenger cars rescind the rules indiscriminately excluding colored persons from the inside of the cars.[38]

It obviously mattered little to the signers that, like Still's letter of 1859, the petition contained some inaccuracies. As noted previously New Orleans segregated Negroes on its streetcars, and in New York City Negroes were subject to occasional discrimination on some of the streetcar lines and were required to ride in a Jim Crow car on the Sixth Avenue line.[39] In mid-June Still, on behalf of the car committee, placed the petition in the hands of the board of presidents of the city passenger cars. He conceded that there were fears that "filthy and degraded" Negroes might obtain entrance to the inside of streetcars if the petition were granted but went on to assure the presidents that *"We make no advocacy for the filthy."* This time, however, perhaps because of the criticism of his 1859 letter, Still acknowledged that it might be possible that "filthy and degraded" Negroes were "rendered so by being compelled to live and rear their children in localities of degradation." Still might have been more effective had he pointed out, as did A. L. Standard, acting editor of *The Christian Recorder,* official organ of the AME Church published in Philadelphia, that the companies had no objection to seating in their cars the recent immigrants from Ireland and other parts of Europe who also were forced to live unsanitary lives in Philadelphia's slums.

Still left the companies' presidents "with sanguine feelings and desires that it may not be long before the prayer will be answered to the satisfaction and honor of all concerned." *The Christian Recorder* also exuded confidence and predicted that the "effort nobly made— we mean wisely and prudently made—in behalf of the colored people of Philadelphia" would bring instant results. "We cannot but believe that such an effort will be crowned with success, for it has touched the sympathies of our white friends."[40]

Unfortunately, it failed to "touch the sympathies" of the presidents of the streetcar lines. They were "touched" by the spectre of declining passenger traffic if their white customers took it into their minds to avoid streetcars which required them to sit next to Negroes. Still had gently raised the point to the presidents that "the companies would actually be gainers, instead of losers." But the companies' inspectors had informed the presidents that passengers had been saying that many of the prominent Philadelphians who had signed the petition travelled about in their own carriages and hence could afford to be quite benevolent about the rights of Negroes on streetcars. So it was, that despite the publicity the petition received, and even the endorsement it gained from the Philadelphia *Press*, "our rights," as Still recalled sadly, "were still denied us."[41]

Throughout the rest of 1862 and nearly all of 1863, the protest movement against streetcar segregation remained dormant even while black volunteers in the Union army were being kicked off the horsecars by white roughnecks coming to the aid of conductors. In fact, John Oliver, a militant black Philadelphian, publicly accused the leaders of the Negro community of being averse to further agitation on the ground "that it will make the case worse and injure our cause—that the white people will become still more prejudiced against us, and therefore it is best to wait until they see fit to treat us better."[42] Whatever criticism might be made of William Still for the manner in which he pleaded the case against segregation on the cars, he was certainly not one of those guilty of what Oliver called "abominable sycophancy." On the contrary, though he saw some wisdom in avoiding incessant agitation on the issue, the "car inhumanity" so angered Still that he refused to remain silent. In December, 1863, he sent a letter to the Philadelphia *Press* relating his humiliating experiences on one of the city cars when, despite his vigorous objections, he was forced to ride on the platform in the dark while it was snowing, until he decided it was safer to get off the car and walk. A year before, an old Negro minister was killed while riding on the platform during a dark, cold, and rainy night. Still walked home in the blizzard, "feeling satisfied that nowhere in Christendom could be found a better illustration of Judge Taney's decision in the Dred Scott case, in which he declared that 'black men have no rights which white men are bound to respect,' than are demonstrated by the 'rules' of the passenger cars of the City of Brotherly Love."[43]

Still's letter was more widely reprinted than his earlier communication and even appeared in the London *Times.* Moncure D. Conway reported from London to the Boston *Commonwealth* that Still's letter describing his experiences on the streetcar had done more harm to the Union cause in England "than a military defeat in Virginia."[44]

During the winter of 1864 the car committee of the Statistical Association continued its efforts through public appeals, visits, and interviews for the abolition of discrimination on Philadelphia's transportation system. At the same time a group of younger and more militant black Philadelphians, including Octavius V. Catto and John Oliver, determined to involve the black people themselves in the campaign. On March 3, 1864, at their instigation a mass meeting of Negroes in Philadelphia was held to consider the whole issue of streetcar exclusion. The resolutions, unanimously adopted by the meeting, noted that petitions and appeals to the presidents of the various companies had produced only evidence that these pleas had not even been considered by the corporations. They called for mounting a mass campaign by the Negroes of Philadelphia to persuade the legislature to "provide by law the right of all respectable colored persons the free use of every city passenger railway car, and by law, provide against the ejection or exclusion from equal enjoyment of all railroad privileges in the City and County of Philadelphia." The plan to seek legislative redress was acknowledged to have been influenced by the action of Senator Charles Sumner in the United States Senate in denouncing the Washington streetcar companies for excluding or segregating passengers on account of race and instructing, in a resolution, the Senate District of Columbia Committee to frame a law barring streetcar discrimination in the district. Apart from *The Christian Recorder,* only the Philadelphia *Press* carried any notice of the Negro mass meeting, a situation which caused the organ of the AME Church to comment bitterly that if only the newspapers of Philadelphia "would come out bold, and speaking against it," streetcar segregation would soon be a thing of the past.[45]

The battle against segregation now continued on three fronts: petitions to the presidents of the car companies; action in the courts; and lobbying in the state legislature. The car committee of the statistical association was once again the driving force in the petition movement. In 1864 the committee had high hopes of success in persuading the presidents of the car companies to change their policy. For one thing, the publication of letters from wounded black soldiers who had been ejected from the horsecars and those of relatives who wished to visit them in nearby hospitals had been too much for even some of Philadelphia's newspapers, and a number which had formerly been silent now began to carry news of the struggle against segregation. For another, New York City and San Francisco both abolished segregation on their street railroads in 1864, and these developments were publicized in Philadelphia. The fact that New York City, less than a year after the bloody draft riots during which wild mobs hanged, burned, and butchered Negroes, had seen fit to end streetcar segregation was pointed to by the friends of equality in Philadelphia as an indication of how far behind their city was in upholding the principles of freedom. The *Press* and the *North American and United States Gazette* reprinted the New York *Tribune*'s sharp editorial denouncing the forcible ejection from an Eighth Avenue car of the widow of a Negro sergeant who had been recently killed in battle. "It is quite time to settle the question whether the wives and children of the men who are laying down their lives for their country . . . are to be treated like dogs," the *Tribune* editorialized, and the foes of streetcar segregation in Philadelphia agreed that nowhere was there a more pressing need to "settle the question" than in their city.[46]

A good deal of publicity was also given to the decision of Judge C. C. Pratt in the Twelfth District Court of California which abolished segregation on San Francisco's streetcars. The case involved a Negro woman who had been forcibly ejected from a horsecar and who applied to the court for redress. The company answered to the court that its rules prohibited a Negro or mulatto person from riding in their cars. The plaintiff moved to strike out this rule.

Judge Pratt approached the subject as one of great public interest and comparatively new to the judicial record. He remarked that "this absence of precedent excited but little wonder when it is remembered in how light esteem negro or mulatto persons have been holden for near two hundred years by the whites, in whose control have been placed and exercised the law-making and law-construing powers of the land." He spoke of the injustice of the Dred Scott decision, and said,

> It has been already quite too long tolerated by the dominant race to see with indifference the negro or mulatto treated as a brute, insulted, wronged, enslaved, made to wear a yoke, to tremble before white men, to serve him as a tool, to hold property and life at his will, to surrender to him his intellect and conscience, and to seal his lips and belie his thought through dread of the white man's power.

Was not the government ordained to defend the weak against the strong, the Judge asked; to exalt right above might, and to assure the rights of each and all, however lowly or exalted, and to make them, as far as possible, inviolate? What was asked by the defendant in this case was nothing less than to make the court an instrument of power to trample upon rights; and, in support of this position, nothing was offered, "except the invocation of prejudices which have no holier origin than in brutal propensities, and a willingness to assist in perpetuating a relic of barbarism."

Conceding that railroad companies had a right to manage their own affairs, Judge Pratt insisted that they had no right to manage the affairs of the general public, which was exactly what they attempted to do by the exclusion of colored people. Where, he asked, did the companies find the right to make such distinctions between one and another on the ground of color? Only if legislation authorized the exclusion of colored people would the companies have the right to adopt rules authorizing the exclusion of passengers because of their color, and until such authorization was given, the color of a man's skin was an illegal reason for expelling him from a car. When the company obtained a railroad franchise, it also took on the responsibility of carrying in its cars

> all persons, whether of high or low degree in social life, the rich and the poor, the popular and unpopular, the Caucasian and the African, and all other civilized people, without distinction based upon classes, race or color. The law, in giving the right of exclusive carriage, enjoined the duty of transporting all who are physically fit, and willing to pay; and

that duty cannot be avoided or successfully evaded to the injury of classes, or individuals of a class, on account of prejudice arising from color or race, although performing its whole duty may tend to lessen the business or profits of defendant. With the *benefit* came the *burden,* and while the *one* is enjoyed the *other* must be borne.

The Philadelphia *Press* published the full text of Judge Pratt's opinion and, in an accompanying editorial praising the San Francisco jurist, predicted that it would be influential in ending "the pro-slavery rule which still disgraces the government of the city railroads." It urged the black community not to despair but keep up their protests. "If the colored people of this city are in earnest, and would maintain their self-respect, they must not cease to urge their civil rights. Not only justice but law is upon their side in this dispute, and their cause will be warmly sustained by all who despise prejudice, and the petty, inconsistent tyranny of these anti-republican rules."[47]

It was, therefore, with considerable confidence that the car committee made its second appearance before the presidents of the companies on December 7, 1864. The committee pointed to the fact that since their last petition to the board of presidents, New York had removed "every vestige of proscription" from all the city passenger cars. They asked if it were possible that there "was more prejudice and less humanity in Philadelphia than in New York?" The number of signatures to their petition, they insisted, gave the answer to this question and had convinced the committee that "should the oppressive and proscriptive rules be changed to-day, the great majority of the citizens of Philadelphia would acquiesce in the change." A change had occurred in public opinion since their last meeting with the presidents, a change the committee attributed to the growing sense of shame over the fact that relatives of wounded black soldiers could not visit their kinsmen and the awareness that due to the regulations of the city railways, "not one mother, wife or sister could be admitted even to see a United States soldier, a relative, although the presence and succor of said mother, wife or sister might save a life." The committee left, expressing the hope that their efforts this time would "meet with a more favorable response than before," and that before many weeks or months had passed, concrete action would be taken to remove the cause of complaint of the Philadelphia Negro community.[48]

This time the walls of prejudice were slightly cracked. The stock-holders of the West Philadelphia and Darby Road unanimously voted "that no discrimination ought to be made in the use of the public cars, to the exclusion of any person, except such as intended to secure good behaviour and general comfort" and requested the board of directors to adopt such regulations as would permit colored persons to ride in the cars. The directors then opened the cars to all passengers without regard to color. The Fifth and Sixth Streets line followed with the announcement that their cars would be "open to all decent and well-behaved persons without regard to complexion." But the other companies refused to budge. The Girard College and Ridge Avenue Road made what they termed "a concession" by agreeing to run special cars every half hour for colored people only, and the Union line, just beginning its operations, went a bit further by putting on separate cars to run regularly but to be labelled, "For Colored Only." The Negro community rejected these so-called concessions.[49]

The same meager results emerged from a meeting between the board of presidents and committees appointed by the Female Anti-Slavery Society and the Pennsylvania Society for the Abolition of Slavery. Not even the threat that the groups would urge a boycott of the cars, unless colored people were admitted as equals, moved the executives. One president was willing to run special cars at half-hour intervals; another to put on every fifth car and mark it "Colored," but the others, in the words of the abolitionist committee, "were cold and indifferent." A visit to several leading stockholders produced the response, "Get the community right, and then we will not object."[50]

Some abolitionists, including members of the Philadelphia Female Anti-Slavery Society, then voted to boycott the cars.[51] Others busied themselves helping to promote public protest meetings. The first developed from a suggestion made by Still to J. Miller McKim. Still proposed calling a mass meeting at the Concert Hall to be sponsored by many of the eminent Philadelphians who had signed the car committee petition.[52] McKim, an ardent foe of the car companies' Jim Crow policy, quickly agreed and rounded up the sixty-three sponsors. Among them were Henry C. Carey, the nationally-famous economist; Phillips Brooks, the young Episcopal minister soon to become famous as pastor of Trinity Church in Boston;

Thomas de Witt Talmage, another famous preacher; Jay Cooke, head of the international banking firm; James Mott and J. Miller McKim, veteran anti-slavery crusaders; clergymen of every religious persuasion in the city; and a large assortment of Philadelphia lawyers. Their names appeared under the notice of the call of a meeting "To take into consideration the question of the Colored People and the Street Cars," and they invited citizens of Philadelphia "who are opposed to the exclusion of respectable persons from the Passenger Railroad Cars, on the ground of complexion, to unite with them . . . to consider the subject, and take such action as may be deemed advisable."

The Concert Hall was full on Friday evening, January 13, 1865. The reporter for the *Press* was "agreeably surprised at the audience," since many of the "most respectable ladies and gentlemen that our city can boast were present." He was surprised, too, by the seating arrangement. Contrary to the usual practice in Philadelphia of assigning Negroes to a separate place in the balcony, if they were allowed to enter a hall, there were "quite a number of genteel colored persons" seated in the midst of the vast audience. On the platform were representatives of the clergy, the legal and medical professions, the mercantile interests, and several members of Congress, and here, too, black and white sat together.[53] Five white and two black Philadelphians addressed the audience, and one of the scheduled white speakers declined, saying "that colored people could speak for themselves." They did. Robert Purvis, the veteran abolitionist, spoke at length and insisted that the meeting demand that Negroes be given the right to ride the cars not as a favor but as a right. "We ask no favors, but in the name of the living God—we ask, 'Give us justice!'" he cried to thunderous applause. The Reverend Alston told the moving story of his inability to take his sick child home on the cars and remarked that though born and reared in the South, he had never before "met with a spirit so satanical as this car question in Philadelphia." The black minister did not confine himself to the car question but also condemned the exclusion of Negroes from the workshops of Philadelphia, pointing out that this was primarily responsible for widespread poverty in the Negro community and especially caused the black youth of the city "to hang their heads and hearts in despair."[54] None of the white speakers touched on this issue, but they did condemn "the higher circles of society" in Philadelphia for "moral cowardice" in having for so long accepted the existing pattern of discrimination against Negroes.

J. Miller McKim moved the audience with the story of how Robert Smalls was forbidden to ride to the Navy Yard to see his famous vessel, the *Planter*. The Reverend W. H. Furness told how he had resolved never again to use the streetcars after he had seen the mother and sister of a Negro soldier forced to stand on the front platform. And he called upon those present to boycott the cars until "they were managed with equal justice."

The meeting closed with the unanimous adoption of a series of resolutions. These expressed "shame and sorrow" over the fact that "decent women of color" had been forced to walk long distances or accept a standing position on the front platform of the cars, "exposed to the clemency of the weather," while visiting at the military hospitals their relatives who had been "wounded in the defence of the country." They also pointed out that "the two main causes" of the nation's struggle for its life were "the enslavement of the black man at the South, and contempt for him manifested at the North"; held it to be "fitting and just that both these great evils should disappear together," and specifically protested "against the assumption that an unchristian prejudice or a fastidious taste may longer be allowed to take precedence of justice and humanity in determining the rights of any class of our citizens to the use of our public conveniences and institutions." The resolutions also asserted that the rights of colored people in the cars should be without qualification or limitation; condemned the recently-instituted practice of running special cars at long intervals "bearing aloft the degrading label of caste," and described this as "a simple substitution of one act of injustice for another, and as much in violation of their rights as is their total exclusion." The heart of the resolutions was the statement of firm opposition to "the expulsion of respectable persons from our Passenger Railroad cars on the ground of complexion," and the request that the directors of the street railway companies withdraw the discriminatory rule in the name of "justice and humanity."[55]

Quite a few of the participants at the meeting were convinced that "the character and high social standing" of the men involved in the protest all but guaranteed that the streetcar issue was settled. Phillips

Brooks assured his father that the meeting would bring a quick end "of our special Philadelphia iniquity of excluding negroes from the cars." But the *Sunday Dispatch*, while agreeing it was high time "the iniquity" was ended, was not so optimistic. "The prejudice against colored passengers in the City railway cars is probably stronger than in any other city in the Union," it reminded the participants in the meeting. "Whether the present movement will result in the dissipation of prejudice and the removal of restrictions remains to be seen." It feared that the voices of Philadelphians who believed "that 'niggers should be kept in their proper places,'" would carry more weight than those of the advocates of removing restrictions on the rights of Negroes to travel.[56]

It turned out that the *Dispatch* knew Philadelphia better than did the young Episcopal minister. A committee, headed by McKim and James Mott, had been appointed at the public meeting to negotiate with those street railway companies which still practiced discrimination. The group immediately requested that the presidents rescind the regulation excluding colored persons from the cars. The companies replied that they could not admit Negroes in opposition to the wishes of their passengers and proposed that the issue be settled by a "poll" in the cars. The committee protested vehemently against this "new method of settling our social questions," but the company presidents were adamant.[57]

While the news of the forthcoming balloting was making the rounds of the city, an incident occurred which demonstrated how low the foes of equality were willing to sink to guarantee a vote against opening the cars to Negroes. On a car of the Fifth and Sixth Street Railway, one of the two lines which had abolished the regulation excluding Negroes from inside the cars, two blacks entered and sat down. A white man accompanying them paid their fare. Their clothes were covered with filth and emitted a foul odor. Several passengers objected, and the men were arrested. Brought before a magistrate, they told their story. They had been working cleaning cesspools when they were approached by Alderman William McMullin and offered a sum of money to go to an address on Fifth and Brown Streets and bring back a box. They were instructed to ride inside the car going and coming, and to stay close to a white man who would accompany them. When they entered the car, they realized that the odor from their clothes was causing resentment among the passengers, and they tried to go forward and stand on the platform. But the white person with them refused to permit them to leave. Before they could get away, they were arrested.

The magistrate, noting that they had violated no law, discharged the two blacks. But black Philadelphians were furious that their enemies, in the attempt to sway the forthcoming vote on the streetcars, had stooped to using innocent, hard-working Negroes as instruments in their diabolical plot. *The Christian Recorder* demanded Alderman McMullin be relieved of his office immediately, an appeal which fell on deaf ears. The *Recorder* saw some consolation for black Philadelphians in the "dastardly incident." Perhaps now even those in the city who had had doubts would finally begin to understand something of "the malignant and disgraceful prejudice exising against the colored people."[58]

NOTES

1. Edward Needles, *An Historical Memoir of the Pennsylvania Society for Promoting the Abolition of Slavery, the Relief of Free Negroes Unlawfully Held in Bondage, and for Improving the Condition of the African Race* (Philadelphia, 1848), pp. 14, 32, 54; Arthur Zilversmit, *The First Emancipation: The Abolition of Slavery in the North* (Chicago, 1967), p. 206; James M. McPherson, *The Struggle for Equality: Abolitionists and the Negro in the Civil War and Reconstruction* (Princeton, N.J., 1964), p. 233. There were two separate abolitionist societies in Philadelphia: the "Abolition Society," founded in 1775; and the better known "Anti-Slavery Society," formed in 1834.

2. Ruth Nuremberger, *The Free Produce Movement* (Durham, N.C., 1942), pp. 119–132; "Free Produce Among the Quakers," *Atlantic Monthly,* XXII (October, 1868), 485–494.

3. U.S. Bureau of the Census, *Negro Population, 1790–1915* (Washington, D.C., 1918), pp. 60–62. The majority of Philadelphia's Negroes lived in South Philadelphia, Southwark, and Moyamensing. (Ellis Oberholtzer, *Philadelphia: A History of the City and Its People, A Record of 225 Years* [Philadelphia, 1912], II, 281–291.) For a seminal study of the place of the Negro in the ante-bellum North, see Leon F. Litwack *North of Slavery: The Negro in the Free States, 1790–1860* (Chicago, 1961).

4. Philip S. Foner, *Business & Slavery: The New York Merchants and the*

Irrepressible Conflict (Chapel Hill, N.C., 1941), p. 1 "Colorphobia is more rampant here than in the pro-slavery, negro-hating city of New York," William Wells Brown wrote of Philadelphia in 1854. (William Wells Brown, *The American Fugitive in Europe: Sketches of Places & People Abroad* [New York, 1855], p. 312.) No publisher was willing to issue *Uncle Tom's Cabin.* (See William Dusenberre, *Civil War Issues in Philadelphia, 1856–1865* [Philadelphia, 1965], p. 21.)

5. *National Anti-Slavery Standard,* December 10, 17, 1859. A committee of Negroes had been appointed at a meeting of sympathy for Brown in a Negro church to meet Brown's body at the railroad station, but Mayor Henry hastily gathered a large police force, banned unauthorized persons from entering the station, and ordered the body sent on from Philadelphia. (Philadelphia *North American,* December 3, 5, 1859; *Pennsylvanian,* November 29, December 1, 3, 1859; Philadelphia *Ledger,* December 3, 1859; Philadelphia *Dispatch,* December 4, 1859.)

6. *Proceedings of the Anti-Slavery Convention of American Women* (Philadelphia, 1839), p. 6; *Friend,* August 1, 1840; Carleton Mabee, *Black Freedom: The Non-violent Abolitionists from 1830 Through the Civil War* (New York, 1970), pp. 92, 94. The reference to the "noble few" is by Samuel Douglass, a black Quaker and is quoted in Benjamin Quarles, *Black Abolitionists* (New York, 1969), p. 73.

7. John Runcie, "Hunting the Nigs' in Philadelphia: The Race Riot of August, 1834," *Pennsylvania History,* XXXIX (April, 1972), 189–190. Philadelphia was again the scene of anti-Negro riots in 1838, 1842, and 1849.

8. Zilversmit, *First Emancipation,* p. 207; James Forten, *A Series of Letters by A Man of Color* (Philadelphia, 1813); *Appeal of Forty Thousand Citizens, Threatened with Disfranchisement, to the People of Pennsylvania* (Philadelphia, 1838); Edward R. Turner, *The Negro in Pennsylvania Slavery-Servitude-Freedom, 1639–1861* (Washington, D.C., 1911), pp. 122, 136, 148, 152–153; Charles M. Snyder, *The Jacksonian Heritage: Pennsylvania Politics, 1833–1848* (Harrisburg, 1958), p. 105. The Pennsylvania legislature considered and rejected proposals to limit the rights of free Negroes in 1805–07, 1813–14, 1819–20, 1831–32, and 1860, Oberholtzer, *Philadelphia,* II, 286–288.

9. *Pennsylvania Laws* (May 8, 1854), p. 623; Ira V. Brown, "Pennsylvania and the Rights of the Negro, 1865–1887," *Pennsylvania History,* XXVIII (January, 1961), 46.

10. Quarles, *Black Abolitionists,* p. 72. Ward, however, came under sharp attack from Frederick Douglass for capitulating to Philadelphia's anti-Negro prejudice by lecturing in the Second Presbyterian Church despite the fact that the notice for the meeting announced that "the lower Saloon will be

appropriated exclusively for our white fellow citizens." Douglass issued a special supplement to *The North Star,* May 23, 1850, headed "Shameful Abandonment of Principle" in which he denounced his fellow abolitionist's "shameful concession to the spirit of slavery and prejudice. . . ." (Philip S. Foner, *Life and Writings of Frederick Douglass* [New York, 1950], II, 121–127.)

11. John Campbell, *Negro-Mania, Being An Examination of the Falsely Assumed Equality of the Various Races of Man. . . .* (Philadelphia, 1851), p. 545.

12. *The Christian Recorder,* October 31, 1863.

13. *Ibid.,* October 6, 1866.

14. *The North Star,* May 30, 1850, reprinted in Foner, *The Life and Writings of Frederick Douglass,* II, 125.

15. *The North Star,* October 19, 1849, reprinted in Foner, *The Life and Writings of Frederick Douglass,* I, 407.

16. *The North Star,* April 12, 1850, reprinted in Foner, *Life and Writings of Frederick Douglass,* II, 119–120. For evidence that Douglass's prediction came true, see speech of Robert Purvis at the American Anti-Slavery Society, May 8, 1860, *Liberator,* May 18, 1860.

Writing to Gerrit Smith in July, 1852, Douglass indicated that in planning to travel to Pittsburgh from Rochester to attend the Free Soil Convention, he deliberately sought to avoid Philadelphia. " . . . I should encounter the 'American demon' [racism] that way, more than by way of Cincinnati." (Frederick Douglass to Gerrit Smith, July 20, 1852, Gerrit Smith Papers, George Arents Research Library, Syracuse University.)

17. *Douglass' Monthly,* February, 1862. See also speech of John S. Rock to the Massachusetts Anti-Slavery Society, January 23, 1862, *Liberator,* February 14, 1862.

18. Gilbert Barnes, ed., *Letters of Theodore Dwight Weld, Angelina Grimke Weld and Sarah Grimke* (New York, 1934), pp. 273, 379–381.

19. Frederic W. Speirs, *The Street Railway System of Philadelphia. Its History and Present Condition* (Baltimore, 1897), pp. 11–17.

20. Brown, *American Fugitive in Europe,* pp. 312–313. For Brown's earlier experience in Philadelphia see "My First Visit to Philadelphia," *Liberator,* September 1, 1848. In this piece Brown complained only of the churches in the city.

21. Philadelphia *Press,* December 22, 1865.

22. Goines vs. McCandless, 4 *Philadelphia Reports,* p. 255; *Twenty-Seventh Annual Report of the Philadelphia Female Anti-Slavery Society* (Philadelphia, 1861), p. 17.

23. The Rev. Robert J. Parvin in Philadelphia *Press,* March 22, 1865. The

Union League of Philadelphia had been reluctant even to organize a company of Negro troops for fear of the hostility to the soldiers in the city. When a company was raised and the Negro troops marched through the city in 1863, Mayor Henry was so fearful that they would be attacked by whites that the Negroes marched without arms. (George Lathrop, *History of the Union League of Philadelphia from its Origin and Foundation to the Year 1882* [Philadelphia, 1884], pp. 75–77, 79–81.) See also Alexander Henry to George Cadwalder, July 30, 1863, Cadwalder Collection, Historical Society of Pennsylvania (HSP).

24. *Thirtieth Annual Report of the Philadelphia Anti-Slavery Society* (Philadelphia, 1864), pp. 23–24.

25. Philadelphia *Press,* August 31, 1864.

26. Philadelphia *Sunday Dispatch,* August 27, 1865.

27. Frances E. W. Harper in Philadelphia *Evening Telegram,* March 20, 1866, and reprinted in *The Christian Recorder,* March 24, 1866.

28. Philadelphia *Evening Bulletin,* January 14, 1865.

29. The Reverend J. Alston in Philadelphia *Press,* July 21, 1864.

30. Speirs, *Street Railway System of Philadelphia,* pp. 22–23; Philadelphia *Sunday Dispatch,* March 13, 1864; New York *Independent,* February 25, 1864; *Free Nation* reprinted in *National Anti-Slavery Standard,* June 3, 1865; *Thirty-Third Annual Report of the Philadelphia Female Anti-Slavery Society* (Philadelphia, 1867), p. 27; Frederick Douglass in the *Alumni Magazine,* Lincoln University, Pennsylvania, I (November, 1885), 124. Jewish rabbis in Philadelphia also refrained from speaking out on the issue. Throughout the battle against streetcar segregation, *The Occident and American Jewish Advocate* appeared monthly in the city, and carried frequent articles condemning discrimination against Jews in this country and abroad. But only one issue dealt with the streetcars, and that, like the concern shown by Christian ministers, dealt with the operation of cars on Sunday. Since religious Jews did not ride on Saturday, the journal called the prohibition of Sunday cars a special blow at the Jewish community. (*The Occident and American Jewish Advocate,* XXIV [1867], 405–419.) *The Occident and American Jewish Advocate* was published and edited by Rabbi Isaac Leeser. For a discussion of the Jewish community on the eve of the Civil War, see Philip S. Foner, *The Jews in American History, 1654–1865* (New York, 1945) pp. 43–50.

31. James M. McPherson, *The Negro's Civil War* (New York, 1965), pp. 255–256. But the issue does not seem to have been important enough to merit even a mention in William Dusinberre's study, *Civil War Issues in Philadelphia, 1856–1865,* published in 1965 nor in Edwin Stanley Bradley's book, *The Triumph of Militant Republicanism: A Study of Pennsylvania*

and Presidential Politics, 1860–1872, published in 1964. Both books were published by the University of Pennsylvania Press.

32. For the details of William Still's life, see James P. Boyd, "William Still: His Life and Work to this Time," in *Still's Underground Railroad* (Revised Edition, Hartford, 1886), pp. i–xiv, and Lara Gara, "William Still and the Underground Railroad," *Pennsylvania History,* XXVII (January, 1961), 33–39. Joseph A. Boromé, "The Vigilant Committee of Philadelphia," *Pennsylvania Magazine of History and Biography,* XCII (July, 1968), 320–351. Still became nationally famous as the author of *The Underground Railroad* (Philadelphia, 1872).

33. Alberta S. Norwood, "Negro Welfare Work in Philadelphia, Especially as Illustrated by the Career of William Still, 1775–1930" (M.A. Thesis, University of Pennsylvania, 1931), p. 4.

34. Roger A. Fischer, "Racial Segregation in Ante Bellum New Orleans," *American Historical Review,* LXXIV (February, 1969), 932; McPherson, *Struggle for Equality,* p, 233 *n.*

35. Philadelphia *North American and United States Gazette,* September 14, 1859.

36. *A Brief Narrative of the Struggle for the Rights of the Colored People of Philadelphia on the City Railway and a Defence of William Still Relating to His Agency Touching the Passage of the Late Bill, Etc.* (Philadelphia, 1867), pp. 1–2.

37. Minutes of the Executive Committee of the Social, Cultural, and Statistical Association of the Colored People of Pennsylvania, *Ms.,* HSP.

38. Philadelphia *Evening Bulletin,* June 11, 1862; *The Christian Recorder,* June 14, 1862. Among the signers were Bishop Alonzo Potter, Horace Binney, Morton McMichael, Gibson Peacock, John Lawlor, Daniel Dougherty, the Reverend Phillips Brooks, and about forty-two other Methodist and Episcopal Church ministers. The original petition with all of the signatures is in the Historical Society of Pennsylvania.

39. New York *Tribune, August 4–7,* 1863.

40. *The Christian Recorder,* June 14, 1862.

41. *Ibid.;* Philadelphia *Press,* June 14–16, 1862; *A Brief Narrative of the Struggle for the Rights of Colored People,* p. 7.

42. John Oliver in *The Christian Recorder,* October 31, 1863.

43. Philadelphia *Press,* December 12, 1863.

44. *National Anti-Slavery Standard,* January 2, 1864; *A Brief Narrative of the Struggle for the Rights of Colored People,* pp. 8–10.

45. Philadelphia *Press,* March 4, 1864; *The Christian Recorder,* March 5, 1864. For Sumner's actions in the Senate on the streetcar segregation in

Washington, see James M. McPherson, *The Negro's Civil War* (New York, 1965), pp. 261–262.

46. Philadelphia *Evening Bulletin,* Philadelphia *North American,* June 23, 1864, quoting New York *Tribune,* June 21, 1864. By the end of June, 1864, both the Eighth Avenue and Sixth Avenue roads had ended exclusion of Negroes, and all of New York City's public transportation was integrated. (New York *Tribune,* June 30, 1864.)

47. Philadelphia *Press,* October 5, 1864, quoting San Francisco *Bulletin,* October 3, 1864; *Liberator,* November 18, 1864; *The Christian Recorder,* November 19, 1864.

48. Philadelphia *Press,* December 8, 1864.

49. *A Brief Narrative of the Struggle for the Rights of Colored People,* p. 11; Philadelphia *Sunday Dispatch,* January 25, 1865; *Thirty-First Annual Report of the Philadelphia Female Anti-Slavery Society* (Philadelphia, 1865), pp. 18–19.

50. *A Brief Narrative of the Struggle for the Rights of Colored People,* pp. 14–15.

51. *Thirtieth Annual Report of the Philadelphia Female Anti-Slavery Society* (Philadelphia, 1864), pp. 23–24.

52. William Still to J. Miller McKim, November 10, 1871, J. Miller McKim Papers, New York Public Library; William Cohen, "James Miller McKim: Pennsylvania Abolitionist" (Ph.D. Thesis, New York University, 1968), p. 305.

53. Philadelphia *Press,* January 10, 1865; see also *National Anti-Slavery Standard,* January 26, 1865.

54. Purvis was described as "a man of wealth and refinement, and he consequently feels very keenly the proscription he has been compelled to submit to upon account of his race." Purvis also recounted his experience during a passage to Europe when he moved freely among Southerners who, because of his light skin, did not know he was a Negro. He became good friends with a Virginia slaveholder of wealth, sharing walks on the deck with him, until he broke the news that he was a Negro. (Philadelphia *Press,* January 14, 1865; Philadelphia *Sunday Dispatch,* January 15, 1865.)

55. Philadelphia *Press,* January 14, 1865; Philadelphia *Sunday Dispatch,* January 15, 1865; *The Christian Recorder,* January 21, 1865.

56. Alexander V. G. Allen, *Life and Letters of Phillips Brooks* (New York, 1900). I, 527; Philadelphia *Sunday Dispatch,* January 25, 1865; *National Anti-Slavery Standard,* January 21, 1865.

57. *Report of the Committee Appointed for the Purpose of Securing to Colored in Philadelphia the Right to the Use of the Street Cars* (Philadel-

phia, 1867), pp. 1–2; *Why Colored People are Excluded from the Street Cars?* (Philadelphia, 1866), pp. 3–4.

58. Philadelphia *Press,* January 19–20, 1865; *The Christian Recorder,* January 21, 1865, *The Evening Bulletin* on January 18, 1865, concluded, after an investigation, that on the lines that allowed Negroes to ride inside the cars, "some of the vulgarest of the negrophobists have hired the dirtiest negroes they could find, to ride up and down all day in order to stir up feeling, and prevent a reformation of the abuse."

4

The Battle to End Discrimination Against Negroes on Philadelphia Streetcars: (Part II) The Victory*

On January 31, 1865, Congress adopted an amendment to the Constitution providing that neither slavery nor involuntary servitude should exist within the United States and sent it to the states for ratification. On that same day, indeed at the very hour that Congress adopted the Thirteenth Amendment, conductors on Philadelphia's streetcars announced that an overwhelming majority of the passengers had voted "no" on the proposal: "Shall colored persons be allowed to ride in all the cars?" Two years later Alfred H. Love, an important activist in the streetcar battle, recalled sadly: "To think that, when the Nation was voting *freedom,* we were voting exclusion of colored people from our cars—the grossest kind of slavery."[1]

The Frankford and Southward Company decided to ignore the poll and began admitting Negroes to its cars. The experiment lasted one month at the end of which the company announced that it had lost white passengers and suffered a decline in revenue. Thereafter it would allow Negroes only in special "Colored" cars.[2]

The Frankford and Southwark Company's experiment pointed out a special difficulty in ending streetcar discrimination. The male workers employed in the navy yard and the women who were working there on government clothing were the chief patrons of the line, and it was their opposition which did much to force the company to abandon its policy. In other words, the white working class of Philadelphia were among the chief supporters of segregation on streetcars. Yet Philadelphia at this time boasted one of the largest

*Reprinted from *Pennsylvania History,* XL (October, 1973), 355–379.

and most advanced labor movements in this country. And it was in this city at this time, too, that the most influential labor paper of the era, *Fincher's Trades' Review,* was published. The *Review,* edited by Jonathan Fincher of the Typographical Union, had on its editorial board representatives of the Molders, Printers, Ship Carpenters, Stone Cutters, Cabinet Makers, Carpenters, Hatters, and Shoemakers unions in Philadelphia. Between June 6, 1863, its first issue, and August 18, 1866, when the last issue came off the press, *Fincher's Trades' Review* appeared every Saturday. Had it concerned itself to any extent with the battle taking place in its own city for the right of a section of Philadelphia's working class to use the transportation facilities in going to and from work, and had the unions which were on its editorial board involved themselves in the campaign to end segregation on the streetcars, the results might have been very different. Unfortunately, although it strongly supported the Union cause during the war, as did all of the unions associated with it, *Fincher's Trades' Review* paid no attention to the streetcar issue. In the scores of editorials, union notices, and articles which appeared in the Philadelphia labor paper during its three years of existence, not a single one even mentioned the battle occurring in the city over the rights of Negroes on the streetcars.[3] But the labor paper did feature an editorial entitled "The Etiquette of Travel" in which it criticized the ladies of Philadelphia for scorning seats in the streetcars offered by "tired, poorly clad" workingmen "worn out by a hard day's work."[4] *Fincher's Trades' Review* called itself "An Advocate of the Rights of the Producing Classes." But it either did not believe black workers belonged to the producing classes, or, if they did, that they did not have any rights.

Many of Philadelphia's white workers received their education on the streetcar issue from the racist Philadelphia *Age,* a Copperhead daily filled with anti-Negro propaganda. Readers were told six days a week from the first issue in March, 1863, that Negroes were "barbarians," so "inclined to rape white women" that to allow them to sit next to Philadelphia ladies was to run the risk of having them attacked right on the floor of the streetcars. In addition to rape, opening the cars to blacks involved the risk of racial intermixture— "Miscegenation," as the editors of the *Age* were fond of calling this social phenomenon. Finally, there was the constant refrain in the

Age that the "bodily odors of Negroes" were enough reason to maintain the existing practice of segregation on the cars.[5] Opinion was so intense that when Mayor Alexander Henry sent a message to the city council bemoaning "the great loss of life on our city railroads," one correspondent in the Copperhead paper said he favored integration on streetcars because it would simply prompt more violence and thereby further reduce the size of the city's black population.[6]

Still seeking to accomplish something at the city level, the Concert Hall committee appealed to Mayor Henry, requesting him to prevent the use of the police to assist conductors in ejecting colored passengers. The mayor rejected the request and went on to uphold the segregation policy, saying that he did not wish "the ladies of his family to ride in the same car with colored people." The committee observed that "except in his more than average frankness," the mayor "well represented our educated, respectable, and religious classes." But the Reverend Elisha Weaver, the usually mild-mannered editor of *The Christian Recorder,* was so infuriated by the mayor's remark and the blank check it gave to Philadelphia's police and the streetcar conductors to manhandle blacks, that he announced: "We do not believe in fighting or taking life, but we greatly fear, that if Mayor Henry does not put a stop to such treatment by the police, and railroad conductors become more civil to persons of color, some of them may appear at the judgment bar of God before they are ready."[7]

It was not so easy to put the Reverend Weaver's policy of self-defense into practice. A few days after his warning to the police and conductors, three Negro men boarded a car of the Walnut and Chestnut Street line during a pelting cold rain. The conductor instantly informed them they could not ride. "You can draft us in the service, and why can we not ride?," one of the blacks asked. The conductor brushed this aside as irrelevant and insisted that the three get out into the rain. "We do not mean to get out; you can put us out if you choose. We came from Boston; we could ride in the cars there; we cannot see why we should not ride here." A white passenger rose to the conductor's defense and shouted in rage, "You know you are not allowed to ride in here." "If we are offensive to the passengers, we will get up and go out," the Negroes replied. "You are offensive to the ladies," the passenger shouted back. The two ladies in the car rose and said, "They are not offensive, but we want no disturbance." At this point the car was stopped, and the conductor called a policeman, who said to the three blacks, "You must leave the car, or be locked up." Asked if it was against the law for Negroes to ride, the policeman replied in the affirmative. One of the blacks shouted back, "It is *not* against the law, and you may lock me up." "Then I will take you first," the officer shouted, grabbing him by the collar roughly. The white passenger jumped to the policeman's assistance. Suddenly from the streets a gang of toughs pushed into the car and began beating the Negroes with clubs.

> "Feeling ourselves, however, to be men and not dogs," the three victims wrote in a signed letter published in the *Press*, "one of us determined to suffer risk of personal injury and the lock-up rather than run. He came in for more than a due proportion of blows, as fists and the billy were applied freely to his person, the head not be spared. We confess that in the excitement of the moment, we felt unwilling to endure the outrage without resentment, and at least one of us dealt a few blows in return. But we were overpowered and taken before an alderman. Here insult was, as it were, added to injury, for grave charges were made against us; and we soon found that we should be sent to the lock-up unless bail could be procured. For the time being, our minds were so much absorbed by reflections upon the outrages heaped upon us that we were not in a condition to think of this; hence we were incarcerated, as threatened, and remained so until a friend kindly came and procured our release. . . ."[8]

While seeking concessions from the companies, the advocates of equal rights had been also attempting to win in the courts. Criminal prosecution was instituted against a number of conductors who had ejected Negroes from the cars. But the grand juries stymied these efforts by refusing to indict. Only in civil cases was there success. In May, 1865, a conductor on the Lombard and South Street line was tried in the Court of Quarter Sessions upon the charge of having violently thrust "a respectable colored woman" from a car. The old woman had been on her way home from church, where she had been engaged in providing comforts for wounded soldiers. After she had been seated for only a few minutes, the conductor came in and told her she must get out, "that no niggers were allowed to ride on that line." She pleaded the lateness of the hour, that there were only two or three passengers in the car, none of whom objected, and finally asserted her right to remain. The conductor called in two friends standing upon a street corner, took off his coat, seized hold of the old woman, struck, kicked, and finally threw her from the car with great force, tearing her clothes and inflicting personal injury.

The usual defense was raised: the conductor was only carrying out the rules of the company which prohibited colored passengers on the cars. Judge Allison, however, charged the jury that, while common carriers could keep out obnoxious individuals of any race or class, they could not make color distinctions. He went further, declaring:

> The logic of the past four years has in many respects cleared our vision and corrected our judgment, and no proposition has been more clearly wrought out by them than that the men who have been deemed worthy to become defenders of the country, to wear the uniform of the soldier of the United States, should not be denied the rights common to humanity.

The jury, probably startled to hear such words uttered in a Philadelphia courtroom, quickly returned a verdict in favor of the Negro passenger and awarded her damages of fifty dollars "for the indignity that had been put upon her."

The *Evening Bulletin* which had the distinction of being one of the two newspapers in the entire city to venture editorial comment on the policies of the streetcar companies—the *Press* was the other—hailed the judge's charge to the jury and the latter's verdict. It was a hard-hitting editorial, and so unusual for Philadelphia that it merits quotation in full:

> The public highways are not the exclusive property of persons of any particular shade of complexion, and the railway companies that have obtained the use of them without cost to themselves, and to the complete exclusion of every other vehicle of public conveyance through the streets, have no more right to refuse to carry well-behaved colored passengers, than the owners of the Penrose Ferry Bridge have a right to forbid black men crossing the Schuylkill by means of their structure. Fastidious persons who do not like to ride with "niggers," can, if they can afford it, loll in their own private coaches, with company of their own choosing. They can exclude blacks from their private halls, forbid them pressing their velvet carpets—but when they take to the public

conveyances, they must submit to such associations, under proper restrictions, as chance throws in their way. The right of transit is not the exclusive privilege of any particular class, and the common carrier has no more right to refuse the privileges he pays for to the colored passenger, than he has a right to block his foot-passage through the common highway, or deprive him of the common blessings of light, air and water. Where a mulet of fifty dollars will be sure to follow every expulsion of a respectable colored person from a city railway car, such expulsions will become very rare, and the strong arm of the law will be found more potent than the influence of common sense or the sentiment of fair play have proved, in breaking down a cruel and unreasonable prejudice.[9]

In the battle against streetcar segregation, optimistic predictions invariably proved to be wrong, and the *Bulletin's* conclusion, that conductors would now think twice about ejecting colored passengers, was no exception. None of the companies changed their regulations, and the difficulty of obtaining white witnesses who would testify against conductors made civil cases ineffective. Like petitions to the companies, the courts proved to be a frail reed for foes of streetcar discrimination to lean on.[10]

Defeated at all levels in the city itself, the champions of equal rights turned to the state legislature. Particularly important in advancing the cause in the legislature was the Pennsylvania State Equal Rights League. The league was an offshoot of the great National Convention of Colored Citizens of the United States, held in Syracuse, New York, October 4–7, 1864, and attended by 144 Negroes from eighteen states, including seven slave states. The convention adopted resolutions calling for equal rights and justice in the reconstruction of the Union, issued an "Address to the People of the United States," written by Frederick Douglass, and organized a National Equal Rights League, with John Mercer Langston of Ohio as president, to work for equal rights and equal opportunities for Negroes.[11] By the beginning of 1865 state leagues had come into existence in eight states, one of them in Pennsylvania. The Pennsylvania league published its constitution in January, 1865, and held its first convention in Harrisburg the following month. The call for the convention emphasized three issues: voting rights, officer commissions for colored soldiers, and equal public schools.[12] But the convention adopted a resolution dealing with civil rights which read: "As the nation has cast off slavery, let them destroy restrictions which prevent colored people from entering libraries, colleges, lecture rooms, military academies, jury boxes, churches, theatres, street cars, and from voting."[13]

The abolition of streetcar segregation became a major early objective of the league. Alfred M. Green, Octavius V. Catto, and John Oliver, already deeply involved in the streetcar battle, represented the organization in lobbying in the state legislature for passage of a law to prohibit street railway companies from excluding persons on account of color.[14]

In this activity the league worked closely with Morrow B. Lowry, senator from Erie and Crawford counties. Lowry was a *rara avis* in the Pennsylvania legislature. Fit to be ranked in many ways with his great predecessor, Thaddeus Stevens, he was described by Garrison as "a most radical abolitionist."[15] Already in 1861 Lowry had introduced a bill in the Senate to prohibit segregation in public transportation, only to see it bottled up in the committee of the judiciary. On January 19, 1865, after conferences with a delegation from the State Equal Rights League, Lowry again introduced his bill, and this time it was considered by the Senate.[16]

The language of the bill was simple. It stated: "That it shall not be lawful for any passenger railway company, within this Commonwealth, to make or enforce any rule, regulation or practice, excluding any race of people from its passenger cars on account of color." But Lowry's speech in favor of his bill was a detailed presentation of the necessity for such legislation, expressed in strong, often passionate, words. "Slavery is the cause of the war," he began, "and it alone made rebellion possible. He is the best friend of the Union, who goes farthest and fullest for the destruction of the Union's great enemy. We can no longer ignore truth. Upon its treatment of the black man, rests the fate of the Republic." It was not enough, he insisted, to make the black man "nominally Free." It was not enough to cease to make him a slave. "We must make him, also, truly a freeman." It might not be possible "to pull down the whole fabric of wrong and outrage at once," but it was possible and necessary to remove "one by one" the disabilities under which black people lived and suffered. One of the most galling of these disabilities was the "wholesale exclusion" of blacks from the passenger railways, especially in Philadelphia. The proposed bill was not the result of rumors, it was the product of his own personal observations:

> I have seen it made impossible, for the friends and families of sick and wounded soldiers, to go to them on errands of mercy and missions of love. I have seen a soldier with but one leg—the other having been given to his country—rudely prohibited from entering the cars, and forced to plod his weary way through storm and darkness, as best he might! Outrages of this nature, are liable to be of daily occurrence. What a spectacle for the civilized world to contemplate! A soldier of the republic, having done heroic battle, and risked his life that his country may live, returning to his home in Philadelphia, scarred, and perhaps permanently disabled, is denied the privileges extended to the very lowest and most repulsive vagabond of the city—denied by men for whose sake and safety he has periled all, even life itself! Can we rationally hope to have the curse of war lifted from our land, so long as we tolerate such wrongs upon the race, to *avenge* whose wrongs "God has let upon us the dogs of war?"

Lowry warned that if a railway company had the legal right to exclude men and women because of the complexion of their skin, it could next exclude those with red hair, short or tall people, or members of any race or religion the managers disliked. Where would it all end? He accused the companies of allowing their policies to be determined not by the decent elements of society, intelligent men and women of character, but by "political hucksters" who catered to what they supposed to be popular prejudice and by the lowest elements in the community—"the swaggering, bullying loafer," the prostitute; those, in short, who sought to elevate themselves at the expense of the Negro.

After a fulsome tribute to the contributions of the Negro to the Union cause, in the course of which he called the blacks "the only loyal class, *as a class,* in the whole land," Lowry remarked bitterly that upon returning to their homes after fighting for the nation, "we drive them from our street cars as though they were ministers of death rather than of life. Behold the spectacle of a people calling upon the black man to help save their government, and then basely denying them civil and social rights under the government which they have helped to save!" He closed his eloquent speech by conceding that he had been subjected to vile attacks because of his crusade for equal rights on the streetcars. But he scorned such critics. They swore by the Dred Scott decision; he by the Golden Rule; they would "re-enslave the Negro after the danger is past and the war over—*I* would reward him with freedom and justice."[17]

The Philadelphia *Press* urged the legislature not to adjourn before enacting Lowry's bill. It was bad enough when Negro men, women, and children were not allowed to ride the streetcars, but increasingly Philadelphians were required to read of their city's "shame" over the exclusion of colored soldiers "by people who care nothing for the struggle in which we are engaged, and who, while realizing fortunes out of profitable enterprises, use their power to insult brave men who are ready to offer their lives for the old flag." Unless the legislature acted, "men who peril their lives for the Republic" would continue to be "insulted under the rules of these companies while on the way to their headquarters."[18]

The state senate passed Lowry's bill by a close vote, but in the house it was smothered in the Passenger Railway committee. Delegations from the Colored People's Union League, the Social, Civil, and Statistical Association of Colored People, and the Pennsylvania Anti-Slavery Society pleaded with the twelve Republicans of the fifteen-member railway committee—eight of them from Philadelphia—to report the bill to the house. They were told that compliance with the request would guarantee their defeat in the next election. To make certain that Lowry's bill never saw the light of day, its opponents resorted to the tactic of having it stolen from the chairman's file so that it could be said that there was no such measure under consideration by the railway committee.[19]

Before the state and municipal elections of 1865, the Pennsylvania Anti-Slavery Society appointed an interracial car committee to query every candidate on whether, if elected, he would use his influence in favor of colored persons riding in the passenger railway cars. The circular letter pointed out: "In view of the momentous issues arising out of the present condition of the Southern States, and the demands made for the abolition of all unjust distinctions on account of complexion, we deem it right to rid ourselves most promptly of the shameful practice of excluding colored persons from our cars, and to have your reply at the earliest moment possible."

A number of Republican candidates indicated they would favor equality in the cars, but all of the Democrats made it clear they would oppose removing the restrictive ban, and several accused the abolitionist committee of seeking to open the doors to "amalgamation of the races."[20] In any event, throughout 1866 neither the Republicans nor the Democrats moved in either the city council or the state legislature to alter the *status quo* on the car issue.

Here is how the situation stood at the end of 1866 almost eight years after the battle to end segregation on the streetcars had been launched. Philadelphians were now spared having to read reports of incidents of mistreatment of blacks, for the simple reason that Negroes rarely entered the cars, knowing that they risked severe beatings and arrests, and, at the very least, humiliation, cruelty, and injustice. The incident that finally convinced Negroes that it was better to walk, hire a carriage, or simply stay at home rather than make an effort to ride the cars occurred in the fall of 1866. Miles Robinson, his wife, and infant entered a car on Spruce street, and being light-skinned, the conductor did not make an objection until he noticed, on asking for Mrs. Robinson's fare, that she appeared to be darker than her husband. Taking no chances, he ordered them to leave the car. The weather was bitter cold, it was night, the walk was long, and the exposure would have been hazardous to their little child, so they refused. This time the white passengers, about twenty in number, supported the Negro family. But the conductor, insisting he would lose his job if the Negroes remained in the car, shouted that he would have to follow company rules, throw the car off the track, and empty it of passengers. This he proceeded to do. When the Robinsons still remained in the car alone, the conductor threw open the doors and windows and even removed the cushions with the aim of "freezing them out." Finally, the Robinsons had to leave the car, and they walked home in the freezing cold, while the following car picked up the white passengers standing in the dark.[21]

Shortly after this incident, the Pennsylvania Anti-Slavery Society met at Franklin Institute for its twenty-ninth annual meeting. Lucretia Mott pleaded for a new campaign to end streetcar segregation. "The hour has come to demand it now," she cried. Several speakers replied that it was pointless to try to change the existing situation. Henry Peterson, editor of the *Saturday Evening Post,* predicted that all efforts and funds expended in the streetcar campaign would be wasted. "Even an army of occupation here could not put the negro into the street cars," he told the black and white delegates to the convention.[22]

Black Philadelphians were almost unanimously of the same opinion. At the December 17, 1866, meeting of the Social, Civil, and Statistical Association of Colored People, Stephen Smith insisted that nothing further would be gained by attempting to change the streetcar regulations since there was nothing to expect in the way of meaningful support from the white people of the city. He had an "entire lack of confidence in them."[23] The Reverend B. F. Barrett stressed the same theme in a sermon to his congregation. "It is the city of Philadelphia, then, that I arraign. . . . It is the community, and not merely the street railway companies, that exclude or eject colored people from the cars; for it is the community that justify and uphold the companies in their wrong and unchristian conduct."[24] A group of white Philadelphians, all of whom had been involved in the streetcar campaign, conceded that the indictment was justified. In a pamphlet published in 1866 entitled *Why Colored People in Philadelphia Are Excluded from the Street Cars?,* they summarized the long and futile battle to end streetcar segregation and observed gloomily:

> We are forced then to the conclusion that this community, as a body, by long indulgence in the wicked habit of wronging and maltreating colored people, has become, like a moral lunatic, utterly powerless, by the exercise of its own will, to resist or control the propensity. And unless it finds an authoritative and sane guardian and controller in the Supreme Court—unless this Court has itself, by chance, escaped this widely spread moral imbecility of vicious type, there seems to be no cure for the disease, nor end to its wickedness. And Philadelphia must continue to stand, as she now does, alone, among all the cities of the old free States in the exercise of this most infamous system of class persecution.[25]

Yet only a few months after this hopeless note was sounded, the street railway corporations of Philadelphia ceased either to exclude or segregate colored passengers. To understand the reason for this remarkable development, one must focus not on Philadelphia but on Washington and Harrisburg. In the two years since Morrow B. Lowry's bill to outlaw discrimination on the streetcars had passed the

Senate but failed in the House, the Radical Republican program of Reconstruction had been moving forward in Congress over the opposition of President Andrew Johnson. The Radical Republicans, under the leadership of Pennsylvania's Thaddeus Stevens and Massachusetts's Charles Sumner, had put through the Civil Rights Act and the Fourteenth Amendment, which conferred state and national citizenship on "all persons born or naturalized in the United States" and provided to any person the equal protection of the law. In February, 1867, the Pennsylvania legislature ratified the Fourteenth Amendment. Thus equal rights for Negroes was now, at least in intent, state policy. On March 2, 1867, Congress overrode President Johnson's vetoes and passed the Radical Reconstruction acts. New governments were to be established in the South by delegates to conventions elected by universal manhood (including Negro) suffrage, and these governments were to guarantee Negro voting and office holding rights, and to ratify the Fourteenth Amendment. It was clear even to a political novice that the Negro in Pennsylvania would soon again be armed with the ballot, and he would have to be reckoned with as a political force. In the fall elections of 1866 the *Age* had raised the spectre of a Haiti-like rule in Philadelphia if the blacks received the vote, and the anti-Negro sentiment was so whipped up by the Democrats that mobs attacked and burned the Union League House. Still the Radical Republicans won a narrow victory, and Negro suffrage now appeared to be certain.[26]

It is to the credit of the Pennsylvania State Equal Rights League that it quickly sensed that developments in Washington would have an important influence in producing a change of heart among the very members of the General Assembly who had refused in 1865 even to report Senator Lowry's bill. In January, 1867, the league's car committee, in cooperation with the committees of the Colored People's Union League and the Statistical Association, began a new and more intensive lobbying campaign in the legislature, pointing out to members of that body that when he received the vote, the black man would know how to use it for his friends and against his enemies, and that how a member of the legislature voted on the car issue would be a major test of friendship.[27] The Equal Rights League's car committee prepared a bill which Senator Lowry introduced into the Senate on February 5, 1867. The measure was more specific and detailed than the one he had sponsored two years before. The bill made it an offense for railroad corporations within the Commonwealth to make any distinction with their passengers on account of race or color and stipulated punishments for corporations, their agents, and employees for the commission of such offenses. The corporation would be liable in an action of debt to the person injured or aggrieved in the sum of five hundred dollars, and any agent, conductor, or employee of any railroad or railway corporation who excluded or allowed to be excluded, or assisted in the exclusion "from any of their cars, set apart for the accommodation of passengers, any person, or persons, on account of color, race, or who shall refuse to carry such person, or persons, on account of color, or race, or who shall throw any car, or cars, from the track, thereby preventing persons from riding, shall be deemed guilty of a misdemeanor, and upon conviction thereof, shall pay a fine, not exceeding five hundred dollars, nor less than one hundred dollars, or be imprisoned, for a term not exceeding three months, nor less than thirty days, or both, at the discretion of the court."[28]

Once again Lowry spoke in favor of equal rights in transportation, repeating many of the points he had made in his speech two years before. But this time he was sharper in his indictment of the City of Brotherly Love. In words that must have caused even calloused Philadelphians to blush with shame, the Senator from northwestern Pennsylvania declared scornfully:

Philadelphia stands disgraced before the world, for her conduct in attempting to block up the highway of the colored man in his great and unequal contest in the battles of life. I arraign Philadelphia, her newspapers, her corporations, her judges, her lawyers, her churches, and her citizens, and pronounce them hostile to the execution of justice between man and man. History will be just toward Philadelphia, and the fact will be recorded to her everlasting discredit, that she left her weak, her poor, and her defenseless citizens to be trodden down by the Copperheads, and the demoralized, the wealthy, the wicked and the strong. Philadelphia, in the face of the judgment of God for our sins of oppression upon a weaker race, is the last city that inflicts this cruel barbarity upon a redeemed race, and denies the right of equal facilities of transportation to black and white. Philadelphia is the only city, where the Lord's prayer is repeated, which compels a respected woman of color to borrow a white baby before she can receive admission into the streetcars. Philadelphia will not permit a colored woman to take her honest-begotten child in her arms into a street car to be carried to a baptismal fount, but a base-born white child will protect her from being kicked into the streets by a conductor. . . .[29]

Democratic senators did not blush. They stoutly defended the practice of excluding Negroes from the cars. W. H. McCandless, Democrat of Philadelphia, said flatly, "I do not desire to ride with them" and charged that the Republicans were supporting the bill simply to get the Negro vote. To "eke out their lease of political power a little longer, they will grovel in the dust before this black god of their idolatry." Senator William A. Wallace of Clearfield, chairman of the state Democratic committee, asked bluntly if the legislature was willing "to give to the most brutal and degraded negro a seat side by side with the cultivated and intellectual lady. Shall the barbarous and brutal negro, just emancipated from slavery, be your equal? Shall he sit side by side with you?" He concluded, "if you are ready for this thing, we are not; and I, as one of the representatives of the people of Pennsylvania, assert that they are not ready for it."[30]

Other Senators shared this view, but not enough to prevent passage of the bill on February 10 by the vote of eighteen to thirteen. Nine days later the car committee reported to the Pennsylvania State Equal Rights League that for the first time in eight years there was reason for optimism. "The prospects for its (the bill's) passage through the House are cheering," said Octavius V. Catto, for the committee. "It will be brought up at the earliest possible moment. The (Committee) are sanguine that the governor will sign it without hesitancy."[31]

For once a prediction related to the car issue came true. In the house the bill was referred to the Passenger Railway committee, but now the very members, who had previously refused to report it to the body for consideration, acted quickly to send it along. On March 18 the bill came up for consideration in the house. The Democrats refused to allow a vote, hoping to force adjournment while they could round up opposition and exhaust time by parliamentary tactics. At a late hour only forty-five Republicans could be found in the house. Since this was not a quorum, the bill could not be acted on. The Democrats remained in their seats, refusing to vote. Very late in the night the Democratic side of the house was declared in contempt for refusing to vote; this was followed by an agreement under which a vote could be taken, and the Democrats purged of contempt. The bill finally went through the house by a vote of fifty to twenty-seven.[32]

In 1773 the Philadelphia reformer, Benjamin Rush, at the suggestion of another Philadelphia humanitarian, Anthony Benezet, published *An Address to the Inhabitants of the British Settlements in America Upon Slave-Keeping.* This remarkable anti-slavery essay, one of the finest products of the Age of Enlightenment, called upon the legislators of America, and especially those of Pennsylvania, to reflect upon the trust imposed upon them, and to "Extend the privileges we enjoy, to every human creature born among us, and let not the Journals or our Assemblies be disgraced with the records of laws, which allow exclusive privileges to men of one color in preference to another."[33] It had taken almost a century before the legislators in Harrisburg moved to apply this great principle. The first important step in this direction was the passage of the law in March, 1867, forbidding railway corporations either to exclude or segregate colored passengers and providing both civil and criminal remedies. Once this step had been taken, it would be easier to move forward in a similar direction. This was discerned by Senator William A. Wallace when he noted, in opposing passage of the car bill: "Are you willing to recognize this equality in the railroad car? If you are, then the next step is, of course, to recognize their equality with you at the ballot-box."[34] Two years later, in March, 1869, the state legislature proved Senator Wallace a good prophet by ratifying the Fifteenth Amendment, thereby restoring to Negroes of Pennsylvania the right to vote, which had been taken away in 1838.[35]

On March 23, 1867, the Philadelphia *Press* carried the following telegraphic item: "Harrisburg, March 22.—Gov. Geary today signed the act requiring railroad and railway companies to carry all passengers, without distinction or color."

Two days later Miss Carrie Lacount, a teacher in a colored school, was refused admission to a city passenger car at 9th and Lombard streets. In response to her signal, the conductor refused to stop and shouted out, "We don't allow niggers to ride." The young teacher immediately complained to a magistrate who told her he knew nothing officially of the passage of the car bill and would not rely on newspaper reports. Miss Lacount went to the Commonwealth Secre-

tary of State who was then in the city, obtained a manuscript copy of
the bill certified by the official, and returned with it to the magistrate.
The conductor was arrested and fined $100. With this incident
segregation on the streetcars of Philadelphia finally came to an end.[36]
An abolitionist journal rejoiced:

> Henceforward, the weary school-teacher, returning from her arduous
> day's labor, shall not be condemned to walk to her distant home
> through cold and storm; henceforward invalid women and aged men
> shall be permitted to avail themselves of a public conveyance, even
> though their complexion may not be white. And their scornful brothers
> and sisters who cannot comfortably sit beside a colored fellow-citizen in
> a car, will have the right to walk, or indulge in the luxury of a private
> carriage, if their purses will afford it, and their prejudice is, in their
> estimation, worth the expense.[37]

The Negro community of Philadelphia celebrated the car victory
with a mass meeting in Liberty Hall, but it was featured more by
discord than rejoicing. While some speakers hailed William Still for
his "self-sacrificing efforts" in behalf of equal rights on the cars,
others raised the cry that he and his fellowmembers of the Statistical
Association's car committee had retarded the day of victory by their
attempts to distinguish between those Negroes who were entitled to
ride in the cars and those who should be excluded because of where,
and the conditions under which, they lived. There was also some
dispute over which of the various car committees of the Negro
organizations—that of the Colored People's Union League, the
Social, Civil and Statistical Association of Colored People, or the
Pennsylvania State Equal Rights League—deserved the most credit
for the final victory. There was agreement only on the fact that the
bill outlawing discrimination on the streetcars was drawn up by the
committee representing the Equal Rights League, and there was
common satisfaction expressed that the Democrats must be morti-
fied to learn *"that a bill drafted by colored men,* passed the Legislature of the Keystone State."[38] Politeness probably kept the speakers
from pointing out that the initiative throughout the battle against
streetcar segregation had come from the blacks themselves; that they
had provided the first committees to challenge existing practices, and
that it was not until after seven years of Jim Crow transportation on
the horsecars that the first important white citizens' committee to

demand a change in the companies' regulations had come into existence.

Disturbed by the tone of the victory celebration, *The Christian Recorder* expressed the hope that the "brilliant success" scored in the legislature would not be tarnished by a feud over who deserved the most credit for the achievement and called for an end to "personal and party feeling."[39] But this did not assuage the critics of William Still who continued to charge that he had denigrated the masses of Philadelphia Negroes in order to elevate the rights of the elite of the black community. A boycott of Still's coal business was launched, and the poorer classes of Negroes were urged to patronize Copperheads rather than the man who had abused and insulted them.[40]

On April 8, 1867, another meeting was held in Liberty Hall, this time to allow Still to defend his role in the streetcar battle. The meeting was chaired by Robert Purvis and was devoted entirely to a two-hour address by Still tracing the history of his contributions in the car campaign from his first letter to the press in 1859 to the passage of the car bill eight years later. The lengthy speech— interrupted at intervals by shouts of disagreement from a group of young Negroes—was later published by Still at his own expense as a pamphlet. The back cover was devoted to an advertisement for Still's coal business and two tributes from the Philadelphia newspapers testifying to his "high reputation" for integrity and promptness in business transactions, the "good quality" of his coal, and the "liberal terms" on which it might be purchased by dealers.[41]

Following the second Liberty Hall meeting, *The Christian Recorder* gave the anti-Still elements a stern lecture. "We must differ among ourselves on many public questions pertaining to men and measures," it began. "But let us differ on fair statements of facts and arguments, and study to avoid violence, selfishness and falsehood." Then it got down to the heart of the whole dispute. The black youth of Philadelphia, it cautioned, should not disdain the advice of older members of the Negro community, nor "throw aside the advice and good wishes of worthy, discreet well-wishers and friends." It became clear that what was really at the root of the conflict was the existence of a real generation gap in the Philadelphia community. During the battle against car segregation younger and more militant blacks, like Catto and Oliver, had voiced scorn for the elitist position of the older leaders of the Negro community, and they had resented their tendency to rely more on the good will of upper class whites than on mobilizing the black masses in the struggle for their rights. Moreover, they had never been too impressed by the fact that so many ministers, merchants, lawyers, and politicians had signed petitions and attended the Concert Hall protest meeting. Only three of these ministers—the Reverends William H. Furness, B. F. Barrett, and Phillips Brooks—had ever dared to express opposition to car segregation in sermons to their congregations. Most of the merchants and lawyers who had signed the petitions had publicly endorsed Mayor Henry, a vicious foe of equality for Negroes in Philadelphia, for re-election. And several of the politicians had bottled up the car bill in the House Railway Committee in 1865 and had only acted favorably when they feared future reprisals at the polls by Negroes armed with the ballot. In short, a conflict had emerged in the Negro community during the battle to end streetcar discrimination which was to increase in intensity as the struggle for equality continued.[42]

On one point all involved in the car controversy agreed. Regardless of color or age, Philadelphia deserved no credit for the success of the long struggle to end segregation on its streetcars. "No thanks to Philadelphia for this thing," wrote the local correspondent of the *National Anti-Slavery Standard:*

> It is no compliment to the community or the churches that the Legislature was at last obliged to interfere in behalf of justice. Indeed, it is mortifying to know that it was a power abroad and not humanity at home that accomplished this act for human rights. How much more worthy the character of an enlightened community had it sprung from a willingness to be just, a voluntary movement unto all their rights.[43]

The Concert Hall Committee, reporting in 1867 on the conclusion of its work, made much the same point. It noted that neither it nor any of the committees organized by the Negro people had received support from the press and pulpit; that of seven daily newspapers, only two had lent their aid to the movement for equality on the cars, that only three white clergymen had ever referred to the question in their pulpits, and that only "the near approach of negro suffrage in the State" had produced the change in the legislature which had made victory possible. Somewhat sadly, it concluded that "love to

the Lord and the neighbor has had little to do with this change."[44]
One commentator noted:

> No laws that can be passed to-day can blot out the wrongs hitherto
> done, or efface the memory of many outrageous scenes of the past. They
> cannot atone for the injuries that the colored people have endured, or
> give redress for their manifold grievances in the years gone by. It
> furnishes another chapter of "man's inhumanity to man," the long
> suffering and patient endurance of the victims.[45]

Still there were some who saw great hopes for the nation from the
triumph. Soon, one commentator predicted, "the presence of colored
persons in railway cars will attract no more attention in Philadelphia
than it does in other cities; and many foolish persons, who have been
horrified by the prospect of such innovation, will wonder at their
own folly, for a while, and then forget it." And if this could happen in
Philadelphia, the most backward city in the North in according
justice to her colored population, then it must be clear that "the equal
rights of man, *as man,* are destined to receive universal acknowledge-
ment and respect." Who, in the light of what had happened in the
City of Brotherly Love, could now "doubt the final glorious result?"[46]

Philadelphia Negroes had doubts, and it did not take long before
these were justified. The year following the enactment of the law
forbidding segregation on the streetcars, the Democrats won the
election. On April 1, 1870, Hiram R. Revels, black senator from
Mississippi, the first Negro to be seated in Congress, was denied the
right to use the Academy of Music for an address. The board of
directors deemed it "inexpedient" for a black man, even though a
Senator of the United States, to use the leading auditorium in
Philadelphia. The Philadelphia *Post* commented:

> Surely a Senator of the United States might be allowed to speak in our
> Academy of Music. But Mr. Revels is a colored man, and this respect-
> able Board has the negrophobia so bad that it cannot bear the idea of
> hearing eloquence from any one who is not lucky enough to be white. It
> has repeatedly refused Frederick Douglass the privilege of lecturing in
> the Academy, although he alone has more brains than almost any six
> members of the Board together.

Of these six directors, all were Republicans except one; the Republicans had cast their votes against Revels as a speaker, while the lone Democrat had voted for him.[47]

In the fall of 1870, when Philadelphia Negroes went to the polls for the first time since 1838, federal troops had to be sent to the city to see that they were permitted to cast their ballots. The following year no federal troops came, and three Negroes were killed by mobs and many injured. Among those killed was Octavius V. Catto, the young colored high school principal who held a commission as a major in the infantry of the Union army·and was one of the leaders of the successful battle to end streetcar segregation.[48]

But even Philadelphia progressed; in 1899 W. E. B. DuBois, in his monumental study of the Philadelphia Negro, noted that while "a deep-rooted and determined prejudice still remained, . . . it showed signs of yielding."[49] The streetcar issue continued to be a disturbing element in relations between black and white Philadelphians, but it now revolved around the opportunities for Negroes to be hired other than as porters and sweepers. The struggle over this issue came to a climax in 1944 following a War Manpower Commission order, enforcing a directive of the Fair Employment Practice Committee, upgrading eight Negroes to platform workers on the streetcars. A wildcat strike of less than 200 men against the order, aided and abetted by the Transit Company and local political leaders, broke out and lasted from August 1 to 7, 1944. It was accompanied by a small riot in the angry Negro community. The strike was broken when President Roosevelt sent 10,000 troops into Philadelphia.[50]

While a goodly number of Philadelphians condemned the strike solely because it interfered with the war effort, others squarely faced the issue of discrimination and racism which had triggered the walkout. On the fifth day of the strike, the *Evening Bulletin* carried an advertisement inserted by a coalition of black and white organizations in Philadelphia, including the A. M. E. Church, American Jewish Congress, Catholic Interracial Council, National Association for the Advancement of Colored People, National Urban League, CIO Committee to Abolish Discrimination, Committee on Race Relations of the Society of Friends, and the Inter-Racial Discussion Group. The signers called for a grand jury investigation of the strike on the ground that it was not only "treason against the American war effort" but also "traitorous to the fundamental principles of American liberty and the right of all men for equal opportunity to live and to earn their living—without discrimination."[51] On October 17, 1944, the *Evening Bulletin* had the following notice: "As a direct result of this summer's Philadelphia Transportation Company strike, a number of Germantown citizens have banded together to form 'The Good Neighbors of Germantown,' an organization set up to promote interracial friendship."

Contradictions between American ideals and the reality of life for black Americans during the ante-bellum and Civil War years were not confined to Philadelphia. What the battle to desegregate the streetcars of Philadelphia reveals, perhaps more so than elsewhere, is that while they gained some valuable white allies, black Americans had to fall back primarily upon their own resources to pierce the ice of indifference and change the pattern of segregation imposed by a hostile, white world.

NOTES

1. Philadelphia *Press,* February 1, 1865; *A Brief Narrative of the Struggle for the Rights of Colored People of Philadelphia on the City Railway Cars* (Philadelphia, 1867), p. 16. The Philadelphia correspondent of the *National Anti-Slavery Standard* wrote bitterly of the car poll: "The farce was so great that it towered into the proportions of an unmitigated humbug. All manner of fraud was perpetrated, and the mean, contemptible sponges of prejudice displayed such eagerness to make the most of this opportunity to vent their contumely towards the colored man, that injustice itself, were it a thing of life, would have blushed for shame for the zeal thus shown by the votaries." (*National Anti-Slavery Standard,* February 25, 1865.)

The contrast between the vote on the car issue and the action in Congress on the Thirteenth Amendment was not really so startling since Philadelphia had been so hostile to the Emancipation Proclamation when it was announced in 1863 that it almost defeated Republican Governor Andrew Curtin. Had not the victory at Gettysburg come that year, it would have undoubtedly unseated Curtin. (William Dusinberre, *Civil War Issues in Philadelphia, 1856–1865* [Philadelphia, 1965], pp. 154–160; Erwin S. Bradley, *Triumph of Militant Republicanism: A Study of Pennsylvania and Presidential Politics, 1860–1872* [Philadelphia, 1964], pp. 152, 178.)

2. Philadelphia *Press,* February 14, 1865; Frederick W. Speirs, *The Street Railways System of Philadelphia, Its History and Present Condition* (Baltimore, 1897), p. 25.

3. This conclusion is based on an examination of copies of *Fincher's Trades' Review* in the Library Company of Philadelphia. For a discussion of the paper, see Philip S. Foner, *History of the Labor Movement in the United States* (New York, 1947), I, 350–352.

4. *Fincher's Trades' Review,* July 11, 1863.

5. Philadelphia *Age,* July 9, 14, October 2, 1863; March 1, 14, 22, 25, April 8, 16, May 3, June 25, July 12, August 25, November 1, 1864. See also Ray H. Abrams, "Copperhead Newspapers and the Negro," *Journal of Negro History,* XX (April, 1935), 135–152, and Forrest G. Wood, *Black Scare: The Racist Response to Emancipation and Reconstruction* (Berkeley, 1968), pp. 21, 34, 35, 43–51, 59, 60, 63–64, 118, 139.

6. Philadelphia *Evening Bulletin,* June 25, 1864; Philadelphia *Age,* June 27, 1864.

7. *Report of the Committee Appointed for the Purpose of Securing to Colored People in Philadelphia the Right to the Use of the Streetcars* (Philadelphia, 1869), p. 2; *The Christian Recorder,* March 11, 1865. The Reverend Weaver had just returned from Washington where he had witnessed the inauguration of President Lincoln and where, he reported, he had "enjoyed the privilege of exercising a freeman's rights, to ride in the cars on the Metropolitan City railroad, among the most refined ladies and gentlemen of Washington, New York, Massachusetts, and elsewhere, who, like ourselves, had journeyed tither to witness the day's proceedings. . . . But when we came back to Philadelphia, the first thing that struck our eyes in looking over the morning papers, was an account of the forcible ejection of some colored gentlemen from the Chestnut and Walnut street cars, and the brutal and cowardly treatment they received at the hands of the conductors and some of Mayor Henry's police." Segregation had been abolished on Washington's streetcars in March, 1865.

8. Miles R. Robinson, James Wallace, and R. C. Marshall in Philadelphia *Press,* March 15, 1865. The letter was reprinted in *Liberator,* March 24, 1865, and may also be found in Herbert Aptheker, ed., *A Documentary History of the Negro People in the United States* (New York, 1951), pp. 505–506. It was William Still who bailed out the three.

9. Philadelphia *Press,* May 10, 1865; Derry vs. Lowry, *Philadelphia Reports,* p. 30; Philadelphia *Evening Bulletin,* May 11, 1865.

10. *Why Colored People of Philadelphia Are Excluded from the Street Cars?* (Philadelphia, 1866), pp. 4–5. An appeal was taken to the State Supreme Court from a verdict in a civil case against a Negro passenger ejected from a car, but no decision was handed down before discrimination on the streetcars was banned by state law.

11. *Proceedings of the National Convention of Colored Men Held in*

Syracuse, New York, October 4–7, 1864 (New York, 1864); Philip S. Foner, *Life and Writings of Frederick Douglass* (New York, 1953), III, 49–51, 408–421.

12. *The Christian Recorder,* January 28, 1865. Jonathan Gibbs, born in Philadelphia and educated at Dartmouth College and Princeton Theological Seminary, was the league's first president. Gibbs later became a member of the Radical Reconstruction convention in Florida and eventually was appointed superintendent of public instruction in that state.

13. *Liberator,* March 3, 1865.

14. Minutes of the Executive Board of the Pennsylvania State Equal Rights League (1864–1872), *Ms.,* Historical Society of Pennsylvania (HSP).

15. William Lloyd Garrison to Helen Garrison, November 5, 1865, William Lloyd Garrison Papers, Boston Public Library.

16. Minutes of the Executive Board of the Pennsylvania State Equal Rights League, *Ms.,* HSP; M. B. Lowry to William Still, March 29, 1867, in *A Brief Narrative of the Struggle for the Rights of the Colored People of Philadelphia,* p. 21.

17. *The Christian Recorder,* January 28, 1865; Pennsylvania *Telegraph,* January 20, 1865; *Liberator,* January 27, 1865.

18. Philadelphia *Press,* March 22, 1865.

19. *Why Colored People of Philadelphia Are Excluded from the Street Cars?,* p. 4; Philadelphia *Press,* February 17, 1865.

20. Minutes of the Society for Promoting the Abolition of Slavery, for the Relief of Free Negroes Unlawfully Held in Bondage, and for Improving the Condition of the African Race, September 28, 1865, *Ms.,* HSP; *A Brief Struggle for the Rights of the Colored People of Philadelphia,* p. 15.

21. *National Anti-Slavery Standard,* February 23, 1867.

22. *Ibid.,* December 1, 1866.

23. Minutes of the Executive Committee of the Social, Cultural and Statistical Association of the Colored People of Pennsylvania, *Ms.,* HSP.

24. *The Christian Recorder,* October 6, 1866.

25. *Why Colored People of Philadelphia Are Excluded from the Street Cars?,* p. 18.

26. Charles D. Cushdollar, "Andrew Johnson and the Philadelphia Election of 1866," *Pennsylvania Magazine of History and Bibliography,* XLII (July, 1968), 379–383; Philadelphia *Age,* September 4, 29, October 2, 3, 4, 1866.

27. Minutes of the Executive Board of the Pennsylvania State Equal Rights League (1864–1872), January-February, 1867, *Ms.,* HSP.

28. *Pennsylvania Laws,* (March 22, 1867), pp. 38–39.

29. *Legislative Record,* (February 5, 1867), Appendix, p. lxxxiv.

30. *Ibid.,* pp. lxxxvii–lxxxviii.

31. Minutes of the Executive Board of the Pennsylvania State Equal Rights League (1864–1872), February 19, 1867, *Ms.,* HSP.

32. Philadelphia *Press,* March 19, 1867. The vote in both houses was almost entirely on party lines, with Republicans in favor and Democrats opposed. Interestingly enough, a bill to permit the streetcars of Philadelphia to operate on Sunday was defeated. During the debate on the "Sunday-car" bill, characterized by predictions that passage of the measure would cause immorality to rise in Philadelphia, one member of the house observed "that these persons who are opposing the passage of this bill on the principle of morality and Christianity are stultifying themselves by their very acts when they refuse respectable colored or any other persons to enter their cars. Now, if there is one spark of humanity in the people of Philadelphia, or any number of those people, or in members of this House, who oppose the passage of this bill on grounds of morality, I appeal to that principle of humanity if this action of theirs is consistent when they would hurl people of color, because they are colored, from the cars and let them lie broken in the streets? Where is your humanity? Where is your Christianity? I cannot see that there is a particle of either in such acts." (Speech of Mr. Pennypacker, *Legislative Record* [February 6, 1867], Appendix, p. xci.) The Philadelphia correspondent of the *National Anti-Slavery Standard* on February 15, 1867, commented wryly: "Our people had all along been so good, so pious that they could not allow the black man to ride in the cars. And so, of course, they were too good to permit the cars to run on Sunday. Now that they have become so bad as to permit that, by-and-by they may come to this." The Philadelphia Female Anti-Slavery Society's comment was equally to the point. It noted that had Philadelphia's churches "made half the effort to abolish this practice (of streetcar segregation), which they made to prevent the running of Sunday cars, it would have ceased long ago." (*Thirtieth Annual Report of the Philadelphia Female Anti-Slavery Society* [Philadelphia, 1867], p. 27.)

33. Benjamin Rush, *An Address to the Inhabitants of the British Settlements in America, Upon Slave-Keeping* (Philadelphia, 1773), pp. 20–22.

34. *Legislative Record* (February 5, 1867), p. lxxxviii.

35. Ira V. Brown, "Pennsylvania and the Rights of the Negro, 1865–1887," *Pennsylvania History,* XXVIII (January, 1961), 52. Segregation in education was not abolished until June, 1881. In May, 1887, the General Assembly passed "An Act to provide Civil Rights for all People, Regardless of Race or Color." It prohibited discrimination by any person, company, or corporation in restaurants, hotels, theatres, concert halls or places of

amusement and on railroads, street railways, and omnibus lines. It provided for a fine of not less than fifty or more than one hundred dollars. (*Pennsylvania Laws* [May 19, 1887], pp. 130–131.)

36. Philadelphia *Press,* March 26, 1867; *The Christian Recorder,* March 30, 1867.

37. *National Anti-Slavery Standard,* March 30, 1867.

38. *The Christian Recorder,* March 30, 1867.

39. *Ibid.*

40. Alberta S. Norwood, "Negro Welfare Work in Philadelphia, Especially Illustrated by the Career of William Still, 1775–1930" (M.A. Thesis, University of Pennsylvania, 1931), p. 63.

41. The pamphlet was entitled *A Brief Narrative of the Struggle for the Rights of the Colored People of Philadelphia in the City Railway Cars; and a Defence of William Still. Relating to His Agency Touching the Passage of the Late Bill, &c. Read Before a Large Public Meeting, Held in Liberty Hall, Lombard St. below Eight, April 8th, 1867.* It was reprinted in 1969 as part of the Afro-American History Series, Historic Publication No. 240, edited by Maxwell Whiteman. However, this edition does not include the back-cover advertisements of the original. The two papers quoted in this advertisement were the *North American and United States Gazette,* February 9, 1867, and the *Press,* April 1, 1867.

42. *The Christian Recorder,* April 13, 1867; *Why Colored People in Philadelphia Are Excluded from the Street Cars?,* pp. 26–27.

43. *National Anti-Slavery Standard,* February 16, 23, March 30, 1867.

44. *Report of the Committee Appointed for the Purpose of Securing to Colored People in Philadelphia the Right to the Use of the Street-Cars,* p. 3; see also *Why Colored People in Philadelphia Are Excluded from the Street Cars?* pp. 4–5.

45. *National Anti-Slavery Standard,* February 15, 1867.

46. *Ibid.,* March 30, 1867.

47. *The Nation,* April 7, 1870; Elizabeth Lawson, *The Gentleman from Mississippi: Our First Negro Senator* (New York, 1960), pp. 33–34.

48. Philadelphia *Public Ledger,* October 11, 14, 1871; Brown, "Pennsylvania and the Rights of Negroes," pp. 53–54.

49. W. E. B. DuBois, *The Philadelphia Negro: A Social Study* (Philadelphia, 1899), p. 43.

50. Philadelphia *Evening Bulletin,* August 1–10, 1944; American Council on Race Relations, *Negro Platform Workers* (Chicago, 1945), pp. 3–20; Joseph E. Weckler, "Prejudice Is Not the Whole Story," *Public Opinion Quarterly,* IX (Summer, 1945), 126–139; G. Gordon Brown, *Law Ad-*

ministration and Negro-White Relations in Philadelphia (Philadelphia, 1947), pp. 122–130. The wildcat strike was condemned by the Transportation Workers Union (CIO).

51. Philadelphia *Evening Bulletin,* August 5, 1944. The other organizations listed in the advertisement were: Allied Veterans Association of Pennsylvania; A. M. E. Preachers Meeting of Philadelphia; Baptist Ministers Conference of Philadelphia and Vicinity; Department of Race Relations of Federation of Churches; Fellowship Commission; Fellowship House; Germantown-Chestnut Hill Ministerial Association; Jewish Peoples Fraternal Order, I. W. O.; National Alliance of Postal Employees; National Bar Association; National Conference of Christians and Jews; National Lawyers Guild; North Philadelphia Civic League; Pennsylvania Baptist State Convention; Philadelphia Industrial Union Council, CIO; Philadelphia Metropolitan Council for Equal Job Opportunity; and South Philadelphia Civic League.

5

Blacks and the Labor Movement
in Pennsylvania:
The Beginnings*

I

It is important to understand the relationship between Black and white labor from the time of slavery to the Civil War in order to understand the position of Blacks in the early labor movement. Since the early trade unions were primarily for skilled workers, the elimination of Blacks from the skilled trades helps explain their absence from the unions. In addition, the conflict between white and Black labor established a heritage which was difficult to overcome even when slavery was abolished.

Blacks in Pennsylvania had enjoyed a favorable position in the craft trades before the end of Pennsylvania slavery. As slaves, they had acquired certain skills. The advertisements for runaway Blacks suggest that a substantial number of slaves were purchased for iron work as skilled laborers. While many served as unskilled laborers, too, they eventually became competent in the specialized tasks associated with iron production. Some of the slaves were described in advertisements as hammermen, liners and keepers, smiths, forge carpenters, and forgemen. These were highly skilled positions at the iron furnace.

In other aspects of Pennsylvania's diversified colonial economy, Blacks performed skilled work. Since trained white craftsmen were in short supply in Pennsylvania as elsewhere in colonial America, slave labor was used in such crafts and trades as the building trades, coopering, milling and baking, sailmaking, barbering, silversmithing, tanning, skinning, and sailing. Sailing was especially appealing

*Reprinted from *Pennsylvania Heritage,* IV (December, 1977), 34–38.

since privateers departing Philadelphia carried many Blacks fleeing slavery, and the shipmasters seldom heeded the admonitions of colonial administrators forbidding Black seamen.

Even after the colonial period, many Negroes continued to work as mechanics. In fact, between 1790 and 1820, a large proportion, and perhaps most, of the artisans of Philadelphia were Black. In many instances, employers hired Black rather than white laborers, since Negroes would work for lower wages.

Quite early, the use of Blacks in these skilled trades aroused some, but not serious, opposition. Some people argued that the skill required to fashion articles of culture or necessity could just as easily be used to fashion weapons that could be turned against the Blacks' own masters and the entire white community. The major protest, however, came from white workers who complained of the depressing and demoralizing effect of skilled Black labor on white labor. As early as 1708, free mechanics in Philadelphia complained of the "want of employment, and lowness of wages, occasioned by the number of *Negroes* . . . hired out to work by the day."

After 1820, however, the combination of immigration and the hostility of white working men, especially the Irish, prevented many of those Negroes who possessed skills from using them, and kept most younger Blacks from gaining apprenticeships and learning a trade. Whites' attempts to gain toeholds in the skilled positions drove Negroes out of employment. *Niles' Weekly Register* of August 30, 1834, carried the following on its front page:

> Though gatherings of large numbers of people at Philadelphia to commit acts of violence, had ceased after the third night—many excesses subsequently took place, and colored persons, when engaged in their usual avocations, were repeatedly assailed and maltreated, especially on the *Schuylkill* front of the city. Parties of white men have insisted that no Blacks shall be employed in certain departments of labor.

"P.O.," a perceptive analyst of the Moyamensing area of Philadelphia, which housed Irish weavers and unskilled laborers, among them numerous Blacks, wrote that by 1849 the Irish had effectively driven the Blacks from the Schuylkill docks: ". . . where a few years ago we saw none but Blacks, we now see nothing but Irish." Indeed, there was a dramatic decline in the number of Black stevedores and hod carriers in Philadelphia County during the latter half of the 1840's. Blacks were also driven from the skilled trades and limited to positions of servants and manual laborers, and even then were often deprived of the opportunity to work.

Between 1820 and 1850, Blacks not only lost their traditional means of employment but they also became the victims of violence. Eight major riots were directed against Black people in Philadelphia, and there were several in Pittsburgh. In each case, white mobs burned and looted Negro churches, meeting halls, and homes, and clubbed, stoned, and sometimes murdered Blacks.

There were various reasons for native-white and Irish intransigence in the 1830's, 40's, and 50's. Even when Irish and native-white workers secured street trades (stevedores, etc.), or gained entrance into consumer industries or sweatshops, their economic position did not improve. In the sweatshops, for instance, vigorous routine emerged, wages declined, and opportunity for advancement was limited. All this made workmen reluctant to admit another source of cheap labor and more competition for wages. Early trade unions were designed as much to protect these exposed trades for white men as to win better working conditions and higher wages for their members. Blacks, naturally, were the scapegoats of the unions and not the new trends in mechanization.

II

Philadelphia proudly boasted that it was the birthplace of the American labor movement. The first authentic strike in American history occurred in Philadelphia in 1786; the first organization to maintain a permanent union was formed in the city in 1792; the first labor paper, the *Mechanics' Free Press,* appeared in Philadelphia in 1827; in the fall of that same year, fifteen Philadelphia unions formed the Mechanics' Union of Trade Associations, the first city central labor body in America; and in 1828, the first labor party in this country was formed in Philadelphia.

But Black workers could take little pride in Philadelphia's reputation as a pioneer trade-union center, for although they were members of the city's labor force, they were rigidly excluded from all of its trade unions. *The National Trades' Union,* official organ of the labor body bearing the same name, and published in Philadelphia, explained in 1835 that Negroes could not belong to unions of white workers since they were inherently inferior to whites, and were actually employers' tools to hinder the growth of unions and keep white workers oppressed. The short-lived Industrial Congress—a national organization of reformers and workingmen—did admit Negro delegates to an 1851 convention, but the Mechanics' Assembly of Philadelphia was so resentful of the admission of Blacks that it voted to sever all ties with the Industrial Congress.

John Campbell, a British Chartist who had risen to prominence as a leader of the Typographical Union in Philadelphia, applauded the stand of the Mechanics' Assembly. Indeed, in a book he published in 1851, with the flaming title, *Negro-Mania,* Campbell summarized the prevailing views of the trade unions in Philadelphia when he wrote:

> Will the white race ever agree that blacks should stand beside us on election day, upon the rostrum, in the ranks of the army, in our places of amusement, in places of public worship, ride in the same coaches, railway cars, or steamships? Never! never! nor is it natural or just that this kind of equality should exist. God never intended it . . .

During the Civil War, anti-Negro sentiment in northern working-class circles grew even more bitter. Opposition to the presence of Black workers, who were accused of accepting wages lower than those paid to white workers, expressed itself in strikes against employers who used Negroes, and often in violence against Blacks. Longshoremen in Philadelphia, as well as in other major northern ports, engaged in periodic clashes with Negro workers over employment on the docks.

Unfortunately, the leading labor paper of the era, *Fincher's Trades' Review,* published in Philadelphia, did nothing to help eradicate this racism from the ranks of white labor. The *Review,* edited by Jonathan Fincher of the Typographical Union, had on its editorial board representatives of the molders, printers, ship carpenters, stone cutters, cabinet makers, carpenters, hatters, and shoemakers unions in Philadelphia. Between its first issue on June 6, 1863, and its last on August 18, 1866, the publication appeared every Saturday. Yet not once did it call upon the unions of Pennsylvania to lower their barriers against Black workers and permit them to enter their ranks and work beside the white workers in shops and factories. Indeed, *Fincher's Trades' Review* paid no attention whatsoever to the fact that Black workers in Philadelphia were deprived of the right to use the streetcars. *Fincher's Trades' Review* may have called itself "An Advocate of the Rights of the Producing Classes," but either it did not believe that Black workers belonged to the "producing classes," or it did not believe that they had rights.

Although they were excluded from white unions even after the end of slavery, Black workers in Pennsylvania were able, on occasion, to join forces with whites in common struggle. In Philadelphia, the Black brickmakers struck jointly with whites in July, 1868, for higher wages. While the strike was largely a failure, it did stimulate the organization of Black workers in the city. By the fall of 1868, there was not only an active Colored Brickmakers' Association, but also a large Hod Carriers' and Laborers' Association, and a Workingmen's Union built by Negroes of Philadelphia.

Elsewhere, too, Black workers were forming their own organizations and going out on strike. Even though some of these walkouts did not end in victory, they did mark the entry of the Black working class into the labor movement—albeit a separate movement of its own.

Meanwhile, a labor-Negro alliance was being discussed by some farsighted labor leaders, headed by William H. Sylvis, Pennsylvania-born head of the Iron Molders' National Union, the outstanding labor leader of the era, and co-founder of the National Labor Union in 1866. Although Sylvis had been a Douglas Democrat before the Civil War, he had helped recruit a company of molders for the Pennsylvania militia in which he served, and after the war he became convinced that either the newly emancipated Blacks had to be enlisted in the labor movement, or they would be used by employers against the white trade unions.

Sylvis warned those unions that excluded Negro workers that their "fanatical bigotry" jeopardized the future of the labor movement, for it was "impossible to degrade one group of workers without degrading all." Besides, he said, labor must realize that as a result of the Radical Reconstruction program of the Republican Party, initiated in 1867, the Negro now had the suffrage in the South, would soon gain the ballot in the North, and even hold the balance of political power in the nation. "If we can succeed in convincing these people to make common cause with us . . . we will have a power . . . that will shake Wall Street out of its boots," he declared. But, Sylvis continued, it was too much to expect the Negro to use his ballot in the cause of a labor movement that denied him not only membership, but even the opportunity to earn an honest living.

Sylvis was not completely free of racist views, and these marred his insight into the crucial issue of Black-white labor relations. But he did understand more clearly than most other white labor leaders the need to build a Black-white labor alliance. Unfortunately, both his advanced views and his organizing genius were lost to the American labor movement when he died suddenly on July 26, 1869. Yet before his death, Sylvis, as president of the National Labor Union, provided that organization's forthcoming convention with a magnificent opportunity to achieve labor unity. In December, 1868, he and the Executive Committee of the NLU met in Washington, D. C., and, in a precedent-shattering action, made the organization's first official overture to the Negro by extending a formal invitation to all persons interested in the labor movement, regardless of color or sex, to attend the organization's annual convention in Philadelphia on August 16, 1869.

Nine Black delegates were present at the 1869 NLU convention, representing unions of Black workers in Maryland and Pennsylvania. Choosen to represent the Black workers of Maryland were Isaac Myers of the Colored Caulkers' Trade Union Society, Ignatius Gray of the Colored Moulders' Union Society, Robert H. Butler of the Colored Engineers' Association, and James W. W. Hare of the Colored Painters' Society. The five delegates selected to represent the Black workers of Pennsylvania were Robert M. Adger and Peter P. Brown of the United Hod Carriers' and Laborers' Association of Pennsylvania, John H. Thomas and James Roane of the United Curriers Union No. 2 of Philadelphia, and Isaiah Wears of the Workingmen's Union of Philadelphia. It is difficult to determine whether there was communication between the Pennsylvania and Maryland delegates before the convention, but once they arrived in Philadelphia, the Black delegates acted as a group, and Isaac Myers spoke for the Pennsylvania as well as the Maryland Black workers in his magnificent address to the convention.

Myers opened by paying tribute to the delegates for their awareness of the need for unity between Negro and white workers: "Silent,
but powerful and far-reaching is the revolution inaugurated by your
act in taking the colored laborer by the hand and telling him his
interest is common with yours." White workers, he assured the
delegates, had nothing to fear from Black laborers, for they desired
just what the whites wanted, and were ready to join in a common
struggle to achieve it. Cooperation had not always existed in the past
because the workshops and trade unions had been barred to the
Negro, and he had, therefore, been compelled to put his labor on the
market for whatever he could get. Myers warned against the continuation of such rivalry; he stressed the desire of the Negro to
cooperate in the future. Even though they were uttered more than a
century ago, his words have lost none of their significance:

> American citizenship is a complete failure if he [the Negro] is proscribed
> from the workshops of this country—if any man cannot employ whom
> he chooses, and if he cannot work for any man whom he will. If
> citizenship means anything at all, it means the freedom of labor, as
> broad and as universal as the freedom of the ballot.

Myers then asked pointedly whether "the minor organizations
throughout the country" would be influenced by the convention's
example in admitting Black delegates. As for the Blacks: "We carry
no prejudices. We are willing to forget the wrongs of yesterday, and
let the dead past bury its dead."

The very presence of Black trade unionists at a white labor
convention in the city of Philadelphia, notorious for its anti-Negro
practices, did not escape national notice. The Philadelphia correspondent of the *New York Times* reported:

> When a native Mississippian and an ex-confederate officer, in ad-
> dressing a convention, refers to a colored delegate who has preceded
> him as "the gentleman from Georgia," when a native Alabaman, who
> has for the first time crossed the Mason and Dixon line, and who was
> from boyhood taught to regard the Negro simply as a chattel, sits in
> deliberate consultation with another delegate whose ebony face glistens
> with African sheen, and signs the report of his colored co-delegate,
> when an ardent and Democratic partisan (from New York at that)
> declares with a "rich Irish brogue" that he asks for himself no privilege
> as a mechanic or as a citizen that he is not willing to concede to every
> other man, white or black—when I say, these things can be seen or

heard at a national convention, called for any purpose, then one may indeed be warranted in asserting that time works curious changes.

And all this was seen and heard in the City of Philadelphia during these August days in this year of grace 1869. Who shall say now, that prejudices, no matter how strongly they may have been implanted in the human breast, may not be rooted out?

The Chicago *Workingman's Advocate,* official organ of the National Labor Union, called upon the labor movement to follow the example of the 1869 convention and honor the memory of the great William H. Sylvis by putting an end to the exclusion of Negroes from trade-unions. But even the NLU did not go that far. Rather, the 1869 convention adopted a resolution encouraging the organization of separate Negro unions to be affiliated with the NLU. In addition, a special committee of five Black delegates was appointed to "organize the colored men of Pennsylvania into labor unions" and report their progress to the president of the NLU.

The Black delegates did not object to the policy of separate unionism. Robert H. Butler of the Colored Engineers' Association of Maryland emphasized that Black workers were not looking for "parlor sociabilities, but for the rights of mankind." Unfortunately, few trade unions were willing to accord Black workers "the right of mankind." Typical was the action of the fifth annual session of the Carpenters and Joiners National Union in September, 1869. The Committee on Colored Labor reported the following resolution, which was adopted by the entire convention:

> Resolved, that we are ever willing to extend the hand of fellowship to every laboring man, more especially to those of our own craft; we believe that the prejudices of our members against the colored people are of such a nature that it is not expedient at present to admit them as members or to organize them under the National Union.

This policy doomed the attempt to "organize the colored men of Pennsylvania into labor unions" and affiliate them with the National Labor Union. At the 1870 convention, the committee appointed to supervise this effort reported that the prejudice against Black workers among the white trade unions of Pennsylvania had rendered the organizing drive stillborn. This outcome came as no surprise to *The Christian Recorder,* the official organ of the A.M.E. Church, published in Philadelphia. While it had praised the actions taken at the

NLU convention, it had warned that "the ineffable meanness as well as the stupidity of the American Trades-Unions in regard to color" was too deeply ingrained to expect action "consistent with common sense and the spirit of our American democracy."

It was to take at least another decade, with the emergence of the Knights of Labor, before these characteristics were to change to any important extent. But even during this development, and the organization of thousands of Black workers into the Knights of Labor, "the ineffable meanness as well as stupidity" of too many trade unions "in regard to color" did not disappear, and the battle to eradicate racism in the American labor movement was to continue— and, indeed, is still being waged today.

BIBLIOGRAPHY

Aptheker, Herbert, ed. *A Documentary History of the Negro People in the United States,* Vol. I. New York, 1951.

Bloch, Herman D. "The National Labor Union and Black Workers," *Journal of Ethnic Studies,* I (Spring, 1973), 13–21.

Brown, Ira V. *The Negro in Pennsylvania History.* University Park, 1970.

———. "Pennsylvania and the Rights of the Negro, 1867–1887," *Pennsylvania History,* XXVIII (January, 1961), 316–29.

Campbell, John. *Negro-Mania.* Philadelphia, 1851.

Commons, John R., ed. *A Documentary History of the American Industrial Society,* Vol. IX. Cleveland, 1910.

Davis, W. W. H. "Negro Suffrage in Pennsylvania in 1837," *Era Magazine,* XXII (1903), 384–87.

Du Bois, W. E. B. *The Philadelphia Negro: A Social Study.* Philadelphia, 1899.

———. *Black Reconstruction in America, 1860–1880.* New York, 1935.

Dusinberre, William. *Civil War Issues in Philadelphia, 1856–1865.* Philadelphia, 1965.

Fisher, Sidney George. *A Philadelphia Perspective: The Diary of Sidney George Fisher Covering the Years 1837–1871,* ed. Nicholas B. Wainwright. Philadelphia, 1967.

Foner, Philip S. *Organized Labor and the Black Worker, 1619–1973.* New York, 1973.

———. *History of the Labor Movement in the United States,* Vol. I. New York, 1947.

———. "The Battle to End Discrimination Against Negroes on Philadelphia

Street Cars: (Part I) Background and Beginning of the Battle," *Pennsylvania History,* XL (July, 1973), 261–92; "(Part II) The Victory," *ibid.,* (October, 1973), pp. 355–80.

———. "A Labor Voice for Black Equality: *The Boston Daily Evening Voice,* 1864–1867," *Science & Society,* XXXVIII (Fall, 1974), 304–25.

———. *The Voice of Black America: Major Speeches by Negroes in the United States, 1797–1971.* New York, 1972.

Geffen, Elizabeth M. "Violence in Philadelphia in the 1840's and 1850's," *Pennsylvania History,* XXXVI (October, 1960), 381–410.

Hershberg, Theodore. "Free Blacks in Antebellum Philadelphia: A Study of Ex-Slaves, Freeborn, and Socioeconomic Decline," *Journal of Social History,* V (Winter, 1971–72), 183–209.

———. "Slavery and the Northern City: Ante-Bellum Black Philadelphia: An Urban Perspective," paper presented to the Association for the Study of Negro Life and History, October 23, 1970.

Litwack, Leon F. *North of Slavery: The Negro in the Free States, 1790–1860.* Chicago, 1961.

Lofton, Williston H. "Northern Labor and the Negro during the Civil War," *Journal of Negro History,* XXXIV (July, 1949), 251–73.

Mann, Albon J. "Labor Competition and the New York Draft Riots of 1863," *Journal of Negro History,* XXXVI (October, 1951), 375–405.

Mattison, Sumner Eliot. "The Labor Movement and the Negro During Reconstruction," *Journal of Negro History,* XXXIII (October, 1948), 426–68.

Memorial of Thirty Thousand Disfranchised Citizens of Philadelphia to the Honorable Senate and House of Representatives. Philadelphia, 1855.

Montgomery, David. *Beyond Equality: Labor and the Radical Republicans, 1862–1872.* New York, 1967.

Oblinger, Carl D. "Alms for Oblivion: The Making of a Black Underclass in Southeastern Pennsylvania, 1780–1860," in John E. Bodnar, *The Ethnic Experience in Pennsylvania* (Lewisburg, Pa., 1973), pp. 94–119.

Price, Edward J., Jr. "Let the Law Be Just: The Quest for Racial Equality in Pennsylvania, 1780–1915," unpub. Ph.D. diss., Pennsylvania State University, 1973.

Report of the Committee Appointed for the Purpose of Securing to Colored People in Philadelphia the Right to the Use of the Street Cars. Philadelphia, 1867.

Runcie, John. "Hunting the 'Nigs' in Philadelphia: The Race Riot of August, 1834," *Pennsylvania History,* XXXIX (April, 1972), 180–98.

Shankman, Arnold. "Draft Resistance in Civil War Pennsylvania," *Pennsylvania Magazine of History and Biography,* CI (April, 1977), 190–204.

Spero, Sterling D., and Abram L. Harris. *The Black Worker: The Negro and the Labor Movement.* New York, 1931.

Turner, Edward R. *The Negro in Pennsylvania: Slavery, Servitude, Freedom, 1639–1861.* New York, 1969.

Wesley, Charles H. *Negro Labor in the United States, 1850–1925.* New York, 1927.

Wright, Richard R., Jr. *The Negro in Pennsylvania: A Study in Economic History.* New York, 1912.

6

William P. Powell:
Militant Champion of Black Seamen

William P. Powell is truly an "unforgettable figure"—but he is also a forgotten figure. One will not find a mention of him in *The American Negro Reference Book, The Negro Almanac, The Negro Heritage Library, The Negro Vanguard, Who's Who Among Black Americans, The Negro Handbook, The Ebony Handbook,* Encyclopedia Britannica's *The Negro in American History, The National Cyclopedia of the Colored Race,* nor in the preparatory volume of W. E. B. Du Bois' *Encyclopedia of the Negro.*[1] Powell's name does not appear in any of the 1,314 pages of William S. Simm's *Men of Mark,* nor in the 550 pages of John Hope Franklin's *From Slavery to Freedom: A History of Negro Americans.*[2] There is no entry for William P. Powell in either the *Dictionary Catalogue of the Schomburg Collection of Negro Literature and History,* or the *Dictionary Catalogue of the Jesse E. Mooreland Collection of Negro Life and History* at Howard University.[3]

Although Benjamin Quarles, Herbert Aptheker, James M. McPherson, Sidney Kaplan, and Dorothy Sterling have noted his existence and dealt with some of his activities,[4] the aim of this paper is to fill out the story on the basis of details that have become available.

William P. Powell was born in New York City, with the exact day and year still unknown. In an application for a passport in 1846, he is described as "of a mulatto colour, but of Indian extraction." In another document somewhat later, Powell described himself as the grandson of Elizabeth Barjona, a cook for the first Continental

88

Congress, and the son of a slave father.[5] Apart from that information, and the fact that he married Mercy O. Haskins in New Bedford, Massachusetts, in 1832,[6] Powell's early life is a blank. His name first appeared in the press during the fall of 1837, when he was a promoter of a meeting of colored abolitionists held in the whaling port of New Bedford. Since he once noted that he had been a seaman for five years,[7] it is possible that his residence in New Bedford was between whaling voyages. At any rate, as reported in the *Liberator,* the meeting was called to nominate "a list of Candidates to be supported as Representatives for the General Court" of Massachusetts. Only those candidates who were in favor of "impartial Liberty and equal rights" were to be supported by the "oppressed and proscribed" people of New Bedford.[8]

Two years later, Powell was back in New York City to stay. The *Colored American* of March 21, 1840, carried the notice of a "Boarding House for Seamen under the Direction of the American Seamen's Friend Society." Bearing the name "Colored Seamen's Home," it was, according to the announcement, located at No. 70 John Street, and was kept by William P. Powell. Finally, there was this additional information: "Cooks, Stewards, and Seamen who come to this house, will have their choice of ships, and the highest wages; and if they are not satisfied after remaining twenty-four hours, no charge will be made."

The American Seamen's Friend Society, the financial supporter of the Colored Seamen's Home, was a Protestant missionary organization dedicated to the salvation of the sailor's soul through the preservation of his sobriety. Its monthly journal, the *Sailors' Magazine,* had a wide distribution among seamen. In 1837, the Society had established a home for sailors in New York City. Two years later, Powell was approached by the Society with a proposal that he start a home for black seamen, some two thousand of whom sailed regularly from the port of New York City. With the Society's financial assistance, Powell launched the Colored Seamen's Home in mid-1839, and for the next quarter of a century, with a decade's interruption, he was to be the keeper-proprietor of the largest home for black seamen in New York City. While the American Seamen's Friend Society was the principal source of outside financial support for the Colored Seamen's Home, Powell provided additional funds out of his own pocket, and on the tenth anniversary of its founding, it was reported that "in a pecuniary point of view, it [The Home] has been to him a source of considerable loss."[9]

From the earliest colonial days, black men had been employed on seagoing vessels. The black seaman was a common sight in colonial New England, and nearly half of the whaling crews were sometimes made up of Negroes. In the bustling port of Philadelphia, slaves serviced the needs of the vessels engaged in trade with many parts of the world, and they also comprised a good part of the crews of these vessels. When a 29-year-old slave was listed in the January 31, 1760, issue of the *Pennsylvania Gazette* as available for sale, readers were informed that all the masters of the ships he had sailed on liked him.

Among other things, sailing offered a hope of escape for those who fought to flee the bonds of slavery. Runaway slaves usually made for a port and attempted to hire on a vessel leaving the colonies. Advertisements frequently referred to a runaway who had made "off in some vessel." While the intolerable conditions on board vessels induced many whites to jump ship, the black runaway slaves had no choice but to stay on, and this made them attractive to shipowners as a labor force. The captains of ships did not delve too deeply into the backgrounds of blacks who wanted to become crew members. Nor did they heed the admonitions (affixed to an increasingly large number of advertisements for runaway blacks) that all vessels were forbidden to carry them.[10]

Probably one-half of the native American seamen who manned the crews of American vessels in 1850 were men of color.[11] Many famous blacks who made their marks in other fields at one time or another sailed on various types of ships—usually when they were younger men. Crispus Attucks, the first American to die in the Revolution, a victim of the Boston Massacre of 1770, was a seaman who had escaped from slavery. Paul Cuffe started out as a sailor and ended as a wealthy shipowner. James Forten was a sailor in the navy during the Revolution before he went on to become a manufacturer of sails, and the employer of many men, both black and white, in Philadelphia. Peter Harvey and Cato Tobias, Jr., were black crewmen on the Connecticut sailing vessels that first sighted Antarctica in 1820.[12] Among the five blacks who took part in John Brown's raid in

1859 was Shields Green, a sailor. Negro seamen were part of the crew of Herman Melville's *Pequod* when it sought the white whale. In his book, *Redburn,* Melville wrote of "the looks of interest with which negro-sailors are regarded when they walk the Liverpool streets." He noted that

> . . . in Liverpool indeed the negro steps with a prouder pace, and holds his head like a man; for there no such exaggerated feeling exists in respect to him, as here in America. Three or four times, I encountered our black steward, dressed very handsomely and walking arm in arm with a good-looking English woman. In New York, such a couple would have been mobbed in three minutes; and the steward would have been lucky to escape with whole limbs.[13]

Once aboard ships, black sailors experienced a somewhat different life than that on American soil. The atmosphere was freer, and in many cases, racism was relatively absent as white and black seamen worked, ate, and slept together. In the nineteenth century maritime industry, all seamen were exploited terriby, regardless of color. In his extensive series, "Colored Seamen—Their Character and Condition," the first comprehensive study of black seamen,[14] Powell pointed out that under the tyrannical maritime laws of the times, the seaman's life was a bitter one. The sailor, whether black or white, he wrote, was treated as "an article of merchandise. Imported and exported from one country to another, and bartered for, sold, transferred from his ship to a rum-selling boarding-house—to the brothel, and those sinks of pollution, where he is exchanged for what he is worth, until, like a depreciated currency, he is shipped at a discount to some foreign port, and passed off as current coin." At sea, the sailor was "wholly at the mercy of tyrant captains and brutal officers."[15]

The black seaman had the additional burden of his color, and if conditions were horrible for white seamen, they were doubly so, Powell noted, for those "erratic philosophers of toil—the colored sons of the ocean."[16] Thousands of black seamen, he pointed out, "enter the mercantile and naval service at an early age, uneducated and unskilled in the mechanical arts or scientific knowledge, and, therefore, have no encouragement to follow the industrial pursuits of landsmen." The black seaman soon became "a mere tool in the hands of evil-disposed persons." Many were "despoiled of their clothing by shipmates, and sometimes by the officers, when crossing the Western ocean. . . ." Subject as he was "to the unholy prejudice" everywhere in his native land because of his color, the black seaman faced special oppression in the slave states. He was "seized upon when entering a Southern port of discharge, and thrust into prison for no other crime than that of his having a colored skin, where in some cases, he is stripped of his hard earnings, and not permitted to depart until he has paid the utmost farthing. . . ." If he was unlucky, he could easily be sold into slavery and remain a slave the rest of his life.[17]

In the ports of Charleston, Savannah, Mobile, and New Orleans, black seamen were taken from the vessels to which they belonged, thrown into prison, and detained there at their own expense. Late in 1822, South Carolina, thoroughly frightened by the Denmark Vesey conspiracy, passed a law forbidding free black seamen to leave their vessels while in her ports. Black cooks, stewards, mariners, or any other blacks on such vessels were "to be seized and confined to jail, until said vessel is ready to sail." At that time, either the seaman or his captain was required to pay the cost of the detention; should either fail to do so, "such free negroes or persons of color shall be deemed and taken as absolute slaves, and sold. . . ." During the years that followed, several other slave states passed similar laws.[18]

No one did more to expose and denounce this vicious practice than Powell. He published articles bitterly condemning "the many brutal outrages committed upon the liberties of these poor defenceless coloured sailors in the Southern ports of their own country, for which country, coloured men poured out their life's blood, to defend against British bayonets." He pointed out that Article IV, Section 2, of the Constitution of the United States, expressly provided that "citizens of each State shall be entitled to all the privileges and immunities of citizens in the several states," and he insisted that since blacks were citizens of a number of northern states, their imprisonment constituted a clear violation of the Constitution. Powell further argued that the state laws under which the acts against black seamen were committed were also in direct contravention of two other provisions of the Constitution: the power of Congress "to regulate commerce with foreign nations and among the several states," and the provision that "all treaties made, or which shall be made, under the authority of the United States, shall be part of the supreme law of the land." He pointed out that when black seamen who were part of the crews of foreign vessels were imprisoned in southern states, such actions came into direct conflict with all the commercial treaties that had been negotiated by the United States with foreign nations.

Powell did more than argue the legal issues involved in the outrages committed against black seamen. He petitioned Congress and memorialized northern state legislatures, challenging them to make known whether they acquiesced in a situation where "free colored people are to be kept in prison, [so] that the slave owners of South Carolina, Alabama, and Georgia may find profitable employment for their slaves," and so that they might sleep free of the fear that "the colored seamen of the North, having experienced the blessings of freedom, might contaminate their slaves, and thus cause insurrection."[19]

It was through the Colored Seamen's Home, however, that Powell made his major contribution to the well-being of black seamen. With the aid of the American Seamen's Friend Society, his enterprise kept expanding, although Powell also put his own money into alterations and repairs.[20] While most boarders paid for their stay, no "destitute black sailors" were turned away, and all received relief in the form of board and clothing.[21] After a visit in February, 1848, Frederick Douglass praised Powell's Colored Seamen's Home as "an *Oasis* in the desert, when compared with the many houses where seamen usually congregate." The banner of temperance floated conspicuously throughout the establishment, and an excellent library and other reading room facilities were available. At meal times, and on every other occasion, Powell led discussions of the issues confronting blacks. Douglass himself had escaped from slavery with the aid of a black seaman who was his height, and who had loaned him his sailor's suit and a sailor's "protection," and he was very much impressed with the discussions held at Powell's home concerning slavery and the need for conducting a continuous struggle against it.[22]

In July, 1849, Powell moved the Home from Cherry Street (where it had been moved earlier) to 330 Pearl Street in order to be closer to the waterfront. In announcing the move, Powell added that he was

compelled to make the first public appeal to the friends of the cause for aid. To procure beds and bedding and furniture, and to pay his additional rent, will sink the enterprise, unless friends voluntarily come to his relief. And this relief he *earnestly* asks, not on his own account, but on account of his brethren, the colored seamen, who may, through the instrumentality of a well regulated home, be saved from wretchedness here and hereafter.[23]

The public response was sufficient to enable Powell to accommodate over seventy black seamen, although he made it a practice to open the place to the general public as well. He believed that the "sailor's occupation necessarily shuts him out of the pale of social, civil, moral, and religious society," and that mingling with the general public would help destroy the image of the sailor as nothing but a drunkard. At the same time, he hoped that the militancy of the black seamen on the slavery issue might influence the general public who met them at the Home. Powell frequently stressed the role that black seamen had played in the anti-impressment riots of colonial America. He kept a portrait of Crispus Attucks in the main room of the Colored Seamen's Home and pointed with pride to the fact that free black sailors had distributed copies of David Walker's *Appeal* to slaves in the South.

Powell also involved the black seamen in his home in anti-slavery work. He was a founder of the Manhattan Anti-Slavery Society, and in November 1840, as its secretary, he announced proudly that the new organization, with over 100 members, was not confining itself to any special group of abolitionists, but was composed of "the real 'lapwater' abolitionists of New York City, and has a platform broad enough to admit ALL without respect to sex or color."[24]

Although Powell did effective work for the Manhattan Anti-Slavery Society at the same time that he was operating the Colored Seamen's Home, it was not until the first case involving the Fugitive Slave Act of 1850 that his activity in the anti-slavery movement became well known. The case took place in New York City and brought home very sharply the inhuman features of the act. James Hamlet, a fugitive slave, had worked for three years as a porter for the firm of Tilton & Maloney. On September 26, 1850, a few days after the adoption of the new fugitive slave law, Hamlet was seized on the streets of New York, arrested, tried before the United States Commissioner, and ordered returned to his former owner. Hamlet left behind him a wife and two children, and a description of the tearful parting from his family before being "hurried off into slav-

ery. . . , probably to wear out his life quickly in severe and unre-
quited labor on a cotton or sugar plantation." This enraged the black
community of New York City, and even moved the commercial
interests.[25]

As secretary of the Manhattan Anti-Slavery Society, Powell,
accompanied by several black seamen from his Colored Seamen's
Home, visited Mayor C. S. Woodhull to find out whether the civil
authorities would protect free colored persons from being carried off
into slavery. It is possible that the news that black seamen were part
of the delegation frightened the mayor, for he was not in his office
when they arrived. Powell left a letter asking the mayor:

> . . . what protection we, the free colored people, may expect under the
> operation of the Fugitive Slave Law. The peculiar position we occupy in
> this State—depending upon the magistery of the People of New York to
> defend her citizens against the operation of an unjust law, requires that
> we solicit in the name of our families that information from you which
> the nature of the case demands. Please answer and address William P.
> Powell, Colored Seamen's Home, 330 Pearl Street.

The mayor's answer did not come for several days, but when it did,
he assured Powell in person that in case of the arrest of a fugitive, he
had ordered policemen or any other officers of the city to refrain
"from assisting the slaveholder in returning the slaves under the late
act of Congress." However, he could not tell free colored people what
course they ought to pursue in the event of seizure. "I assured his
Honor," Powell reported, "that in the event of my friend Robert
Hamilton [who was present] being arrested under the Fugitive act
with the intent to reduce him to Slavery, that we would not allow him
to be taken out of the city—to which the Mayor made no reply."[26]

Powell made this report to a mass meeting called at Zion Chapel
Church on October 1, 1850, for the purpose of asking colored men
the questions: "Shall we resist oppression? Shall we defend our
Liberties? Shall we be *Freemen* or *Slaves?*" In addition to presiding
at the packed meeting, Powell delivered a militant speech, asking:

> Shall the iniquitous Fugitive Slave bill, which subjects every free
> colored man, woman and child, to be seized upon, handcuffed, and
> plunged into perpetual Slavery, be resisted or acquiesced in? Shall the
> blood-thirsty slaveholder be permitted by this unrighteous law to come
> into our domiciles, or workshops, or the places where we labor, and

carry off our wives and children, our fathers and mothers, and our-selves, without a struggle—without resisting, even if need be, unto death? Or, shall we sit down and tamely submit our necks to the halter, and our limbs to the shackles, and every step which we may take, whether it be backwards or forwards, will be followed by consequences too vast, too momentous to be considered by any one present; upon your decision this night hangs suspended the fate of millions. . . . When the mother country imposed on the infant colonies the three-and-a-half per cent tax, and the Stamp Act, the first blood that was shed in resistance of the odious act was shed by Attucks, a colored man, and he was the first to receive the fire of the British soldiery, and throughout the revolutionary and late war, colored men stood side by side with white men, and achieved a most glorious victory in the name of liberty. We have met this night to decide, not whether we will pay the govern-ment a three-and-a-half percent tax or an impost duty, but whether we will suffer ourselves and families to be made slaves. . . . You are told to submit peaceably to the laws; will you do so? You are told to kiss the manacles that bind you; will you do so?[27]

Shouts of "No! No! No!" greeted each of these questions. Later, the meeting resolved to help raise enough money to redeem Hamlet from slavery. By October 3, the purchase price of $800 had been raised, and within a day, Hamlet was back in New York City, restored to his family, his friends and supporters, and his job as porter.[28]

On Saturday, October 5, 1850, at twelve noon, New York's blacks met for the first time in a public park. Five thousand people gathered to welcome James Hamlet home. William P. Powell opened the meeting by welcoming the audience and thanking them for being present "to honor a man, the first victim arrested under an unconstitutional act, and brought to trial without due process of law." He then read the resolutions which thanked those who had "so generously contributed to the emancipation of James Hamlet"; joyfully hailed his restoration to freedom, and predicted that his return would "be the time of our complete enfranchisement." In his speech, however, Powell was not so confident that Hamlet's return signified a victory over slavery, since he had been redeemed, "not by the irresistible genius of universal emancipation, but by the irresistible genius of the almighty dollar." Nevertheless, he said with deep emotion: "In the name of Almighty God and his holy angels, beneath an October sun, and in the name of humanity all over the earth, I welcome you, James Hamlet, back to your wife, your children and your home once made desolate by an awful abduction of your person but now to be made happy by your speedy return, not as a slave, but as a *Freeman*." At this point, Powell shook Hamlet by his hand amidst an outburst of cheers, mingled with sobs and tears.[29]

While he continued his involvement in the struggle against the Fugitive Slave Act,[30] Powell was growing more and more discouraged at the prospects for his seven children in the United States. He had had several personal encounters with racism. In the mid-1840s, while travelling to Canada with his family on board a lake steamer, he was told by the captain that he could not eat at the same table with white people because he was colored. "I told him," Powell recalled, "I did not think it any honor to eat with them as white people, nor neither was it his place to decide what I considered to be a question of *right* and not of *principle*—that my money for first class fare, which I had paid, had *settled* that question both ways, and all he had to do, as the servant of the travelling public, was to serve them without regard to *color*." A year later, he gave the same reply to a conductor in the Harlem cars who had ordered Powell and his wife to sit "in the place for colored people."[31]

In August 1850 Powell stirred a storm in the New York City pro-slavery press by having "the impudence to walk arm and arm through Cherry Street with a white man." While explaining that he had been helping a "poor miserable drunkard by the arm and led him home to his wife and children," he told the press that it was no business of theirs with whom he walked. What particularly angered Powell was the fact that Horace Greeley of the New York *Tribune* rebuked him for his conduct, and had reminded Powell that this was not his country. Powell shot back angrily:

I will endeavor to tell this modern Philosopher and wily Politician, what we have done for *his* country, for we are told this is not our country. Our fathers have toiled and labored and their children have levelled your forests, tilled your lands, enriched the soil with their sweat and blood, cultivated the three greatest staple commodities upon which your *commerce* is based, viz., *Cotton, Rice, and Tobacco*. They have fought your battles, manned your ships of war, mingled their blood with that of your fathers, laid down their lives as a free will offering on the altar of freedom, and secured your Independence from British rule. For more than two hundred years, by the profits of their unpaid labor our fathers have launched this nation with treasures untold. All they have received in return are whips, chains, perpetual Slavery and *imprisonment* whenever a free colored man sets his foot on slave territory. The whole world knows that we have done enough for you, and so does the *Honorable Horace Greeley,* editor of the New York *Tribune* know that we have done enough. But this cowardly editor dares to tell us how to conduct ourselves because this is not our country![32]

On July 31, 1851, *Frederick Douglass' Paper* carried the following announcement under the heading "The Shame of America":

Mr. William P. Powell of New York, an educated and highly respectable man, though of an unconstitutional color, intends to remove to England with his large family to give his children a better chance than they have in this caste-ridden country.

In an interview, Powell explained that although he himself had been successful in the United States, this success had been "in spite of the obstacles which every day of my life have been thrown in my way because of my complexion." He had no way of knowing, he went on, that his children would be blessed with equally good luck, or that energy and enterprise would bring them success:

I have decided to remove to another country where my children will not, because of their color alone, be compelled to fight the battle of life at a disadvantage, which I too well know how to appreciate. I do not feel I would be discharging a parental duty by retaining them in a land which though theirs by birth, makes them alien to the protection of its laws and the benefits of its social relations.[33]

Although he had the means to move to England with his wife and seven children, before leaving, Powell chose to present claims to the New York legislature which had been denied him from his birth. He sent a petition to the legislature requesting aid to assist him in the removal of his family to a new home. He set forth the facts that his grandmother had been a cook for the first Continental Congress and had thereby helped to form the glorious Union of the United States; that his father had been a slave in New York, and through his unpaid labor, had also contributed to the welfare of the nation; and that they had been entitled to receive the benefits of the Declaration of

Independence, but had been denied them because of their color, with the result that the contract embodied in the Declaration guaranteeing to all "life, liberty and the pursuit of happiness" had been broken. Inasmuch as the New York legislature had taken favorable action to aid blacks "emigrating from this country to Liberia," Powell insisted that it make good what was owed to his grandmother and father by enabling him to give his own children "those opportunities for a livelihood and a respectable position in society, to which, as human beings, and as American citizens they are entitled, by making it possible to take them to the kingdom of Great Britain, where character and not color—capacity and not complexion, are the tests of merit."[34]

Powell sent his petition to the member of the state legislature from his district, but that individual refused even to present it. "Had Mr. Powell asked permission to sell his children at auction to the highest bidder," commented the *National Anti-Slavery Standard,* "we have no doubt he would have gained a hearing, but a petition for aid to remove them where the buying and selling of their brethren would not consign them to contempt and degradation, was not deemed proper by his representative even to present to the Legislature."[35]

In his parting letter to his associates in the anti-slavery movement, Powell urged them to be "true to principle, to be true to the slave." As for himself, he pledged to remain faithful to those still "in the bondage of American slavery."[36] He lived up to this pledge. In the ten years Powell spent in England, he spoke regularly at meetings sponsored by the various anti-slavery societies, and did much—especially to counter the argument prevalent in British working-class circles that the chattel slaves of the South were far better off than the wage slaves in the British mines and factories, and that therefore the abolitionists should concern themselves solely with the problems at home. Powell hammered away at the theme that "the systems of free and slave labor are as far [apart] as the Poles." Bad as conditions were in the mines and factories he had visited in England, the workers there

> . . . are not chattels personal, subject to corporal punishment, ships and chains, and separated, parents from their children, and husbands from their wives. But not so with the supposedly "sleek, comfortably clothed, well fed, fat and saucy southern slaves." Are there any laws

regulating the price of slave labor or the hours of slave work as there are Parliamentary enactments for the workers in British mines and mills? Are there any laws forbidding corporal punishment of slaves for non-performance of tasks? Are there laws punishing with death the master, overseer, or driver, for murder, rape or *violence* committed daily upon the defenceless slaves? And yet we are supposed to believe that the American negro slaves are better off than the operatives in the cotton factories and coal mines of England!

British abolitionists reprinted Powell's attack on the defenders of chattel slavery and distributed it widely in British labor circles.

Continuing a struggle he had waged so vigorously while in America, Powell also sought to mobilize public opinion to pressure the British government to take firmer steps to protect black seamen from England who were jailed in southern ports in the United States. He published facts in the British press about the vicious practice and played an important part in making the issue a significant one.[37]

Early in 1861, feeling that the approaching Civil War would bring about a major change for his people, Powell returned to New York City. He quickly resumed two of his former activities. For one thing, he immediately rejoined the anti-slavery movement in the Empire City and, soon after the outbreak of war, demanded the immediate abolition of slavery. He was disappointed to discover that the Lincoln Administration was unwilling to move in that direction. In a letter from Boston to a West India Emancipation Celebration meeting on August 1, 1861, in New Bedford, Powell (who was described as "recently of Liverpool") praised the British for having freed the slaves in the West Indies almost thirty years earlier. He continued bitterly:

But how stands the record in our unfortunate distracted country? Alas! tell it not in heathen lands, publish it not in the highway of the worlds progressive civilization that cotton is still king—the lords of the lash, though in open rebellion with armed resistance against the best slave-holding government that ever cursed the world. I say the lords of the lash still live as a terrible power.[38]

As early as August 1861, Powell insisted that the preservation of the Union was impossible without the abolition of slavery:

Will the government prosecute this war of subjugation, and bring the rebel States—slavery and all,—back to their allegiance? Ah! sir, if that is the sole aim of the government of President Lincoln and the federal army, they will be surely and shamefully beaten. This war, disguise it as they may, is virtually nothing more nor less than perpetual slavery against universal freedom, and to this end the free States will have to come. . . .

Never was there a greater opportunity for the American nation to put an everlasting end to negro slavery than now. . . . Without going into detail, I propose that Congress, at its next session, instantly abolish slavery by proclamation, without compensation, in all the rebel States . . . repeal the Fugitive Slave Law—form a new treaty with Great Britain, to effectually break up the African slave-trade—abolish slavery in Maryland and Virginia by compensation, and thereby make the capital free territory, as it should have been at the foundation of the government.[39]

The second activity Powell resumed after his return was reported in the *Sailors' Magazine:* "On Mr. Powell's return from England, whither he had been for the education of his children, because the foolish and wicked prejudices of Americans would not permit them to enter our institutions, he has again opened a Sailors' Home for the seamen of his race."[40] The Home was reopened at 2 Dover Street, and as its superintendent, Powell reported regularly on its affairs to the American Seamen's Friend Society. Powell's reports pointed up new problems confronting black seamen in addition to those which had previously existed. Not a few of the stewards, cooks, and sailors who boarded at the Colored Seamen's Home were "wholly destitute of money and clothing," having formerly been "slaves of rebel masters . . . liberated by the government and taken into the United States naval service. Subsequently they were discharged, and arrived at this port. Unfortunately, they fell into the hands of white and black land-sharks, and were stripped of all their clothes and money." In this predicament, "they found their way to the Home, and were kindly welcomed and cared for." Sixty-one black sailors, shipwrecked and destitute, some of them former capatives of the "pirate Alabama," came to the Home in 1862–1863. Others, "who had been discharged from Government service, fell among a gang of runners and landlords, and were made to pay $4 each for breakfast, with an intimation, (when they expressed dissatisfaction), that they must each pay $7 more before they could leave the premises." However, they "escaped and with some difficulty, managed to save their luggage, and were brought to the Home."[41]

"Gentlemen," Powell stated in concluding one of his reports to the Board of Trustees of the American Seamen's Friend Society, "these facts, though of everyday occurrence, tend to confirm the existence of a widespread evil, from which, notwithstanding all the safeguards the Society may throw around the unsuspecting, confiding sailor, and all the vigilance we may use, it seems almost impossible for him to escape."[42] By now Powell was convinced that much as temperance and religion could accomplish for the black seamen, they could not really solve their fundamental problems. So long as the seamen were forced to accept whatever wages and conditions were offered them, and had no control over their labor, they would remain at the mercy and under the absolute and despotic domination of ship masters and shipowners while at sea and loan sharks and rent-gouging landlords while on land. Powell, himself a deeply religious man, felt that while the concern for sailors' souls was a good idea, it was no substitute for concern for their temporal well-being.[43]

The answer, Powell concluded, lay in the formation of an organization of black seamen which would protect and uphold their rights. Although there was some tradition before the Civil War for black workers to unite for protection and for the alleviation of their conditions, such societies resembled fraternal lodges more than trade unions, emphasizing "the need to relieve the distressed, and soften the forms of poverty by timely aid to the afflicted."[44] As Charles H. Wesley has pointed out: "Their special features were benevolence and protection. They cared for the sick and the infirm, and helped the unemployed to secure employment."[45] So far as we know, there is no history associated with them of economic pressure of a trade union nature.

Another type of organization in existence before the Civil War is exemplified by the American League of Colored Laborers, organized in New York City in July 1850, with Frederick Douglass as a vice-president. Its main objective was to promote unity among mechanics, foster training in agriculture, industrial arts, and commerce, and assist member mechanics in setting up business for themselves. Clearly, the league was interested in industrial education rather than trade union activity; moreover, its orientation was toward the self-employed artisan.[46]

In March 1863, William P. Powell and a handful of black seamen created what Sidney Kaplan correctly describes as "a pioneer organization on a quasi-trade union basis"—an organization which stood somewhere between the "old style benevolent society and the Negro labor unions that burgeoned during the five years following the end of the Civil War."[47] This was the American Seamen's Protective Union Association, the first seamen's organization of any kind or color in the United States.

The American Seamen's Protective Union Association was organized at William P. Powell's Colored Seamen's Home on December 31, 1862. Reverend Amos C. Beman, a black minister, was present on the occasion, and he reported remarks "by Mr. Powell upon the importance of Union among our seamen and modes in which their condition might be improved and their welfare secured. A committee was appointed to prepare and present a suitable constitution for an organization."[48] In March 1863, a constitution was adopted and, on April 15, the Association was incorporated. Its constitution, consisting of a preamble and seventeen articles, has been lost. However, the *Sailors' Magazine* did note receiving a copy and reported that it provided for a president, twelve vice-presidents, a secretary, treasurer, chaplain, physician, and nine counsellors. Its tenth article restricted the membership to stewards, cooks, and seamen.[49]

Although the editor of the *Sailors' Magazine* chided the founders for having omitted the word "colored" from its name and constitution—after all, it noted, the Association "is for the benefit of *colored* seamen"—he had nothing but praise for its principles and found its list of officers and counsellors "very respectable." "We heartily rejoice," he concluded, "in any movement which this most useful class of men is making toward their own elevation and improvement, or which their friends are making in their behalf."[50]

By May 1863 the ASPUA was "in successful operation." Already the Association was using the Colored Seamen's Home as a "shaping-up" hall from which black seamen would be hired to ship out without having to pay bribes or special fees to land-sharks and landlords. Although the shaping-up hall had been "bitterly opposed by a combination of colored sailor landlords," the operation had continued and was now successful. Powell reported that meetings were held every Wednesday at the Colored Seamen's Home, and although the organization was only two months old, it already had 55 members. He predicted that

> . . . the time is not far distant when ample arrangements (growing out of this organization) will be made to meet the "ills of earth"!—when the colored sailor shall have thrown around him all needed safeguards for his moral and social elevation.[51]

Powell's optimism was shared by the *Sailors' Magazine* which, in the same month of May 1863, lauded the ASPUA as a "beneficial self-protective Society for colored seamen . . . organized among themselves, which promises good to that class and to the interests of commerce, so far as affected by the improvement of our colored seamen."[52]

Unfortunately, however, any hope that the American Seamen's Protective Union Association could do any more at this point to solve the economic grievances of black seamen was shattered during the riots of July 1863, when for four frightful days a mob roamed the streets of New York, killing, burning, and looting. The rioters were protesting the new Conscription Law, which drafted the poor, but permitted rich men to escape military service by paying for a substitute. However, most of their anger, stirred up by the Copperheads, was directed against blacks. Dozens of blacks were lynched, the Colored Orphan Asylum was burned to the ground, and the Colored Seamen's Home was attacked, "rifled of all its furniture, clothing and books," and the building partly damaged. Powell barely managed to save himself and his family from the mob. He published the following hair-raising account:

> . . . My family, including my invalid daughter, took refuge on the roof of the next house. I remained till the mob broke in and then narrowly escaped the same way. This was about 8½ p.m. We remained on the roof for an hour. It began to rain, as if the very heavens were shedding tears over the dreadful calamity.
>
> How to escape from the roof of a five-story building with four females—and one a cripple—without a ladder was beyond my *not* excited imagination. But God came to my relief in the person of a little deformed, despised Israelite who, Samaritan-like, took my poor help-

less daughter under his protection in his house. He also supplied me with a long rope. Though pitchy dark I took soundings with the rope to see if it would touch the next roof, after which I took a clove-hitch around the clothesline which led from one roof to the other over a space of about one hundred feet. I managed to lower my family down to the next roof and from one roof to another, until I landed them in a neighbor's yard. We were secreted in our friend's cellar till 11 p.m. when we were taken by the police and locked up in the station house for safety. In this dismal place we found upward of seventy men, women and children—some with broken limbs—bruised and beaten from head to foot. We stayed in this place for 24 hours, when the police escorted us to the New Haven boat. All my personal property to the amount of $3000 has been scattered to the four winds . . . My oldest son is now serving my country as a surgeon in the United States army, and I myself had just received a commission in the naval service. . . . I am now an old man, stripped of everything which I once possessed, of all the comforts of life; but I thank God that He has yet spared my life, which I am ready to yield in defence of my country.[53]

Operations at the Colored Seamen's Home, which was the headquarters of the American Seamen's Protective Union Association, had to be suspended for three months while repairs were being made. In November 1863, the *Sailors' Magazine* announced that the Home was "thoroughly repaired, newly painted, and re-furnished with new furniture, beds and bedding," and was ready to operate once again as a home "for our colored seamen." In a tribute to its proprietor, the magazine declared:

Mr. Powell is well known in the business community, as an enterprising, intelligent, and worthy citizen, though [sic] of dark complexion, as his ancestors, on one side, come from Africa. He is entitled to great credit for his persistent efforts in behalf of our colored seamen, and to the protection of the Law, and the patronage of the friends of humanity.[54]

The Colored Seamen's Home continued to operate even though it had lost in the riot nearly all the clothing it kept for destitute colored seamen. In the summer of 1866, Powell reported that the Home was prospering, but a year later he ventured the opinion that "a permanent location" was needed for the more than 3,000 colored seamen shipping out of New York's port. Notwithstanding the many obstacles it had had to overcome since its formation in 1839, the Colored Seamen's Home, Powell declared proudly, had become an "indispensable institution" for black seamen—"a necessity, in all that appertains to the well-being of our colored brethren of the sea."[55] It was with special pride that Powell pointed to the fact that, as superintendent, he had been instrumental in persuading colored seamen to deposit their savings in the Seamen's Savings Bank, and during the five years from 1862 through 1867, he had remitted over $5,000 to the families and friends of seamen. He had also collected claims from the United States government amounting to more than $40,000 due to colored seamen and soldiers in the government service. Salvage money amounting to $27,500 had been paid to Negro captain-owner Mott Johnson and the crew of the Bahamian schooner *Carelton* "for saving from shipwreck the United States gunboat *Claucus* when off the Bahamas." The money had been shared by "colored men."[56]

During the summer of 1865, Powell was appointed a Notary Public in New York City—the first black to be so commissioned. Perhaps remembering Powell's bitter attack on him, Horace Greeley sought to make amends by praising Governor Fenton for the appointment of so "well educated a man who had accomplished so much for sailors of a black complexion."[57]

The American Seamen's Protective Union Association, too, had apparently survived the draft riots of 1863, for seven years later, in a survey of "Labor in New York," Powell reported that there was still functioning in the port of New York an organization "known as the American Seamen's Protective Union Association with an accumulating capital." That is all we learn about the organization, but Powell did add the fact that the annual wages earned by the 3,500 colored seamen in the mercantile-marine service, sailing to and from the port of New York, amounted to $1,260,000, that the seamen were now generally "self-supporting," and that "there is now no invidious discrimination as to color, wages or grade of service, as there was in the days of slavery."[58] Undoubtedly, the Colored Seamen's Home and the American Seamen's Protective Union Association had played an important role in this development.

Powell concluded his survey of "Labor in New York" with the following observation:

> What we most need, next to a plenty of work, in New York, as well as in other Northern States, is the elective franchise. Figuratively speaking, it

lubricates the corroded hinges upon which swings wide open the portals of the temple of industry, closed against the Northern colored man's right of labor, and which can only be opened by the talismanic word of two syllables, viz: the ballot.[59]

Unfortunately, the ballot, secured for black men in the Fifteenth Amendment shortly after this was published, did not prove to be the "open sesamé" to black employment. Indeed, the last time William P. Powell's name crops up in the records of New York City is in October 1873, during the depression of that year, when, as chairman of the New York Civil Rights Committee, he sent a petition to the president and members of the Board of Commissioners of Parks urging the granting to black unemployed of "their share of public employment," so that they could avoid starvation in the midst of plenty.[60]

Powell's name does appear in the black press of San Francisco for a few years thereafter, for he visited California en route to Hawaii, and on his return, remained in San Francisco. He was reported as one of the signers of a call for a civil rights meeting in 1876. Our last evidence of William P. Powell is in 1879, when he is reported to have participated in a William Lloyd Garrison Memorial Meeting in San Francisco.[61]

Our information on the career of William P. Powell is still inadequate. But we know enough already to understand why the *National Anti-Slavery Standard* referred to him as "a leading man among the colored people of New York City, and deservedly well known for his character, for his intelligence, integrity, enterprise, industry and selfless devotion to the well-being of all who are denied the rights of freedom and American citizenship for no color of crime, but for the crime of color."[62] Or why the *Sailors' Magazine* paid tribute to Powell "for his persistent efforts in behalf of our colored seamen. . . ."[63] We can therefore reasonably ask that in all future editions of Negro Handbooks, Encyclopedias of the Colored Race, Negro Reference Books, and histories of Black Americans, the existence of William P. Powell be acknowledged and his distinguished contributions duly noted.

NOTES

1. *The American Negro Reference Book* (Englewood, N.J., 1970); *The Negro Almanac* (New York, 1976); *The Negro Heritage Library* (Yonkers, N.Y., 1965); Richard Bardolph, *The Negro Vanguard* (New York, 1959); *Who's Who Among Black Americans,* (Northbrook, Ill., 1975–1976); *The Negro Handbook* (Chicago, 1969); *The Ebony Handbook* (Chicago, 1974); Encyclopedia Britannica, *The Negro in American History* (Washington, D.C., 1969); *The National Cyclopedia of the Colored Race* (Montgomery, Ala., 1919); Du Bois, *Encyclopedia of the Negro,* prep. vol. (New York, 1946).

2. Simm, *Men or Mark* (New York, 1887; reprinted New York, 1968); Franklin, *From Slavery to Freedom* (New York, 1974).

3. *Dictionary Catalogue of the Schomburg Collection* (Boston, 1962); *Dictionary Catalogue of the Mooreland Collection* (Boston, 1970).

4. Benjamin Quarles, *Black Abolitionists* (New York, 1969), pp. 98, 99, 201, 212. Herbert Aptheker, ed., *A Documentary History of the Negro People in the United States* (New York, 1951), pp. 173, 625. James M. McPherson, ed., *The Negro's Civil War* (New York, 1965), pp. 40, 73. McPherson, however, incorrectly calls Powell a New York physician. Sidney Kaplan, "The American Seamen's Protective Union Association of 1863: A Pioneer Organization of Negro Seamen in the Port of New York," *Science & Society,* Vol. XXI (Spring, 1962), pp. 154–59. Dorothy Sterling, ed., *Speak Out In Thunder Tones: Letters and Other Writings by Black Northerners, 1787–1865* (New York, 1973), pp. 337–38.

5. Letter of James Buchanan, Secretary of State, to George D. Cooper, Notary Public, New York and Washington, Nov. 6, 1846, in *National Anti-Slavery Standard,* Sept. 6, 1849: "Memorial of William P. Powell to the Honorable the Senate and House of Assembly of the State of New York," *National Anti-Slavery Standard,* July 17, 1851.

6. James de T. Abajian, *Blacks in Selected Newspapers, Censuses and Other Sources: An Index to Names and Subjects* (Boston, 1977), p. 96.

7. Letter of William P. Powell in *National Anti-Slavery Standard,* Nov. 2, 1846.

8. *Liberator,* Nov. 17, 1837 and reprinted in Aptheker, *op. cit.,* pp. 173–74. In introducing the report of the meeting, Garrison commented: "We commend the course marked out by our colored friends in New Bedford" (*Liberator,* Nov. 17, 1837).

In a letter to William Lloyd Garrison, July 10, 1839, Powell made clear his support of the position adopted by the editor of *The Liberator* on anti-slavery issues as well as his own opposition to colonization (*Journal of Negro History,* Vol. X, July, 1925, pp. 430–31). For evidence of his later opposition to colonization, see the report of the "Great Anti-Colonization Mass Meeting of the Colored Citizens of the City of New York," where William P. Powell is listed as one of the secretaries (*The Liberator,* May 11, 1949). After Frederick Douglass' break with Garrison in 1849–1850, Powell sided with Garrison, and Douglass described him as using his "wit" to defend Garrison (*Frederick Douglass' Paper,* Sept. 9, 1853). For a discussion of the split between Douglass and Garrison, see Philip S. Foner, *Life and Writings of Frederick Douglass,* Vol. II (New York, 1950), pp. 48–65.

9. *National Anti-Slavery Standard,* April 5, 1849.

10. Philip S. Foner, *History of Black Americans: From Africa to the Emergence of the Cotton Kingdom* (Westport, Conn., 1975), pp. 228, 247, 261, 308, 309, 310–12; Peter Olsen, "The Negro Maritime Worker and the Sea," *Negro History Bulletin,* Vol. XXXIV, Feb. 1971, pp. 38–39.

11. James Freeman Clarke, *Condition of the Free Colored People of the United States* (New York, 1859), p. 23.

12. Sidney Kaplan, "Negro Seamen Present at the Discovery of Antarctica," *Negro History Bulletin,* Vol. XIX, Jan. 1956, p. 80.

13. Herman Melville, *Redburn* (Boston, 1849), p. 203.

14. In its 1845 survey, "Labor in New York: Its Circumstances, Conditions and Resources," the New York *Tribune* included a detailed discussion of "The Sailors," but said nothing at all about black seamen. (See New York *Tribune,* Nov. 17, 1845.)

15. *National Anti-Slavery Standard,* Nov. 12, 1846.

16. *Ibid.,* Nov. 19, 26, 1846; *Sailors' Magazine,* March 1863, p. 201; May 1863, p. 271.

17. *National Anti-Slavery Standard,* Oct. 8, 15, 1846; *Sailors' Magazine,* March 1863, p. 201; May 1867, p. 245.

18. "Free Colored Seamen. . . ," *House Reports No. 50,* 27th Cong., 3rd Sess., Jan. 30, 1845, pp. 21–23.

19. *National Anti-Slavery Standard,* Nov. 12, 19, 26, 1846.

20. *Sailors' Magazine,* Feb. 1842, p. 197; *National Anti-Slavery Standard,* Feb. 24, 1842.

21. *The North Star,* April 7, 1849.

22. *Ibid.,* Feb. 11, 1848. For the story of Douglass' escape from slavery, see Philip S. Foner, *Life and Writings of Frederick Douglass,* Vol. I (New York, 1950), pp. 22–23.

23. *The North Star,* April 7, 1849.

24. *National Anti-Slavery Standard,* Nov. 5, 1840, Nov. 12, 1846, Nov. 12, 1850.

25. New York *Tribune,* Oct. 1, 1850; New York *Evening Post,* Oct. 1, 1850; *Liberator,* Oct. 3, 1850; Philip S. Foner, *Business and Slavery: The*

New York Merchants and the Irrepressible Conflict (Chapel Hill, N.C., 1940), p. 35.

26. *National Anti-Slavery Standard,* Oct. 10, 1850.

27. *Ibid.; The North Star,* Oct. 17, 1850.

28. Foner, *Business and Slavery,* p. 36; Quarles, *op. cit.,* p. 198; *Journal of Commerce,* Oct. 1, 6, 8, 9, 1850. New York merchants contributed to the Hamlet fund, and the *Journal of Commerce* set up a collection agency in its office (Foner, *Business and Slavery,* pp. 35–36).

29. *National Anti-Slavery Standard,* Oct. 10, 1850; *The North Star,* Oct. 17, 1850.

30. *Frederick Douglass' Paper,* Oct. 19, 26, 1850.

31. *National Anti-Slavery Standard,* Aug. 22, 1850.

32. *Ibid.*

33. *Ibid.,* July 17, 1851.

34. *Ibid.*

35. *Ibid.*

36. *Ibid.,* Nov. 27, 1851.

37. *Ibid.,* July 12, 19, 26, 1853; June 5, 12, 19, 1856; *Times* (London), April 15, 18, 1857; William P. Powell to Maria Weston Chapman, Liverpool, n.d., Anti-Slavery Letters to Garrison and Others, Vol. VII, p. 33, Boston Public Library, Rare Book Department.

38. *New York Weekly Anglo-African,* Aug. 10, 1861.

39. *Liberator,* Aug. 30, 1861; also reprinted in part in McPherson, *op. cit.,* p. 40.

40. *Sailors' Magazine,* Aug. 1862, p. 365.

41. *Ibid.,* March 1863, p. 201; May 1863, p. 271; Feb. 1865, p. 169.

42. *Ibid.,* March 1863, p. 201.

43. *Ibid.,* p. 312.

44. Philip S. Foner, *Organized Labor and the Black Worker, 1619–1973* (New York, 1974), pp. 10–11.

The New York African Society for Mutual Relief, founded in 1808; the Coachmen's Benevolent Society and the Humane Mechanics, organized in Philadelphia in the 1820s, and the Stewards' and Cooks' Marine Benevolent Society, established in New York in the 1830s, were examples of such organizations.

45. Charles H. Wesley, *Negro Labor in the United States, 1850–1925* (New York, 1927), p. 203.

46. Foner, *Organized Labor and the Black Worker,* p. 11.

47. Kaplan, "The American Seamen's Protective Union Association," p. 155.

48. *Sailors' Magazine,* March 1863, p. 202.

49. *Ibid.*, p. 200.

50. *Ibid.*

51. *Ibid.*, May 1863, p. 271.

52. *Ibid.*, p. 272.

53. *Liberator*, July 24, 1863. Also reprinted in part in McPherson, *op. cit.*, pp. 73–74, and Sterling, *op. cit.*, pp. 337–38.

54. *Sailors' Magazine*, Nov. 1863, p. 83.

55. *Ibid.*, Feb. 1864, p. 163.

56. *Ibid.*, Aug. 1867, pp. 282–83.

57. New York *Tribune* reprinted in *Sailors' Magazine*, Aug. 1865, p. 378. That same summer Powell was appointed a notary public for Connecticut, and the following winter he received a similar commission for New York State.

58. *New National Era*, Feb. 17, 1870.

59. *Ibid.*
Powell was a delegate representing black labor in New York at the founding convention of the Colored National Labor Union held in Washington, D.C., December 1869. See *Proceedings of the Colored National Labor Convention Held in Washington, D.C., on December 6, 7, 8, 9, 10, 1869*, Washington D.C., 1870.

60. New York *Herald*, Oct. 11, 1873, reprinted in Aptheker, *op. cit.*, pp. 624–25.

61. *San Francisco Elevator*, March 21, April 4, 1874; *San Francisco Pacific Appeal*, Jan. 8, 1876, June 11, 1879.

62. *National Anti-Slavery Standard*, Oct. 24, 1850.

63. *Sailors' Magazine*, Nov. 1863, p. 83.

7

A Labor Voice For Black Equality:
The *Boston Daily Evening Voice*, 1864-1867*

This article deals with only one of the many labor publications which emerged at the close of the Civil War, and it concentrates on only one of the many issues with which this journal concerned itself. The newspaper is the *Boston Daily Evening Voice* and the issue is the role of white labor with respect to black workers—especially the newly-emancipated four million black slaves. Of all the labor periodicals of the period, the *Voice* was the only one to champion the cause of unity of black and white labor in all areas of American life on the basis of equality. It was not only unique among the labor papers of its time, but it stood far ahead, in its social vision, of the vast majority of labor publications ever since.

The outbreak of the Civil War extinguished most of the trade unions which flourished during the 1850s. By the middle of 1862, and particularly after 1863, workers again began to move into unions. The early war depression was over, and business and industry were prospering as never before. Workingmen failed to reap any benefits from the good times that began late in 1862. Soaring prices rendered the vast majority worse off than they had been in 1860. Organization became a matter of urgent necessity. "Organize! Organize!" appealed Jonathan Fincher, editor of *Fincher's Trades' Review,* in December, 1863, "organize in every village and hamlet, and become tributary and auxiliary to district, county, state and national trade organizations."[1]

Long before this call was issued the revival of trade unionism had

*Reprinted from *Science & Society,* XXXVIII (Fall, 1974), 304–325.

started in earnest. Beginning in early 1863, scarcely a week passed without the formation of a new union in some part of the country. Between December, 1863 and December, 1864, the number of local unions (as reported to *Fincher's Trades' Review*) increased from 79 to 270. The national unions also expanded—21 new national unions were created in the decade 1860 to 1870, with the largest upsurge coming during the 1863–1865 period. Until 1865, however, the real center of organizational activity was not the national union but the city trades assembly. The city-council of labor unions, the key institution of the labor movement of the 1830s, became once again the agency for organizing mutual strike assistance, giving direction to labor's political activities, and supporting the labor press.[2]

The wartime revival of trade unions and city assemblies was helped by, and in turn stimulated, the reemergence of a labor press. In all about 130 daily, weekly, and monthly journals representing labor and advocating labor reform were launched between 1863 and 1873.[3] Of these several outstanding ones were formed by the printers themselves, usually during lock-outs. Perhaps because of the greater education necessary to pursue their trade, and certainly because they possessed the particular skills, printers took the lead as labor journalists.[4] Among the papers they established were the *Workingman's Advocate* of Chicago, the *Daily Press* of St. Louis, the *Union* of Detroit, and what George E. McNeill in his 1888 work, *The Labor Movement,* called "the most important" of the labor papers, "the *Daily Evening Voice* of the Boston Typographical Union."[5]

The *Voice* was a product of the employers' offensive which got under way late in 1863 to destroy the newly-formed unions. In November, 1864 the morning newspapers in Boston discharged their union printers. The Printers' Union answered the lock-out with a strike.[6] During the strike, the locked-out printers organized the "Voice Printing Company" to publish a newspaper under the title *Boston Daily Evening Voice*. Three union printers were elected to act as trustees: Henry L. Saxton, Wm. Knollen, and Abram Keach. The first issue of the *Voice* appeared on December 2, 1864, carrying a "Prospectus" which informed the public that "a number of practical workingmen, skilled in the art of printing and publishing a newspaper," had undertaken the publication of a daily evening paper "in the columns of which the rights of Labor—without distinction of sex, complexion or birthplace, shall be advocated, and the 'wrongs' asserted before the bar of an enlightened public opinion." They had been compelled to take this step by the necessity of earning a living. Because they were members of a trades union, which they had every right to form, they had been "thrown on the street." While they sought to win support from all members of the community, they were especially anxious to obtain the backing of the working class. "We speak the language of the laborer, and if we are understood by him, we are content."

The *Voice* company capitalized itself at $20,000 and issued shares. Seven trades' unions and six individuals invested, and in April, 1865 the company assured the public that if a sufficient number of additional shares were taken up to enable the officers to purchase "the necessary implements of Press, etc., and to open an office in some good business locality, there is not the slightest reason for doubting its entire success."[7]

The *Voice* company purchased a press and offices were set up at 77 Washington Street. Here, until the fall of 1867, the paper "published in the interests of workingmen" was put together and printed, and commercial printing, mainly for trades unions and eight-hour leagues, was performed. On March 31, 1866 the *Boston Weekly Voice* made its appearance, composed of selected material from the week's daily issues. The daily sold for two cents per copy; the weekly for five cents per copy. Subscribers paid $6 a year for the daily and $2 for the weekly.[8]

The *Voice* claimed "a larger *circulation* among the workingmen of New England than any other publication." Its appearance coincided with the re-emergence of the struggle for the ten-hour day by the factory workers of New England. By championing their cause the paper secured a fair circulation among the mill workers. But its subscribers were mainly members of the organized trades unions and eight-hour leagues in and around Boston. The Boston Trades' Assembly adopted it as its official organ, and the Grand Mass Meeting of workers in Faneuil Hall, Boston, November 2, 1865, hailed the paper as "a fearless and able advocate of our cause, and consider it the paramount duty of the workingmen of Massachusetts to sustain this paper, as the only true and legitimate organ of labor published in the State."[9]

The *Daily Voice* had four large pages, several columns to the page. (The *Weekly Voice*, issued every Thursday, had the same format.) The front page was usually devoted to national and international news, articles on labor subjects, speeches and public documents, and poetry and songs. Editorials, trade union news, correspondence, reprints from other papers, advertisements, notices of trade union and eight-hour league meetings, made up the rest.[10] Reminding its readers that the labor movement was "no local or temporary thing" but international in scope, the *Voice* paid attention to news of labor activities in England, France, and Germany. "The zeal of our transatlantic brethren should kindle our own," it counseled.[11]

The cause of the working classes, the *Voice* repeatedly emphasized, was in every sense, "conducive and essential to the GENERAL WELFARE." An eight-hour day for men and women workers, the key demand of the labor reform movement, would benefit the community as a whole. The "independence, intelligence, and moral development of the masses" were "the only sure foundation of our Republican System of Government."[12]

Convinced that the education of the working class was essential for the preservation of American democracy, the *Voice* constantly called for labor schools, classes in political economy, libraries, and reading rooms.[13] The paper noted the fact that the public libraries of Boston were closed on Sundays, and readers were urged to vote only for mayoralty and city council candidates who would pledge to open these facilities when workers could best make use of them.[14] The *Voice* was deeply concerned about the public schools of Boston, carrying a series of articles pointing up the inadequacies of the curriculum, the poor quality of the teachers, the antiquated books and equipment and concluding that too many children were graduated at the age of fifteen "with no better instruction than they should have had at twelve."[15] The *Voice* opened a discussion on the need for free colleges. "If we think so much of free schools," it declared, "why do we not carry out the system and have our colleges free?"[16]

Although it was one of the best-edited of the many labor papers of the 1860s, the positions adopted by the *Voice* on such issues as the shorter working day, mass education of the working class, political action, and labor reform in general were similar to those of many other papers.[17] But in a number of respects the *Voice* was unique.

It was, for example, far in advance of most of the labor papers in championing the cause of women workers. While some other labor papers carried news about the plight of women workers and commented sympathetically on their special difficulties, the *Voice* did more. It called upon male workers to assist women to organize and to open their unions to women. It congratulated New York trade unionists who established a library to which working women could have access at a nominal charge. But it reminded them that this was only a preparation for the "next step," which was to assist the working women to organize and secure higher wages and shorter hours: "till they do this they will have but little time and not much money to patronize their library."[18] These two sentences sum up the *Voice's* position: "The laboring classes never will be elevated without the elevation of women—never. While woman is obligated to work like a slave to earn her bread, the country is as hopeless of any progress as Sahara of vegetation." Late in its career, the *Voice* called on labor to consider the demand of women for the right to vote so that "equal suffrage" could read "regardless of sex," and that no distinction of preference should exist in the United States founded on "sex."[19]

However, the thing that most sharply distinguished the *Boston Daily Evening Voice* from the rest of the labor press of its day was its position on two fundamental issues: Reconstruction and black-white labor unity.

At the conclusion of the Civil War, organized labor was faced with a number of serious problems: how to cope with the unemployment arising from demobilization, the sudden cessation of war contracts, the renewal of large-scale immigration, and the post-war depression, which began late in 1865 and lasted until well into 1867. It was necessary to determine how, under these conditions, to strengthen the trade unions and advance the movement for an eight-hour day without a decrease in pay. To these questions, the *Boston Daily Evening Voice* of May 2, 1866, added another: "Can white workingmen ignore colored ones?"

This question had to be faced. Slavery as a labor system had been eliminated, and several million blacks had been added to the nation's free labor supply. How were these millions of ex-slaves to earn a living? Were they to be given the right to vote, or were they to be in effect enslaved again? Were they to be used to strengthen the power of the employers or of the labor movement?

One issue was immediate: the use of black strikebreakers. Employers were refusing the demands of unskilled workers, confident that they could replace strikers with blacks, and at lower pay. In the spring of 1866, the labor press reported that an emigration company was being organized for the purpose of shipping 200,00–300,000 Negro workers from the South to the manufacturing centers of New England, thus enabling employers to lower their labor cost and defeat any move to raise wages or reduce working hours.

The threat of Negro competition was a problem for skilled workers as well. Before the Civil War, free blacks in the South had been engaged in many occupations requiring a high degree of skill. Many ex-slaves who had gained experience in the army, freedman's camps, and relief associations during the war were added to the reservoir of skilled black workers. On an inspection tour of the South in 1868, John M. Langston, an agent for the Freedmen's Bureau, reported that there were at least two Negro craftsmen for every white one in Mississippi, and six Negro mechanics for every white mechanic in North Carolina.[20]

While acknowledging that the bulk of the freedmen were primarily an agrarian population, the *Boston Daily Evening Voice* noted that there was already a large enough group of skilled black workers to constitute a threat to northern urban workers unless they were organized. Moreover, even the agrarian blacks could become allies of northern labor, if not precisely in the trade unions, at least in a political movement to achieve reforms in American society of value both to urban and agrarian workers. But to achieve this goal, the *Voice* insisted, the white workers would have to alter their traditional policies toward black workers.[21]

Before the Civil War white workingmen had systematically excluded Negroes from their crafts, and this situation changed only slightly after the war. Some national unions, like the Cigar Makers, the Carpenters and Joiners, and the Coopers excluded blacks from membership until 1871. Most national unions, however, left the matter of qualifications for admission entirely up to the locals, with the result that exclusion of black workers was the standard pattern in the American labor movement. Where the unions had agreements with employers that only union members could be hired, this pattern resulted in excluding the black worker from the workshop as well as from the union. In some cities the unions sought actively, sometimes by the use of violence, to drive all Negroes out of the skilled trades.[22]

Some white labor leaders understood that union policies of racial exclusion only provided employers with a supply of strike-breakers, and they urged the unity of labor regardless of race and color as the only practical solution. William H. Sylvis, president of the Iron Molders' International Union, and Andrew C. Cameron, editor of the Chicago *Workingmen's Advocate,* emphasized that self-interest dictated cooperation between white and black labor.[23] But the advanced position of Sylvis and Cameron on the question of accepting blacks into the labor movement, a minority position among labor leaders of the era, was never advocated consistently and was never made a key issue in their program for labor reform. Moreover, Sylvis and Cameron, along with the vast majority of white trade unionists, had no understanding of the problems facing the freedmen during Reconstruction.

In addition to the legal freedom set forth in the Thirteenth Amendment, the freedmen demanded political and civil rights, and a material base for their freedom—forty acres and a mule. To the freedmen ownership of land meant freedom from masters and overseers, from the system of control that characterized slavery. "We will still be slaves," was their common refrain, "until every man can raise his own bale of cotton, and say: 'This is mine.' "[24]

With rare exceptions, however, the blacks did not get land and they received no political and civil rights immediately following the Civil War. Instead, under the Reconstruction policies of President Andrew Johnson, they received the "Black Codes." The "Black Codes," the Freedmen's Bureau reported to Congress, "actually served to secure to the former slaveholding class the unpaid labor which they had been accustomed to enjoy before the war."[25]

Negro conventions met during the summer and fall of 1865 to protest against the Johnson Reconstruction policy. They won the support of former white abolitionists and Radical Republicans who were determined to stop the President from returning the slaveholding elements in the South to political power and the ex-slaves to a status closely resembling slavery. Allied with them in this campaign were sections of the industrial and financial class in the North who feared that under Johnson's program an alliance of northern and southern Democrats and groups of discontented farmers of the West would unseat the Republican Party and eliminate many of the gains they had obtained during the Civil War when the southern states were out of the Union. Protective tariffs might be reduced; the national banking system might be abolished; and the currency system might give way to cheap money.[26]

In this struggle against Johnson's Reconstruction policy what was the position of the labor movement? A few trade unionists and leaders of eight-hour leagues condemned Johnson's program, and called upon all white workers to understand that the men who were seeking to crush the black workingman in the South would, if they were victorious, soon destroy the rights of the white laboring man.[27] But these were solitary voices. The majority of white workers and trade unionists endorsed Johnson's Reconstruction program. Most white workers thought of Andrew Johnson not as the President who was restoring the former slaveowners to power and reestablishing a form of slavery for black workers in the South, but as the poor tailor of Tennessee who had introduced a Homestead Bill in Congress in the 1850s and fought for its passage in 1862. They hailed the presence in the White House of one who had been a worker, believing with the Philadelphia Trades' Assembly that "he will exercise the prerogatives of his office for the maintenance and advancement of the General Government, and *also for the benefit of the working classes.*"[28]

At the same time white workers were suspicious of elements in the alliance which was fighting Johnson's policies. The fact that sections of the industrial and financial classes were part of this coalition was enough to alienate a large segment of organized labor, for to many workers the immediate enemy was not the old slaveowning oligarchy, but the new industrial one. The strategy of the industrialists and financiers, argued the *Workingman's Advocate,* was to divert the attention of the workers from the "struggle between capital and labor" by riveting it on the events in the South and thus "distract the public mind from matters of vital importance to the toiling masses." Meanwhile the financiers and industrialists would continue their seizure of the public lands, and impose an unjust monetary system on the nation. By the time the workingmen woke up and turned their attention from events in the South to developments in the North, the conspiracy would have succeeded, and instead of a Republic, America would be a land ruled by financial and industrial monarchists.[29] When Andrew Johnson denounced the Radical Republicans for attempting to use the Negro in the South as a tool to enhance the power of a new oligarchy of financial and industrial capitalists, the majority of the labor papers applauded. "All honor to the President for his practical sympathy with labor," declared the *National Workman.*[30]

Thus most white workers thought the answer to the threat of the use of black labor as strikebreakers was to exclude Negroes from their unions and the trades; and their response to the struggle of the Negro people in the South for political, civil and economic rights, was at best one of indifference. Moreover, even those white labor leaders who did urge that Negroes be organized into the trade unions, did not indicate any sympathy for a radical program of Reconstruction. Both groups agreed that the Thirteenth Amendment had settled the status of the Negro, and that the federal government should now turn its attention to other issues.

While labor historians have pointed to the support given to Johnsonian Reconstruction by the labor movement and to its policy of excluding black workers, few have noted that there was a labor voice in this period which stood for both Radical Reconstruction and black-white labor unity—the *Boston Daily Evening Voice.* Since we do not know much about the men who founded and conducted the *Voice,* we cannot explain with complete accuracy why they should have been so unique in the labor movement of that period. However, we do know that the men who founded the *Voice* belonged to the group of northern workers who before the Civil War were associated with the abolitionists. For one thing, the editors referred to their close friendship with George E. McNeill, the son of John McNeill, a shoeworker who was one of the early supporters of William Lloyd Garrison. The younger McNeill was himself prominent in the New England abolitionist movement on the eve of the war.[31] For another, the editors of the *Voice* referred on several occasions to the fact that they had at one time been in the minority on the slavery issue because of their association with the Boston abolitionists, whereas the majority of the workers, fearing the competition of freed slaves who might come North, had not been friendly to the abolitionists.[32] They insisted, however, that while prejudice died hard, the war had helped create a climate in Boston more friendly to the Negro, and that a number of white workers had returned from the war with their views about blacks changed.[33] Such workers, they said, were ready to back a paper which supported a plan of Reconstruction that offered blacks more than mere legal freedom and advocated black-white labor unity. Moreover, the editors believed that by educating the workers on the necessity of endorsing such a twin policy, they could build firm support for the paper, even though their views were far in advance of prevailing opinion in labor circles.[34]

This educational campaign took the form of news reports, dispatches from the South and the nation's capital (the latter from the *Voice's* own correspondent), editorials, extracts from speeches, statistical material, even poetry—all aimed at informing and convincing white workers that it was necessary to oppose Johnson's Reconstruction policies, to rally behind a program that would insure meaningful freedom for the emancipated slaves, and to understand that unity of black and white labor was essential for the success of the labor movement.

Day after day the *Voice* attacked Johnson's Reconstruction policies as designed to keep the freedmen "under a despotism worse than slavery itself." "No workingman," it warned, "should be found with that party."

> Leaving the question of Negro suffrage to the whites of the former rebel states is an abandonment of the cause of the defenceless freedmen by the Government he has served. . . . There should be no reconstruction without the full recognition of the Negro's manhood, and there should be an energetic superintendence of affairs in the late rebel states till they may be trusted with government.

Day after day, too, the *Voice* attacked those ready to surrender, gave clear arguments to the confused, and led its readers in the struggle against Johnson's policies.

> We ask workingmen to consider that this [Johnson's] plan will degrade black labor and cheapen it, and will consequently cheapen white labor. . . . Put the black laborer in a position to act like a *man*, and he

will get a fair price for his work, in which case we will risk but that his white competitor will get a fair price too; but make a dog of him, and he'll get a dog's pay, and we white men, compete as best we may, will not get much better.[35]

The *Voice's* educational campaign also featured stories about the contributions black soldiers had made to Union victory, reports of speeches of prominent blacks like Frederick Douglass, extracts from the proceedings of Negro conventions in the South, and news about the rise of a southern Negro press. The purpose was to convince white workers that blacks, including the recently liberated slaves, were quite as capable as whites of playing a constructive and intelligent role in the American body politic.[36] The campaign also sought to convince white workers that Garrison and other abolitionists, and not Johnson and his allies, were the true friends of labor. The *Voice* was aware that many Boston workers believed that the anti-slavery men, with some notable exceptions like Wendell Phillips, had been unsympathetic to labor's cause before the Civil War.[37] It pointed out that during the Civil War a number of prominent abolitionists had endorsed the eight-hour day, and some had contributed financially to the shorter-hour movement. It featured on its front page a letter from Garrison to Ira Steward, the eight-hour spokesman, in which the abolitionist leader announced that he supported the labor reformers on "the same principle which has led me to abhor and oppose the unequalled oppression of the black laborers of the South."[38] By presenting evidence that many of those who were championing full freedom for the ex-slaves were also sympathetic to the labor reform movement, the *Voice* sought to break down the long-standing hostility of many white workers towards the abolitionists.

The *Voice's* educational campaign revolved around two principles: justice and self-interest. The two were interrelated. In order to succeed, the labor reform cause must have a good case; it must appeal to the sense of justice which, if not universal, is latent in a great many people. That it had a good case was clear; its demand for improvement in the conditions and status of workers in American society was a continuation of the movement to end slavery, a cause which had triumphed because it was based on justice. But how, asked the *Voice,* could white workers expect to convince the community that their demands were based on justice when they were guilty of denying justice to other workers simply because of the color of their skin? Such an attitude might satisfy their prejudices, but it was shortsighted even from the point of view of enlightened self-interest. It would, in the end, wreak havoc with the campaign for labor reform and doom it to failure.[39] Hence white labor could not afford to be indifferent to the merited claims of black labor for an equal place in American society. Nor could it ignore the fact that under the policies of the so-called friend of labor, Andrew Johnson, the American political community was being defined as one which excluded Negroes, exactly, in short, as Justice Roger B. Taney had defined it in the notorious Dred Scott decision of 1857. Was it to sanctify the Dred Scott decision that white workers had fought and sacrificed so much for the Union cause during four terrible years of war?[40]

As the *Voice* saw it, labor had the duty of rectifying past errors and flaws in American democracy. The founding fathers had made a tragic mistake in their conception of political liberty. "As apprehended by our fathers," the *Voice* editorialized on October 3, 1865, "political liberty meant only the liberty of their own white race; and for nearly ninety years the practical slavery of a whole race stood side by side among us with the freedom of the Anglo-Saxon, and that in the face of the theoretical dogma that 'all men are created equal.' " The inevitable consequence of this error had been a devastating civil war. Failure to eliminate every vestige of inequality based on race or color from American life meant that the war had been fought in vain, and that a new internecine conflict might be required to make the principles of the Declaration of Independence a reality. Labor had the duty to prevent such a tragedy by allying itself with all who stood for a policy of equality for black Americans. The *Voice* conceded that there were those who advocated equality for blacks for the political or economic benefits they hoped to derive from the Negro vote, but it insisted that labor could not remain aloof from alliance with these groups even though it had no admiration for the motives behind their program of Reconstruction. Indeed, if white workers would unite with the aristocrats of wealth to assure the Negro the right to vote, the combined political power of white and black labor could then be used to unseat the men of wealth from power and usher in a new social order for the benefit of all workers, white and black.[41]

Given citizenship and the right to vote, the *Voice* argued, black labor in the South could become the political ally of white labor in advancing the cause of labor reform. But it was too much to expect that the enfranchised black voters would use their power at the ballot-box to aid the labor reform movement if they were convinced that white labor was in alliance with their worst enemies—Johnson and his ex-slaveowning cohorts. Nor could black labor be expected to throw its political support behind a labor reform movement based on trade unions which excluded black workers and sought to drive them out of the workshops. Common sense, if not tragic experience, should convince white workers that if they proved to black labor that they were the enemies of black workers, then black labor would line up with the class enemy of white labor, and its economic and political strength would be used by the employers to weaken and disrupt both the unions and labor reform politics.[42]

The *Voice* warned white workers not to view the employers' threat to bring black labor North to replace white labor at lower wages as sheer propaganda. It pointed out that Irish railroad workers in Cambridge, Massachusetts, who stopped work when two blacks were hired, soon found themselves all replaced by colored workmen, and that several strikes of white workers had already been broken by the use of Negroes imported from the South.[43] How could this threat be met? Certainly not by rioting against the black workers; such action would only lead to the arrest of the rioters, and, in the end, the replacement of the entire white force by black labor. The only correct way, as the *Voice* saw it, was for white labor to fight for a Radical Reconstruction policy which included political and civil rights for economic security—land distribution for the freedmen and decent wages and working conditions for southern agricultural labor. Then black labor, even though it had the right to migrate as did any other worker, would have no reason to move North in search of a better life. If wages for blacks in the South were kept low, moreover, they would set the standard for the nation. The blow aimed at blacks in the South would strike white labor in the North within short order. Then again, southern black workers who received decent wages would provide a market for goods produced in the North and thus would help keep white labor employed.[44]

The *Voice* repeatedly insisted that white labor must realize that exclusion of blacks from their organizations played into the hands of the employers. It cited cases where white workers went on strike, and blacks, excluded from the union, continued to work, causing a defeat for the whites. It prominently featured the experience of the white workers of New Orleans who had organized an eight-hour league which rigidly excluded blacks from membership. When white laborers struck for an eight-hour day in the spring of 1866, Negroes did not hesitate to act as scabs and break the strike. "How many kicks like that which the workingmen of New Orleans have received," the *Voice* asked, "will be required to give them the hint that they cannot ignore the stubborn fact that the colored laborer of the country is henceforth in competition with the white; and if the white will not lift the colored up, the colored will drag the white down?"[45] Labor had to establish a common front, regardless of color, against the common enemy.

The *Voice* had only scorn for those in labor's ranks who argued that the battle for democracy in the South was of no concern to the labor movement, that it was, in fact, a "non-labor issue." These elements—and they represented the majority of white trade unionists —insisted that the Thirteenth Amendment had settled the Negro question, and that by continually harping on black-white labor unity and the need to support a Radical Reconstruction policy, the *Voice* was putting the interests of black labor above those of its readers and the labor movement as a whole. The *Voice* answered the charge: "We could certainly be tender of the people's prejudices, but . . . we are engaged in great work, in which the question of Negro manhood suffrage—of universal freedom, of consistent democracy—is fundamental and vital. We *must* teach truth—We *must* walk in the light or we are sure to stumble and come short of our aim."[46] And what is this truth? The *Voice* replied:

> If the workingmen have learned anything, it is that there can be no hope of their success but in union—the union of all who labor. How mad and suicidal, then, to hold up one hand for the degradation of the Negro, while the other is raised for the elevation of the white laborer! Capital knows no difference between white and black laborers; and labor cannot make any, without undermining its own platform and tearing down the walls of its defence.
>
> The whole power of labor is necessary to the successful resistance of

the united power of capital. Otherwise, those left out of the union are forced, in self-defence, to take a position antagonistic to their brethren of class, and become co-operators with the enemy. If the Trades Unions of white men exclude black men, black men are obligated to underwork, and thus injure the cause of the white men. On the same principle, it is a damage to the cause of white labor that black labor should be ignorant and degraded.[47]

The *Voice* made it clear that the Republican program of Reconstruction was more limited than the policy it advocated. It was critical of the fact that the Fourteenth Amendment did not include Negro suffrage,[48] and it was dismayed because the Congressional Acts of Reconstruction adopted over Johnson's veto in March, 1867, did not provide for land distribution among the freedmen.[49] The *Voice* published speeches by Thaddeus Stevens and Charles Sumner warning that failure to include land distribution would doom Radical Reconstruction since it would leave the freedmen at the mercy of the former slaveowners.[50] Editorially it expressed agreement with this interpretation, and to make the point even stronger, it featured reports of the insurrection of blacks in Jamaica who in 1865 rose up in revolt against conditions not far removed from slavery, a revolt brutally suppressed by British troops. Noting that investigations had revealed that "by the tenancy-at-will system, introduced by the planters after emancipation in the island, the negroes are little better than slaves," operating as they did under a vicious system of sharecropping, the *Voice* warned that failure to distribute land among the ex-slaves in the United States would produce the same conditions in this country. "It is to be hoped that the reconstructionists in this country may learn wisdom from the experience of the Jamaica planters; and instead of placing restrictions upon the negro population, and pursuing a policy to keep them degraded, hold out every opportunity and encouragement to them to make something of themselves." The lesson of the Jamaican insurrection was that half-freedom was practically no freedom at all![51]

When the Congressional Acts of Reconstruction showed that their framers had not learned the lesson of Jamaica, the *Voice* praised those measures which enfranchised blacks in the South but simultaneously urged a campaign to add land distribution. It reminded its readers that "the noble legislator, Hon. Thaddeus Stevens, believed [this measure] . . . to be essential to preserve the freedom of the ex-slaves."[52] But it soon became clear that the paper could not rally much support in labor circles for this more advanced position. The *Voice* abandoned the campaign, explaining that it was yielding to the inevitable; at the same time it justified its retreat with the argument that the Congressional Acts of Reconstruction, incorporating suffrage for Negroes in the South and providing for ratification of the Fourteenth Amendment, had achieved for the freedmen nearly all that the labor paper had been calling for since the end of the war. "The old issues are dying out, the reconstruction problem which has been the mooted topic during the past year or two is practically solved." It was time to turn to making the labor reform program a reality.[53]

Actually, of course, the "reconstruction problem" was far from solved. But the *Voice* had gone about as far as it could in pushing for a radical policy in the South without losing all labor support. More and more it was charged with sacrificing labor reform to the cause of a more complete freedom for Negroes, and with weakening the labor movement by its insistence on having "labor reform so comprehensive in its scope as to include black as well as white workingmen."[54] More serious, these charges were causing a decline in the paper's revenue as workers, influenced by what the *Voice* editors dubbed "colorphobia," stopped renewing subscriptions.[55]

It is to the credit of the editors that they refused to bow to the racists. In an effort to gain new subscribers, they inserted advertisements in various newspapers and issued circulars in which they openly proclaimed that the *Boston Daily Evening Voice*

recognizes no distinction of race or color, but maintains that justice to the freedmen is as essential to the salvation and prosperity of the nation as justice to the white laborer. We contend that their interests are identical, and that the workingmen of the North cannot consistently expect sympathy or protection until they are ready to extend the same, so far as they are able, to the less fortunate colored laborers of the South. The oppression of any large number of workingmen in any section of the country cannot fail to exert a depressing influence upon the condition and privileges of workingmen in other sections. Our strength and success, we believe, depends on unity of action and ideas. The Freedmen are forced to toil for their support as we are, and we cannot but look upon them as entitled to the same rights which we as laboring men claim for our class. The question of political liberty for the negro, is one which all other labor papers have sedulously avoided, fearing to create dissension and division in the labor movement, but the founders of the *Voice* . . . feeling that they could not sincerely defend their cherished principles, without first declaring for equal rights to all, determined not to defer to the mistaken views or prejudices of any particular number of their class, but to take a bold and unselfish position, demanding not only the full enjoyment of what we considered justly due to us, but the same treatment for the freedmen of the South, who without our advantages, were forced not only to contend with the ordinary opposition of encroaching capital, but the brutality of their former masters.[56]

As might be expected, so straightforward a declaration of equalitarian principles only intensified the criticism of the *Voice* in labor's ranks and added to the cancelled subscriptions. Nevertheless, the editors announced that they would not "subtract" a single sentence from the declaration.[57]

But the days of the *Boston Daily Evening Voice* were numbered. Its financial situation was rendered even more precarious by the economic decline of the winter and spring of 1866–1867. Lay-offs and wage-cuts in Boston made it more difficult to raise funds from even those who still stood by the principles of the labor paper. Efforts to sustain the *Voice* by issuing new stock, organizing *Voice* clubs, and establishing a cooperative to publish the paper, staved off the day of doom for a few months. But on October 16, 1867 the editors announced that this was to be the last issue. In a "Valedictory" they recounted the paper's contribution to the working class and observed: "We have every reason to be satisfied with the moral results of our work, disastrous as it has proved to us pecuniarily."

So far as the issue of greater freedom for the Negro people in the South was concerned, this assertion can not be contested. The *Voice* had battled Johnson's Reconstruction policies and had seen them replaced by the era of Radical Reconstruction. It had contributed, in no small measure, to the change. As the *Voice* passed from the scene, the country was taking the first steps which, with all their limitations, were destined to usher in a new and more democratic way of life for blacks and poor whites in the South.

On the issue of black-white labor unity, which the *Voice* had advocated from its inception, there was less progress to report. As the paper was ending its career, the National Labor Union was holding its second convention in Chicago. The first convention of the federation of national and local trade unions, trades assemblies, and eight-hour leagues in 1866, had completely ignored the issue of black labor. At the second convention, there was at least a heated discussion of the issue, but the final decision once again was to ignore "the subject of negro labor."[58]

Terming the decision "very discreditable to a body of American labor reformers," the *Voice* declared angrily:

> The question should not have come up at all, any more than the question of redheaded labor, or blue-eyed labor. Of course the negro has the same right to work and pursue his happiness as the white man has; and of course, if the white man refuses to work with him, or to give him an equal chance, he will be obliged, in self defence, to underbid the white, and it is a disgrace to the Labor Congress that members of that body were so much under the influence of the silliest and wickedest of all prejudices as to hesitate to recognize the negro. When we need to get rid of prejudices and learn to take an enlightened, forward-looking view, they have nailed their prejudices into this platform. We shall never succeed until wiser counsels prevail and these prejudices are ripped up and thrown to the wind.[59]

"We shall never succeed till wiser counsels prevail and these prejudices are ripped up and thrown to the wind." This was the last statement of the *Boston Daily Evening Voice* on this crucial issue. It was far ahead of its time in advocating this principle, but as the history of the labor movement since 1867 has demonstrated, it was truly prophetic.

NOTES

1. *Fincher's Trades' Review,* December 26, 1863.
2. Lloyd Ulman, *The Rise of the National Trade Union* (Cambridge, Mass., 1955), p. 306; John R. Commons *et al., History of Labor in the United States* (New York, 1918), Vol. II, pp. 21–26, 58–60.
3. Philip S. Foner, *History of the Labor Movement in the United States* (New York,1947), Vol. I, p. 349.

4. Frank Luther Mott, the distinguished historian of American journalism, makes the point that most early American journalists were printers. (*American Journalism,* New York, 1941, p. 313). His book, however, is a good example of the neglect of labor papers in works on the history of American journalism. Mott mentions briefly only two English language labor papers, the *Workingmen's Advocate* (p. 205) and the *Alarm* (p. 487). He also mentions the *Arbeiter-Zeitung* (p. 487).

5. George McNeill, *The Labor Movement: The Problem of Today* (New York, 1888). p. 127.

6. *Boston Daily Evening Transcript,* December 1, 1864. The strike ended in a defeat for the Printers' Union.

7. *Boston Daily Evening Voice,* April 17, 1865.

8. The cost per hundred for the daily was $125. Five, ten, and twenty copies of the weekly for the same address cost $9, $17, and $30 respectively.

9. *Boston Daily Evening Voice,* November 3, 1865. The meeting was called to launch a campaign for the eight-hour day.

10. The fact that the notices at times included meetings of unions in cities as far west as San Francisco indicates that the paper had some national circulation.

11. *Boston Daily Evening Voice,* September 25, 1865.

12. Ibid., September 12, 1866, April 3, 1867. For a discussion of the labor reform movement, see David Montgomery, *Beyond Equality: Labor and the Radical Republicans, 1862–1872* (New York, 1967), pp. 91, 113, 123, 125, 369, 373, 411, 422, 426, 446.

13. *Boston Daily Evening Voice,* May 20, October 6, 1865; June 20, 27, 1867.

14. Ibid., November 22, 1866. See also issues of May 12, 1865; February 27, 1866.

15. Ibid., September 9–October 2, 1865.

16. Ibid., October 3, 1865.

17. *Fincher's Trades' Review,* however, opposed political activity by labor.

18. *Boston Daily Evening Voice*, May 2, 1865.

19. Ibid., January 27, December 27, 1866.

20. *Workingmen's Advocate,* March 24, 1866; *Boston Daily Evening Voice,* February 26, April 3, 1866; *Christian Recorder,* August 11, 1866.

21. *Boston Daily Evening Voice,* November 28, 1865; January 27, 1866.

22. Sumner Eliot Matison, "The Labor Movement and the Negro during Reconstruction," *Journal of Negro History,* Vol. XXXIII, October, 1948, pp. 426–42; F. E. Wolfe, *Admission to American Trade Unions,* Baltimore, 1912, pp. 114, 123, 131.

23. Foner, *op. cit.,* Vol. I, pp. 396–97.

24. *Atlantic Monthly,* February, 1866, p. 606.

25. James S. Allen, *Reconstruction: The Battle for Democracy* (New York, 1937), pp. 57–59. Foner, *op. cit.,* Vol. I, pp. 390–391. Under the codes, adopted in all of the Southern states, a Negro who was not at work was arrested and imprisoned. In order to pay off the prison charges and fines he was hired out. If a Negro quit work before his contract expired, he was arrested and imprisoned for breach of contract and the reward to the person performing the arrest was deducted from his wages. Some of the codes also provided that if a Negro laborer left his employer he would "forfeit all wages to the time of abandonment." Negro children whose parents were considered too poor to support them were bound out as apprentices, girls until 18 years of age and boys until 21. In Mississippi the code provided that if a Negro could not pay taxes to care for the poor, he would be regarded as a vagrant and hired out; it clearly asserted that the laws under chattel slavery were to be in full force again "except so far as the mode and manner of trial and punishment have been changed and altered by the law."

26. New York *Herald,* August 10, 1865; Allen, *op. cit.,* pp. 73–78; W. E. B. DuBois, *Black Reconstruction in America* (New York, 1935), pp. 230–33; Howard K. Beale, "The Tariff and Reconstruction," *American Historical Review,* Vol. XXXV, January, 1930, pp. 276–94; *The Nation,* January 11, 1866.

27. Foner, *op. cit.,* Vol. I, pp. 299–300.

28. *Fincher's Trades' Review*, May 6, 1865.

29. *Workingman's Advocate*, August 11, 1866.

30. *National Workman,* October 20, 27, 1866.

31. McNeill organized a club of subscribers for the *National Anti-Slavery Standard* among Boston workers. In forwarding the subscriptions, he wrote to the *Standard:* "Now that the black man has come out of the bondage of chattel slavery, as his white brother, centuries ago came out of villeinage, it is well that you, who have so earnestly and faithfully worked for his enfranchisement, should unite him to us his fellow workers in unity of purpose and harmony of action." (*National Anti-Slavery Standard,* April 9, 1870.)

McNeill showed his support for the *Boston Daily Evening Voice* by getting subscribers, soliciting advertisements, and forming *Voice* clubs. When the labor paper ceased publication in October, 1867, the staff presented McNeill with one of the only two complete sets of the paper. (*Labor Standard,* July 28, 1877.)

32. *Boston Daily Evening Voice,* October 11, 1866.

33. For evidence that this view was not an exaggeration, see Donald Martin Jacobs, "A History of the Boston Negro from the Revolution to the Civil War," unpublished Ph.D. thesis, Boston University, 1968, pp. 362, 369–70.

34. *Boston Daily Evening Voice,* March 11, 1865.

35. Ibid., December 28, 1865; January 24, April 19, 1866.

36. Ibid., January 31, February 2, May 3, November 9, 1865; March 21, May 2, July 26, September 7, 1866.

37. Bernard Mandel, *Labor: Free and Slave* (New York, 1955), pp. 90–91, 136–37, 139–40.

38. *Boston Daily Evening Voice,* May 2, 1866. David Montgomery criticizes labor historians, myself included, for giving the impression that among "the anti-slavery men of the Bay State Wendell Phillips alone was sympathetic to labor's cause. . . ." (*Op. cit.,* pp. 223–24.)

39. *Boston Daily Evening Voice,* September 2, October 5, 1865; March 10, 1866.

40. Ibid., August 27, 1867.

41. Ibid., September 22, December 13, 18, 1865; March 21, June 20, 1866.

42. Ibid., October 14, November 14, 15, 1865; April 19, May 15, 1866.

43. Ibid., May 7, 1866.

44. Ibid., February 26, March 15, 24, April 3, 16, August 22, 1866.

45. Ibid., March 30, May 7, 21, July 20, 1866.

46. Ibid., January 11, 12, 20, February 2, March 23, November 14, 17, 1866. The leading labor critic of the *Voice* was the Detroit *Daily Union,* which accused the Boston paper of causing division and conflict in labor's ranks by agitating for Negro suffrage.

47. *Boston Daily Evening Voice,* January 13, 1866.

48. Ibid., January 24, June 4, November 17, 1866.

49. Ibid., January 19, October 3, 1866.

50. Ibid., January 19, September 3, October 3, December 29, 1866.

51. Ibid., December 2, 18, 1865; May 15, 1866.

52. Ibid., March 5, 1867. While historians have traditionally interpreted the Reconstruction Acts of 1867 as radical measures, more recent scholarship has begun to view them as essentially conservative, since they marked the triumph not so much of the Radical Republicans as of the more conservative elements in the Republican Party. The task of enforcing the Reconstruction Acts was placed in the hands of the army, and since President Andrew Johnson was the commander-in-chief, the task of enforcement was in his hands. In short, the Radicals had not succeeded in taking Reconstruction completely out of the hands of a president hostile to their program.

53. Ibid., March 12, 1867.

54. Ibid., November 1, 1866.

55. Ibid., November 3, 1866.

56. Ibid., November 1, 17, December 1, 1866.

57. Ibid., December 1, 1866.

58. *Workingman's Advocate,* August 24, 31, 1867. During the debate on the Negro question at the 1867 NLU convention, William H. Sylvis urged that Negroes be admitted to the unions so as to strengthen the labor movement. He insisted that there was no time for further delay: the use of white scabs against blacks and black scabs against whites had already created an antagonism that would "kill off the Trades Unions" unless the two groups were consolidated. "If the Workingmen of the white race do not conciliate the blacks," he warned, "the black vote will be cast against them." This was a reference to the fact that under Congressional Reconstruction, Negroes in the South would soon gain the vote.

Andrew C. Cameron endorsed Sylvis's position in the *Workingman's Advocate.* However, unlike the *Boston Daily Evening Voice,* neither Sylvis nor Cameron understood the problems facing the Negro people in the South. Both had supported Johnson in his battle with Congress, and had opposed the Reconstruction Acts passed by Congress in March, 1867. Moreover, both Sylvis and Cameron viewed with disdain the Southern governments established under Congressional Reconstruction, in which blacks played an important role. They saw in them proof that the Reconstruction measures adopted by Congress over Johnson's veto were "disastrous" both for the South and the nation as a whole. See *Workingman's Advocate,* August 25, 1866, August 3, November 30, 1867, March 20, 27, May 8, 1869, and James C. Sylvis, *The Life, Speeches, Labor and Essays of William H. Sylvis, late President of the Iron Molders' Union and also of the National Labor Union* (Philadelphia, 1872), pp. 334–42.

59. *Boston Daily Evening Voice,* August 27, 1867.

8

Black Participation in the
Centennial of 1876*

So long as slavery existed, most blacks refused to participate in a celebration of the Fourth of July on July 4th, setting aside July 5th for the purpose. In his July 5, 1832 address in the African Church, New Haven, Connecticut, Peter Osborn declared: "Fellow Citizens: On account of the misfortune of our color, our fourth of July comes on the fifth; but I hope and trust that when the Declaration of Independence is finally executed, which declares that all men without respect to person, were born free and equal, we may then have our fourth of July on the fourth." Frederick Douglass, the ex-slave and black abolitionist, summed it up succinctly in his great speech, "The Meaning of July Fourth for the American Negro," delivered in Rochester, New York, July 5, 1852: "I am not included within the pale of this glorious anniversary! This Fourth of July is *yours*, not mine. You may rejoice, I must mourn. . . ."[1]

Twenty-four years later, on May 10, 1876, marking the opening of the long-awaited Centennial Exhibition in Philadelphia, Frederick Douglass was one of the dignitaries seated on the main platform in the company of President Ulysses S. Grant, Secretary of State Hamilton Fish, members of Congress, governors, and ministers of foreign countries. But it was only by a miracle that the gray-headed Douglass was there. The police of Philadelphia had refused him admittance, unable to conceive that a Negro—they used a more pejorative term—would be allowed entrance to this august company

*Paper read at the ASALH Atlanta meeting, October, 1975. Reprinted from *Negro History Bulletin,* XXXIX (February, 1976), 533–538.

on this august occasion. In vain, Douglass had remonstrated, showing his ticket of admission to the platform. "It is feared he might have gone out with the crushed and fainting," said the New York *Herald* correspondent, "if Senator Conkling had not seen him, and vouching for his right to be present, enabled him to pass the line. As he reached the platform, he was loudly cheered."[2]

There would undoubtedly have been many more cheers had Douglass been one of the many speakers. But the greatest orator in the nation, whom Abraham Lincoln had said was the "most remarkable man" he had ever met,[3] had not been invited to be heard— only to be seen. Yet even this, as we shall see, was more than was typical of the general nature of black participation in the Centennial of 1876.

As the nation throbbed with preparations to celebrate its one hundredth birthday, there were not a few Americans who viewed the forthcoming celebration as "an overgrown and spread-eagle Fourth of July," "a gigantic fraud to enrich some people," an opportunity for "mindless patriotism and commercial exploitation." With millions unemployed as a result of the business depression that had started in 1873, with the scandals of the Grant administration coming to light, and revelations of corruption in government and business increasing steadily, the argument was that there was indeed little for Americans to celebrate. Better, far better, that the funds to be spent on the Centennial Exhibition be used to provide food, clothing, and shelter for the starving and homeless.[4]

Such bitter thoughts, inspired by the approaching Centennial, seem not to have been shared by most blacks. For one thing, a number of black spokesmen felt that the Centennial offered an opportunity to show the American people the contributions of black Americans to the creation and building of the nation, a subject ignored in nearly all history books then in use in the schools and colleges. "We have been hypocrites and liars with respect to our real history long enough," insisted Robert Purvis, veteran black abolitionist and civil rights leader of Philadelphia in May, 1873, as he called for making the truth available "on the 4th of July, 1876." This truth "would reveal that it was an incontestable fact that the blood of a Negro was first shed for liberty in the Revolution, and that blacks had taken an active part in the War of 1812 and in our late civil war for freedom." Perhaps, Purvis argued, white Americans, made aware of these contributions, would use the Centennial as the occasion to eliminate whatever remained of color prejudice. In that event, Negroes, having defended the flag on the battlefield, "would have one to glory in at the Centennial."[5]

Speaking in the House of Representatives on May 7, 1874, on the bill calling for Congress to appropriate $3,000,000 in aid of the Centennial celebration,[6] black Congressman Josiah T. Walls of Florida criticized those who sneered at the approaching celebration. On behalf of himself and a people who had lived to witness "the tardy but in the end the full and complete vindication of the sublime simple announcements of the Declaration of Independence," Congressman Walls urged the swift adoption of the bill. He argued that the Centennial would bring the nation together for the first time since the Civil War, and "discourage and extinguish all feelings of sectionalism." Moreover, it would help eliminate the "remaining bitterness" still rankling in the breasts of those Southern "irreconcilables" who regretted the abolition of slavery, and refused to accept the Negro as a full-fledged American citizen. Walls closed on a note of exultation and prophecy as he predicted that the Centennial celebration would become the occasion for "a common and patriotic demonstration of a hundred years of popular government for the political necessities of the races." It would be the occasion, too, for the expression of "the spontaneous joy of a free people at their unbroken Union and the restored unity of their nationality." And none would "hail the glorious old banner—the Stars and Stripes—with more joy than the men of the South."[7]

The *New National Era*, black weekly published in the nation's capital, hailed Congressman Walls' speech as proving "that colored Congressmen are alive to everything tending to promote the general welfare of the country." It urged blacks throughout the nation to mobilize their forces to assure that the Negro was at least as well represented at the Philadelphia Exhibition as he was in the halls of Congress where there were seven Negroes, six in the House and one in the Senate. To be sure, all of course were from the South, but the black weekly argued that it was not outside the realm of reason to hope that the Centennial celebration, by helping, in Congressman Walls' words, to "extinguish all feelings of sectionalism," would usher in an era when many states in the North and West would send blacks to the halls of Congress.[8]

Spurred by such optimistic outlooks, the Convention of Colored Newspaper Men, meeting in Cincinnati, August, 1875, adopted an ambitious Centennial program. It envisaged the publication of eighteen volumes "to be known as the 'Centennial Tribute to the Negro,' " which would serve "to let the coming generation know our true history." The first three volumes would trace the history of the Negro people from their "Ancient Glory" in Africa to their intro- duction to the New World. These would be followed by fourteen volumes covering such themes as "One Hundred Years with the Negro in Battle," "One Hundred Years with the Negro in the Schoolhouse, or as an Educator," "One Hundred Years with the Negro in the Pulpit," "One Hundred Years with Negro Lawyers and Doctors," "One Hundred Years with the Negro's Muse," "One Hundred Years with the Negroes' Pen, and Scissors and Press," "One Hundred Years with the Negro in Business," "One Hundred Years with the Negro as a Farmer and Mechanic," "One Hundred Years with the Negro Statesman or Politician." The final volume was to be simply entitled, "Negro Martyrs."

The black newspapermen also appointed a committee to be known as the Centennial Committee, whose duty it would be to correspond with the Centennial Commissioner, and urge upon him "the necessity of having the productions of the colored race represented at the Centennial Exposition," and, in particular, to make certain that the "religious, literary, educational, and mechanical interests of the Negro would be fully represented." The committee was also em- powered to procure a statue from Edmonia Lewis, the famous black sculptress then residing in Rome, and arrange to have the work exhibited at the Centennial Celebration, "in the name of the colored women of America." Further, to assure that following the Expo- sition, the work of art would be placed permanently in some public building or park in the city of Washington.[9]

The question of financing this ambitious project was left vague. All that was suggested was that the Centennial Committee, if it found it necessary, organize a movement "among our ladies" to carry the program into being.[10] Needless to say, with such loose provision, not much of the project could be realized. With the assistance of the

African Methodist Episcopal Church, funds were raised for "two works of art by Edmonia Lewis."[11] But the project for an eighteen-volume "Centennial Tribute to the Negro" never got off the ground.

A few blacks served on the local committees which every state, almost every large city, and many smaller ones set up to prepare their exhibit. Unfortunately, we know very little about this aspect of the Centennial of 1876 since few white newspapers reported such activity; few black newspapers of the period have survived, and the Centennial Commission Papers in the Archives of the City of Philadelphia contain nothing about the role of blacks in the preparations for the celebration.[12] One clue is the following sentence in the *People's Advocate* of Washington, D.C., one of the few black weeklies which has survived: "Colored men were appointed to the several local committees created by the Centennial Commission, prior to the opening of the Exhibition, with the same authority to act as their white *confreres*." But this is certainly distressingly indefinite; it mentions "local committees," but gives no names, no places, and no working details.[13] We may conclude that the appointments, if they occured at all, probably took place in a Southern area, still in Republican hands, or in an area, North or South, with a strong black school system, such as Cincinnati and Philadelphia.

We do know something of the participation of Negro women. The Women's Pavilion at the Philadelphia Exposition was the creation of the Women's Centennial Committee, originally a group of thirteen appointed in 1873 by planners of the Exhibition. Subcommittees were organized in all the states and large cities of the country to raise funds for the Pavilion.[14] In this connection, black women were invited to participate on the Philadelphia subcommittee. However, it was made clear to these women that they were to operate as a separate committee, and solicit subscriptions among blacks only; that they had "no right to work among white people," and that the "whole work of the group be confined to colored people alone." When the black women objected, charging that this was nothing less than segregation by color, they were informed by a representative of the Women's Centennial Committee that this was in keeping with the laws of the land, and if they did not approve of them, they could emigrate to Africa. At this the black women resigned from the committee, and drew up a set of resolutions denouncing the

Women's Centennial Committee for attempting a "revival of the bitterest colored prejudices."[15]

The incident was widely publicized in the Philadelphia press and in the *New National Era;* and the Women's Centennial Committee, somewhat startled by the publicity, beat a hasty retreat. An apology was delivered to the black women, in the form of resolutions assuring them that no "distinction" would be made between races in the raising of funds, and urging them to continue to serve. The apology was accepted, and the Philadelphia sub-committee of the Women's Centennial Committee functioned with black women represented. But it had taken a struggle and considerable publicity for these women even to win the right to serve on the basis of equality.[16]

The reluctance to allow blacks to participate as equals to whites was evidenced again in Philadelphia a year later. To help raise funds for the Centennial Exhibit, the police of Philadelphia sponsored a benefit at the Arch Street Theatre on the night of April 16, 1874. The event was widely publicized, and all Philadelphians were urged to purchase tickets and attend. Evidently forgetting that the City of Brotherly Love was the most racist city in the North,[17] Pusey A. Peer and his wife, a black couple, decided to attend. They purchased tickets, but when they presented themselves at the theatre, the policemen sponsoring the event insisted that they would not have the "Centennial Benefit" stained by "nigger money." Mr. Peer vehemently insisted on his right to attend. "Throw them niggers out," was the cry that arose from the police, and the black couple was forcibly ejected from the theatre. In the process, both sustained severe bodily injuries. In addition, Mrs. Peer was robbed of her fur cape and her husband of his watch! Not a single Philadelphia paper rebuked the police editorially for this vicious conduct, or pointed out that it made a mockery of the "Centennial Benefit."[18]

It came as no surprise then that the Philadelphia Exhibition, during its construction and operation, provided an example of the restricted opportunities for black workers. Nearly two hundred Centennial buildings were constructed between May, 1875 and the opening the following year. (One, the Memorial building, was said to be the largest building in the world, occupying 21.27 acres.)[19] But not a single black worker appears to have been employed during this huge construction at a time when perhaps seventy per cent of the blacks of Philadelphia were unemployed.[20] On the eve of the opening of the Exhibition, Robert Lowry of Iowa, a Vice President of the Centennial Commission, called upon the body at least to allow Negroes to have positions as guards. Nothing came of the suggestion.[23]

Visiting the Centennial city after the Exhibition opened, a black Georgian wrote that he "could not discover among all that mass of people one single Negro in the discharge of any duty save as restaurant waiters and barbers in the hotels."[22] The fact that this observation was criticized because it did not mention that "a few black messengers, janitors, etc, are now employed in the Memorial building," only added weight to the black visitor's discouraging comment.[23]

The paucity of Negro exhibits in number and substance also discouraged black visitors. In the entire exhibition, one wrote, he could find only one exhibit devoted to the American Negro—the statue of "The Freed Slave" in Memorial Hall, a heroic figure of a male black holding aloft the parchment of the Emancipation Proclamation with broken chains at his feet.[24] But this was not even the work of a black artist. Indeed, apart from the trinkets and other artifacts in the exhibits of the Gold Coast, West Africa, Liberia, and the South African Orange Free States, only one work of art by a black artist was in the entire exhibition—Edmonia Lewis' sculpture, "Death of Cleopatra."[25]

A number of newspaper editorials argued that nothing else could be expected since the Negro had too recently shed his shackles to show proficiency in the arts and sciences.[26] But Colonel J. W. Forney, Philadelphia's leading journalist, was more to the point when he voiced regret on the eve of the Fourth of July that "the great show of the American people's industry and independence will close the one link in the chain of its complete history left out. Although the chains of slavery have been broken from the limbs of an entire race in the blaze and fire of our advancement, and the Negro stands before the law a freeman, covered with the habiliments of citizenship, yet, the prejudice against him, the results of his previous condition, have prevented him from taking any part or having a prominent part of this marvelous undertaking in celebration of one hundred years of American independence, save that of a menial, the water-drawers and hat-takers, to the assembled races now to be found there."[27]

Shocked by this observation, Pennsylvania Judge William D. Kelly, a long-time champion of civil rights, pleaded with the Centennial Commission to fill this serious gap in the Exhibition by inviting Frederick Douglass to read the Emancipation Proclamation after the Declaration of Independence was read on the Fourth of July. Later that same day, he should deliver an address from the platform of Memorial Hall, portraying the contributions of Black Americans in the War for Independence and for the preservation of the Union during the Civil War.[28]

As might be expected, nothing came of this suggestion. Instead, Reverend J. T. Jenifer, minister at the St. John's African Methodist Episcopal Church, Pine Bluff, Arkansas, was invited to deliver an address on July 4th on the occasion of laying the base of the Richard Allen monument. The monument itself was being completed by Edmonia Lewis in Rome and was scheduled to be veiled in the Centennial grounds on September 23, the anniversary of the issuing of the preliminary Emancipation Proclamation by President Lincoln—in short, just before the Centennial Exhibition closed.[29]

While Reverend Jenifer did not fulfill the role Judge Kelly had had in mind—not mentioning the American Revolution or the Civil War and black participation in these conflicts,[30] he must have struck what must have been a strange note at an Exhibition, a major theme of which was the new harmonious relations between the North and South. For he referred to the "outrages and murders" committed against Negroes in the South by the "Ku Klux Klan and White Leagues," charged that they were "the fruits of wanton prejudice, hatred and hellish passions," and accused the federal government of "weakness" in yielding to the lawless foes of black Americans. Calling upon the government to spend as much money to provide education for the freedman of the South as it did for internal improvements and military appropriations,[31] he predicted that if this were done, the blacks, along with the immigrant and the capitalist, would make their contribution to transforming the South into a "land of peace and plenty."[32]

None of the white speakers at the Centennial Exhibition on July 4, 1876 mentioned the Negro, and very few outside of Philadelphia did in the orations delivered that day throughout the nation. One, however, did, and his reference is an interesting barometer of the existing viewpoint among large sections of the white population. In the course of his centennial oration at Covington, Kentucky, Hon. W. E. Arthur told Negroes in the United States how fortunate they were that their ancestors had been taken from Africa into slavery in this country. But for that they would be living in a continent with "scarce any society superior to that of the gorilla and monkey," existing on the edge of "the dividing line between man and brute," practicing "the lowest vices of both," and spending their lives in "chaos without change." Thus the black American had a special reason to celebrate the one hundredth anniversary of a nation which had rescued him from all this horror and permitted him to partake of the fruits of civilization.[33]

While the vast majority of American communities were deprived of the opportunity to hear any oration outlining the contributions of the Negro to the creation of the nation, some were not. In Boston, the distinguished black abolitionist and civil rights spokesman, Lewis Hayden, delivered an historical paper before the Colored Ladies Centennial Club; in Portsmouth, Virginia, Professor John M. Langston of Howard University delivered an historical address before the Banneker Lyceum, and in Avendale, Ohio, the future black historian, George Washington Williams, delivered an oration entitled, *The American Negro from 1776 to 1876.*

In his address Langston paid tribute to two individuals: one of the Revolution and the other of the post-Revolutionary era. The first was Crispus Attucks, and the second, Benjamin Banneker. Black Americans, he pointed out, should celebrate not only the Declaration of Independence, but also a man like Crispus Attucks, "brave and courageous who gave up his life one hundred years ago on the sacred soil of Massachusetts in order to make the Independence we now celebrate possible." Nor should they forget that it was America's first black man of science, Benjamin Banneker, who had played so important a role in the creation of the city of Washington, D.C., the nation's capital.[34] A distinguished teacher himself, Langston hailed the state of Virginia for having established a common school system, and not allowing her sons and daughters, as in the days of slavery, to grow up "in ignorance, to a heritage of crime and degradation. . . ." "To-day," he noted, "your schools, a double system, white and black, are better than none. But I trust the day is not distant when they will be one—a common school system, standing open for all regardless of race or color."[35]

Langston's speech in Portsmouth, Virginia, July 4, 1876, had the distinction of being the only oration by a black American included in the close to 900 page *Orations, Addresses and Poems, Delivered on the Fourth of July, 1876, in the Several States of the Union.* Unfortunately the volume published in 1877 and edited by Frederick Saunders, contains not a single clue as to who Langston was.

The orations of Lewis Hayden and George Washington Williams covered a larger canvas. Hayden dealt not only with Crispus Attucks, but with Peter Salem and Salem Poor of the Battle of Lexington and Concord and Bunker Hill as well as with other blacks who had fought with the Patriots in the War for Independence. He went on to depict the contributions of the Massachusetts 54th and 55th Black Regiments during the Civil War, describing the heroism of black soldiers at the battles of Port Hudson, Milliken's Bend, and Fort Wagner. Unfortunately, Hayden noted sadly, slavery and racism had "closed the eyes of this nation to its indebtedness to the colored race."[36]

It had closed its eyes to black women as well as men. For black women, Hayden emphasized, had not been idle during the American Revolution. For one thing, there was Deborah Gannett, the black female soldier who fought in the Continental Army disguised as a man under the name of Robert Shurtleff.[37] After describing other contributions of black women of the American nation, Hayden said to the members of the Colored Ladies Centennial Club:

> E'er another Centennial rolls around, may you be possessed of these rights for which your sisters during and after the War for Independence fought to achieve not alone for men, but for women as well. Since it is written, "There is no rest for the wicked, saith my God," who can doubt that ere another century shall spread its pages before the world, even *this* wrong will be repaired, and that our country will stand forth triumphantly as the living exponent of the principles of self government, liberty, justice, and humanity for all its people—women as well as men![38]

George Washington Williams began his Fourth of July Centennial oration with the statement: "If any class of people in our composite nationality have claims upon the Union, if any class of people after the Puritan, can justly claim a part in establishing the colonies as independent states, it is the American Negro." He then proceeded to prove his assertion, citing the role of Crispus Attucks, Salem Poor,

Peter Salem, and the Black Regiment of Rhode Island, and other blacks who fought in both the Continental Army and Continental Navy during the War for Independence. Moving on to the War of 1812 and the Civil War, Williams urged the Republic to remember that "its most precious stones were cemented by the blood of her negro soldiers whose devotion to the flag was deathless and whose fame will never fade." He also called upon Americans to remember that when almost 200,000 blacks fought in the Union Army to preserve the Union—the vast majority of them fugitive slaves—they, in the process, became their own liberators from slavery, so that it was not just the Emancipation Proclamation but the black slaves themselves which broke the chains of slavery. "The American negro," Williams cried, "deserves the admiration of the civilized world for melting off his chains in the fires of rebellion, and for helping to establish a free government without a single slave under the fold of its flag."

If the blacks in Colonial America helped to create the first Republic in the New World, Williams noted, it was the black slaves of the French West Indies who built the second Republic. For Haiti was brought into being "on the ruins of slavery, and it was the slaves themselves who ratified its benign and humane principles with their own blood." Slavery, he observed, was overthrown in the French West Indies by the military efforts of the slaves themselves. "This is the negro's place in history—his own deliverer," Williams insisted. Continuing, he observed:

> Daniel O'Connell said to Ireland, "Hereditary bondsmen know ye not, that he who would himself be free, must first strike the blow?" The French West Indian negro anticipated O'Connell, and when he rose he made even the mighty Napoleon tremble!

In closing Williams pointed to Phillis Wheatley, poet, Benjamin Banneker, scientist, Charles L. Reason, mathematician, James McCune Smith, physician, Peter H. Clark, teacher, Henry Highland Garnet, Alexander Crummell, James W. C. Pennington, theologians, William C. Nell and William Wells Brown, historians, Charlotte Forten, and Frances E. Harper, literary figures, and Frederick Douglass, orator and statesman. He then asked the "Negro-haters" whether it was true, as they charged, that "the negro can not compete with the white races, that he cannot endure the highest forms of civilization; that he can not master the intricate and subtle problems of the college curriculum!" He ended his great oration with the plea:

> I ask the American people to call to remembrance the valor, military skill, and endurance of the negro in the Wars for Independence, of 1812, and the Civil War! I ask the many schools, academies and colleges open to the race, if the negro has not shown the largest capacity for the severest culture. I ask the American Congress which has listened to the eloquence of Elliott, Lane, Lynch, and others, if the negro is a monkey or a man![39]

While the Fourth of July Orations delivered by blacks dealt mainly with the past, July 4, 1876 also was the occasion for the presentation of a document which concerned itself primarily with the present and future. This was the "Negro Declaration of Independence" read in Washington, D.C. on the Fourth of July, 1876. Drawn up by the Negro National Independent Political Union, with Reverend Garland H. White of North Carolina as President and Howard L. Smith of Virginia, as Secretary,[40] this new Declaration of Independence was modelled after the original document drawn up by Thomas Jefferson. However, instead of George III being the target of specific grievances, in the "Negro Declaration of Independence," it was the American government. It was charged with having evaded compliance with laws necessary for the Negro's welfare; imposed taxes on the Negro without protecting their Constitutional rights; turned a deaf ear to pleas for protection against blacks "being lynched, tortured, harassed and imprisoned without just Cause"; "refused to teach the heritage of the negro, and the magnificent contributions to the life, wealth and growth of the nation made by the negro people," and "refused to provide work for negro labor faced with unemployment, misery and starvation through no fault of its own." The document concluded:

> For these and other reasons too numerous for enumeration, we feel justified in declaring our independence of all existing political parties, and we hereby pledge to each other our Lives, our Fortunes, and our Sacred Honor that we will, in the future, support only those parties whose fidelity to the original Declaration of Independence is unquestioned, and who will make certain that we, the negro people, like all other Americans, will in the second century of our independence, be

assured of FULL AND EQUAL JUSTICE BEFORE THE LAW, PROTECTION FOR
ALL OUR LIVES AND PROPERTY AGAINST LAWLESSNESS AND MOB VIOLENCE,
AND FULL EQUALITY IN ALL ASPECTS OF AMERICAN LIFE!!!![41]

In the voluminous reports in the contemporary press of events
surrounding the celebration of July 4, 1876, the one hundredth
anniversary of the Declaration of Independence, not a single white
newspaper mentioned the new Declaration of Independence, the
"Negro Declaration of Independence."[42] It was an indication of how
blind white Americans were toward the grievances of black citizens
in their midst as they celebrated their Centennial. As the Centennial
year advanced, fresh evidence of this indifference emerged. The
bloody massacres of Negroes in Hamburg and Elton, South Carolina, which *The Colored Radical,* published in Kansas, called "the
darkest chapters in American history," were accepted as part of the
normal way of life in the America of 1876.[43] By the end of the
Centennial year, the fate of blacks in the South had been sealed in the
nefarious bargain following the disputed election of 1876, by which
the South agreed to give Rutherford B. Hayes the presidency over
Samuel J. Tilden in return for the removal of the remaining Federal
troops and the restoration of home rule—a euphemism for the right
to reduce the Negro to a new form of slavery.[44]

Two years before, in urging congressional support for the Centennial Exhibition, black Congressman Walls had predicted that this
show of national harmony would destroy the power of the few white
irreconcilables in the South who refused to accept the Negro as an
equal citizen. Vain hope! In fact, of the Centennial of 1876, only two
positive results for blacks emerged. One was the awarding of $900 as
compensation for damages sustained by Pusey A. Peer and his wife,
the black couple ejected from the Philadelphia police "Centennial
Benefit" at the Oak Street Theatre in 1874. The case was finally
settled in 1881, and in sustaining the damage award, Judge Sterrett of
the Pennsylvania Supreme Court said:

> Whether the tickets conferred merely a license or something more is
> immaterial. If they gave only a license to enter the theater and remain
> there during the performance, it is very clear that the agents of the
> defendant had no right to revoke it as they did; and summarily eject
> Peer and his wife from the building in such manner as to injure her. We
> incline to the opinion, however, that as purchasers and holders of the

tickets for particular seats they had more than a mere license. Their right was more in the nature of a lease, entitling them to peaceable ingress and egress, and exclusive possession of the designated seats during the performance on that particular evening.

The case is famous in the history of the enforcement of civil rights in Pennsylvania, and helped break down restrictions against blacks in public facilities of the state.[45]

The other positive result was the influence of the Centennial on the emergence of George Washington Williams as a distinguished black historian. Williams became absorbed in Negro history while doing research on the Oration he delivered celebrating the one hundredth anniversary of the Declaration of Independence. He tells us that he was surprised to discover the abundance of material which existed on the Negro. After he had delivered the oration, he retired as a minister and lawyer in Cincinnati, in order to devote all his time to writing a general history of the Negro in the United States. After seven years, he published his great work, *A History of the Negro Race in America from 1619 to 1880.* The work, in two volumes, is divided into nine parts, with a total of sixty chapters, tracing the Negro from the African background, through the Colonial, Revolutionary era, down to the Civil War and Reconstruction. In each volume several chapters are devoted to social and cultural history.[46]

With the publication of *A History of the Negro Race in America from 1619 to 1880,* the Centennial of 1876 had produced, even if indirectly and belatedly, what the Negro newspaper men had envisaged in 1875 when they had projected the idea of a multi-volume "Centennial Tribute to the Negro" which would serve "to let the coming generations know our true history."

Yet even this did not grow out of the official Centennial Exhibition. The story of black participation in that tremendous, world-wide exposition was summed up by Colonel Forney, the Philadelphia journalist, when he said: ". . . the prejudice against him, the results of his previous condition, have prevented him from taking any part or having a prominent part of this marvellous undertaking in celebration of one hundred years of American independence, save that of a menial, the water-drawers and hat-takers, to the assembled races now to be found there." How completely the black American was the invisible man at the Centennial Celebration is illustrated by the fact that when a delegation of French workers to the Philadelphia Exhibition submitted a questionnaire to American Socialists on conditions of workers in this country, both men and women, they did not include blacks among their queries. Not one of the 34 questions submitted concerned itself with the black worker.[47]

In the historical accounts dealing with the Centennial Exhibition of 1876, the black American is also the invisible man. Three full-length books, one article in a scholarly journal, one doctoral dissertation have been written on the Philadelphia Exhibition of 1876. But in none is there even a mention of the fact that in the preparations for the Exhibition and the event itself, blacks were discriminated against and kept from making their contributions.[48]

I will close with an observation on a prophecy delivered by a black American on July 4, 1876. In ending his address that day at the Philadelphia Centennial Exhibition, as part of the ceremonies marking the laying of the base of the Richard Allen monument, Reverend J. J. Jenifer said:

> We shall not be here at the national anniversary marking the American bicentennial, but our children and grandchildren will be. They will not come as we have come here, but they will come greater—come with their productions. They will come in their arts, their sciences, their literature, and in their philosophy, in all of which they shall excel. Color lines will then be wiped out, caste will be gone; the American citizen, whether white or black, will be honored and loved, and mind and moral excellence will alone be the measure of the man.[49]

The first part of this prophecy was to be realized in 1976. I leave it to the reader to judge how accurate a prediction is the second part.

NOTES

1. *The Liberator,* December 1, 1832; Philip S. Foner, *The Life and Writings of Frederick Douglass,* New York, 1950, Vol. II, pp. 188–89.

2. New York *Herald,* May 11, 1876.

3. Philip S. Foner, *Frederick Douglass: A Biography,* NewYork, 1964, pp. 224.

4. *Workingman's Advocate,* Chicago, March 6, 1875; Philip S. Foner, *History of the Labor Movement in the United States,* New York, 1947, Vol. I, pp. 439–74.

Estimates of the number of unemployed varied from 3 to 4 millions, or twice the percentage of unemployed in the Great Depression of the 1930's.

5. *Philadelphia Press,* May 14, 1873.

Robert Purvis (1810–1898) was the son of a white South Carolina merchant and a Moorish-Jewish woman whose mother had been a slave. Independently wealthy and so light-skinned that he could have passed for white, he was educated in private schools of Philadelphia, and finished his education at Amherst College. But he left college to devote himself to the anti-slavery movement and at the age of seventeen made his first public speech against slavery. A founder of the American Anti-Slavery Society, Purvis was also a militant fighter against all forms of discrimination against blacks.

6. In early 1874 President Grant sent Congress a message urging Congressmen to support the Centennial Exhibition. He felt strongly that the failure of the United States to celebrate properly its one hundredth anniversary would be a disgrace. (*New York Times,* February 14, 1874.) Congress did not actually pass a Centennial Appropriation bill until early in 1876, and then as a loan of $1,500,000, and not as a contribution. (*Ibid.,* January 26, 1876; *The Nation,* Vol. XXII, February 17, 1876, p. 105.)

7. *Congressional Record,* 43rd Congress, 1st Session, Appendix, pp. 250–53.

8. *New National Era,* May 21, 28, 1874.

Two of the black Congressmen were from South Carolina, one each from North Carolina, Florida, Alabama, Mississippi, and Louisiana. In the Senate, former slave Blanche K. Bruce, still represented Mississippi.

9. *Proceedings, Convention of Colored Newspaper Men, Cincinnati, August 4, 1875,* Cincinnati, 1875, p. 4. Pamphlet in Cincinnati Historical Society.

10. *Ibid,* p. 5.

11. The two works of art were the sculpture, "Death of Cleopatra," and the monument of Richard Allen. For the details on the raising of the funds for these works of art, see *The Christian Recorder,* June 15, 1876. *The Christian Recorder,* published in Philadelphia, was the official organ of the African Methodist Episcopal Church.

12. *See* United States Centennial Commission Papers (Record Group 230), Archives of the City of Philadelphia.

13. *People's Advocate,* July 8, 1876.

14. Dee Brown, *The Year of the Century: 1876,* New York, 1966, p. 139.

15. *Philadelphia Press,* April 5, 17, 1873; *Philadelphia Times,* April 27, 1873; *New National Era,* May 22, 1873.

16. "Chairman" of "Colored Centennial Committee," in *New National Era,* June 5, 1873.

There are reports of the Women's Centennial Committees of the 2nd, 12th, 15th, 22nd, and 27th wards of Philadelphia in the Historical Society of Pennsylvania, but none of them mention this dispute or the role of black women on the Committee.

17. *See* Philip S. Foner, "The Battle to End Discrimination Against Negroes on the Streetcars of Philadelphia, 1859–1867," *Pennsylvania History*, July and October, 1972, and W. E. B. DuBois, *The Philadelphia Negro*, Philadelphia, 1899.

18. *Philadelphia Press* April 13, 17, 1874; Philadelphia *Evening Bulletin*, April 14, 17, 1874; Philadelphia *North American*, April 15, 17, 1874.

About $15,000 was realized by the sale of tickets for the Police Centennial Fund. (Philadelphia *Evening Star*, April 16–17, 1874.)

19. *Scientific American*, Supplement, vol. I, No. 9, February 26, 1876; *New York Times*, October 13, 1875; *Philadelphia Ledger*, February 15, 1875.

20. Philadelphia *Evening Bulletin*, February 15, 1876.

21. Robert Lowry to United States Centennial Commission, March 12, 1876, United States Centennial Commission Papers, Record Group 230, Archives of the City of Philadelphia; *People's Advocate*, May 27, 1876.

22. "Red Cloud" in *People's Advocate*, July 1, 1876.

23. Editorial in response to "Red Cloud" in *ibid.*, Juy 8, 1876.

A study of the Centennial Board of Finance Minutes (Record Group 231, Archives of the City of Philadelphia), which contains the records of the funds disbursed to workers during the construction and operation of the Exhibition is not helpful, since there is no mention of color or race.

24. A full-page reproduction of the statue of "The Freed Slave" appears in *Frank Leslie's Historical Register of the Centennial Exposition, 1876.* Edited by Frank B. Norton, New York, 1877, p. 133.

25. James J. Johnson in *People's Advocate*, July 1, 8, 1876. In the Pennsylvania Educational Hall, however, photos, plans, and catalogues of Lincoln University, the first black college in the United States (founded as Ashmun Institute in 1854) was exhibited, and there were also photos of African students showing changes among them since coming to Lincoln. (Lincoln University, "Minutes of the Executive Committee of the Board of *Trustees, 1865–1877*, March 2nd, 1876 and December 7, 1876," manuscript copy in Lincoln University, Pennsylvania Archives.) I am indebted to Sophie Cornwell, librarian of the Special Negro Collection, Langston Hughes Memorial Library, Lincoln University, for calling this document to my attention.

26. *Philadelphia Press*, June 4, 1876; Philadelphia *North American*, July 12, 1876.

27. *Philadelphia Press* reprinted in *People's Advocate*, July 1, 1876.

28. *People's Advocate,* July 15, 1876.

29. The monument stood on a granite platform eighteen feet high, with a bust of Richard Allen on it. An effort was made to have the monument placed in Fairmount Park after the Exhibition closed as a permanent tribute to the blacks of Philadelphia. But the move did not bring any results. (*See The Christian Recorder,* June 15, 22, 29, 1876.)

Richard Allen, the first Bishop of the African Methodist Episcopal Church, was the founder of Mother Bethel Church in Philadelphia, and a leading figure in the black community during the years from the 1790's to his death in the early 1830's. He presided at the first National Negro Convention held in the Bethel Church in 1830.

30. In a Centennial Sermon, "1876 vs. 1776," which he delivered at his church in Pine Bluff, Arkansas, July 9, 1876, Reverend Jenifer did deal to some extent with the events of the American Revolution and the role of blacks in the creation of the American nation. (*See The Christian Recorder,* August 31, 1876.)

31. Reverend Jenifer also criticized the fact that the federal government gave "millions to feed and clothe Indians who are too lazy to add one iota to the productive resources of the country." This was unusual, since ordinarily blacks expressed deep sympathy for the Indians and their plight. (*See,* for example, Philip S. Foner, *The Voice of Black Americans: Major Speeches of Negroes in the United States, 1797–1972.* New York, 1973, pp. 212–13, 224–25.)

32. *The Christian Recorder,* July 8, 1876; *People's Advocate,* July 8, 1876.

In inviting the capitalists to the South, Reverend Jenifer emphasized a point made popular later by Booker T. Washington: "They will find the affable and strong Negro to welcome them," Reverend Jenifer said. "In him they will find one who is willing and ready to work hard." Washington added that they would find a Negro who shunned labor unions and strikes. (Louis R. Harlan, *Booker T. Washington: A Biography,* New York, 1973, Vol. I, p. 322.)

33. Frederick Saunders, editor, *Our National Centennial Jubilee: Orations, Addresses and Poems Delivered on the Fourth of July, 1876, in Several States of the Union,* New York, 1877, pp. 530–31.

34. Actually, the centennial of the "Boston Massacre" during which Crispus Attucks was one of five killed by the British troops, occurred on March 5, 1870. For Benjamin Banneker, *See* Silvo A. Bedini, *Life of Benjamin Banneker,* New York, 1972.

35. *People's Advocate* July 15, 1876; Saunders, *op. cit.,* pp. 257–69.

36. Hayden himself fought long and hard against both slavery and racism.

A fugitive slave from Kentucky, he settled in Boston and his home soon became a famous rendezvous for runaway slaves. He was a leader of the Boston Vigilance Committee and many of its meetings were held at his home. During and after the Civil War, he continued to work actively for the cause of equal rights.

37. Recent research indicates that Deborah Gannett was a white indentured servant. *See* Julia Ward Stickley, "The Records of Deborah Sampson Gannett, Woman Soldier of the Revolution," *Prologue,* Vol. IV, Winter, 1972, pp. 26–42.

38. *The Christian Recorder,* July 8, 1876. The text of the address was originally published in advance of the Fourth of July in the issues of May 4, 11, 1876 and reprinted following its delivery.

39. *Centennial. The American Negro. From 1776 to 1876. Oration Delivered July 4, 1876, at Avondale, Ohio, by Rev. Geo. W. Williams,* Cincinnati, 1876, Pamphlet in Cincinnati Historical Society.

Williams, a graduate of Howard University and Newton Theological Seminary, served as minister, newspaper editor, and government clerk in New England before moving to Cincinnati, Ohio, where he was a minister and also studied law.

40. Other signers of the Declaration were Robert D. Mortimer of Rhode Island, A. Alex Jones of Massachusetts, N. J. Booker of Pennsylvania, Daniel Lewis of the District of Columbia, Dr. Riley of Arkansas, and C. L. Vincent of Illinois.

41. "Negro Declaration of Independence, 1876," four page leaflet, Copy in Huntington Library, San Marino, California; *The Christian Recorder,* July 15, 1876.

42. This conclusion is based on a study of newspapers of July 5–6, 1876 in the newspaper division of the Library of Congress and includes papers from all parts of the country.

43. *The Colored Radical,* Leavenworth & Lawrence, Kansas, August 24, 1876.

44. C. Vann Woodward, *Reunion and Reaction: The Compromise of 1877 and the End of Reconstruction,* Boston, 1951.

45. Drew *vs.* Peer, 12 Norris, 234; *Philadelphia Press,* October 26, 1881; *New York Times,* October 26, 1881.

46. John Hope Franklin, "George Washington Williams, Historian," *Journal of Negro History,* Vol. XXXI, January, 1946, pp. 60–90; Earl E. Thorpe, *Black Historians: A Critique,* New York, 1969, pp. 46–47.

47. *Vorbote,* Chicago, July 29, 1876. The paper weekly, organ of the German Socialists, announced in the opening of the article: "The French Workers' Delegation had handed the Socialists gathered in Philadelphia the following questionnaire in the French language."

48. The books are S. Edgar Trout, *The Story of the Centennial of 1876,* New York, 1929; Dee Brown, *The Year of the Century: 1876,* New York, 1966; William Pierce Randal, *Centennial: American Life in 1876,* New York, 1969; the article is Faith K. Pizor, "Preparations for the Centennial Exhibition of 1876," *Pennsylvania Magazine of History and Biography,* Vol. XCIV, April, 1970, pp. 113–32; and the doctoral dissertation is Dorothy E. C. Ditter, "The Cultural Climate of the Centennial City: Philadelphia, 1875–1876," unpublished Ph.D. thesis, University of Pennsylvania, 1947.

49. *The Christian Recorder,* July 8, 1876; *People's Advocate,* July 8, 1876.

9

Peter H. Clark: Pioneer Black Socialist*

On March 26, 1877, at a socialist meeting at Robinson's Opera House in Cincinnati, Ohio, the first Black American to identify himself publicly with socialism announced his support of the Workingmen's Party of the United States, the first Marxist political party in this country.[1] This pioneer Black socialist was Peter H. Clark, principal of the Colored High School in Cincinnati.

American socialism had had a long history before 1877, but it had never before been able to recruit any Black adherents. The reasons are not difficult to understand. During the pre-Civil War period, the vast majority of Blacks were slaves and they were hardly potential members of any organized political movement. In addition, an important wing of the socialist movement—the Utopian socialists of the ante-bellum years—showed little interest in gaining converts among free Blacks. Robert Owen attacked prejudice and encouraged the education of Negroes, but in his own colony at New Harmony, Indiana, Negroes were excluded except as helpers "if necessary," or "if it be found useful to prepare and enable them to become associated in communities in Africa."[2] In the communities founded by the Associationists, based on the Utopian socialist principles of Charles Fourier, Blacks were not even included as "helpers." In the Utopian society to be created in the United States under the operation of the land reform program of the National Reformers, led by George Henry Evans, there was to be no room for Blacks. They

*Reprinted from *The Journal of Ethnic Studies,* Vol. V, no. 3, pp. 17–35.

would have to be separated from the rest of society, either through colonization to Africa or by being settled in their own communities somewhere in the West.

The Utopian socialists' approach to the slavery question served to further alienate Blacks. Owen retreated gradually from his earlier insistence upon the absolute necessity of speedily eliminating Negro slavery. During his second visit to the United States in 1845, Owen addressed a convention of the New England Anti-Slavery Society and announced that, while he was still opposed to Negro slavery, he no longer felt that its swift eradication was a matter of prime importance. He had, he said, seen even worse slavery in England than the chattel slavery in the South, and he was now dedicating himself to the struggle to end the more evil form of slavery—"to contend for the liberty for the white man, who was bound by the most arrant slavery of all."[3]

The view that the condition of White wage slaves under capitalism was either as bad as or worse than that of Black chattel slaves became a common dictum for all Utopian socialists, whether they were Owenites, Associationists, or National Reformers. George Henry Evans, for example, echoed the Southern apologists for slavery by arguing that to free the Negro people in order that they might enter wage slavery would be a great disadvantage to the slaves, since it would mean exchanging their "surety of support in sickness and old age" for poverty and unemployment. At the same time, he maintained that the abolition of slavery would harm the northern worker by throwing millions of Blacks onto the labor market and thus driving down the wages of the entire working class. Under these circumstances, he insisted, the correct solution was to first abolish wage slavery. One of Evans' disciples, Thomas Devyr, put it this way: "Emancipate the white man first—free him from the thraldom of his unsupplied wants and the day this is done, we'll commence the manumission of the much wronged black man within our borders."[4]

Black abolitionists bluntly accused the Utopian reformers of allying themselves with the Southern apologists for slavery. Nothing enraged them more than the cry that wage slavery was either as bad as or worse than chattel slavery. William P. Powell, a Black militant in New York City, who took his family to England in 1851 to remove them from the scourge of American racism, encountered the same arguments as those advanced by Utopian reformers when he addressed meetings condemning Negro slavery in the United States. He unloosed a blast against the theory that the condition of White workers in English factories and mines was worse than that of the Black slaves on Southern plantations. On the contrary, he insisted, "they are, in effect, as far apart as the Poles." While the White workers had the protection of laws, where, they asked, were the laws that protected Black slaves of the South. No White worker, he maintained, was subjected to the unlimited power that the master class had over the Southern slave.[5]

Black abolitionists had no difficulty in deciding which form of slavery—wage or chattel—should be abolished first. They condemned the Utopian socialists for weakening the struggle against Negro slavery by raising the issue of priorities. In so doing, they claimed they furnished the Southerners with ammunition with which to defend their "peculiar institution," and made it increasingly difficult to plead the cause of the slave without first considering the issue of abolishing the wage system.[6]

The approach of the Marxists to Blacks and the slavery question during the period before the Civil War differed sharply from that of the Utopian socialists. On October 25, 1857, some former members of the European Communist League in the United States, all of them disciples of Karl Marx and Frederick Engels, formed the Communist Club of New York, the first one in the Western Hemisphere. The Club invited Blacks to join as equal members. Its constitution required that all members "recognize the complete equality of all men—no matter of what color or sex."[7] At a meeting held in New York on April 22, 1858, which was sponsored by the Communist Club, the following declaration was adopted unanimously:

> We recognize no distinction as to nationality or race, caste or status, color or sex; our goal is nothing less than the reconciliation of all human interests, freedom and happiness for mankind, and the realization and unification of a world republic.[8]

Slave owners could have joined the communities organized by the Owenites, Associationists, and National Reformers as equal members, and they were not required at any time, once they had joined, to dispose of their human property. On the other hand, the Communist

Club of New York not only prohibited membership to slave owners, but expelled any member who manifested the slightest sympathy for the slave owners' point of view.[9] In fact, the Communist Club insisted, as did all Marxists, that while wage slavery was an evil which must be abolished, the abolition of chattel slavery must take priority. They maintained that the heart of the slavery controversy was the struggle between the industrial and slave economy, and that the success of the former through the abolition of chattel slavery would inevitably create new possibilities for the development of free labor. They also held that wage workers could not advance any further in American society until chattel slavery was eliminated, that the working class must play an important role in hastening its downfall, and that this, in turn, would likewise strengthen their organization for its subsequent fight against capital. To put it as Marx did: "Labor cannot emancipate itself in the white skin where in the black it is branded."[10]

Yet for all of their stand on equality of Black and White, and their activity in the struggle against Negro slavery, the Marxists were not able to recruit any more Blacks before the Civil War than did the Utopian socialists. One reason is that the Marxists, in the main, spoke and wrote only German and operated almost exclusively among the German-Americans. Indeed, many of them even refused to learn English on principle, viewing it as an inferior language of a theoretically backward working class.[11] Even after the Civil War, this sectarian policy continued to dominate large sections of the American socialist movement. As John Swinton, a leading post-Civil War American progressive journalist, pointed out:

> The German-Americans . . . of the country at large have not one tenth of the social, moral, or political influence they would have if they would all learn to speak, read, and write the American language. Multitudes of them are isolated from the general life of their community by their inability to do so. What a stream of new thought they would pour through the country if they commanded the country's tongue! We are aware that the German is a rich, ripe, delicate, subtle and mellifluous language, but so also is the American which is spoken by over fifty million of our progressive population, white and black.[12]

Frederick Engels agreed wholeheartedly with this criticism. He believed that in order for the socialists to play an important role in

America, "they will have to doff every remnant of foreign garb . . . [and] to become out and out American. . . . And to do that, they must above all things learn English."[13]

It is not surprising that the socialists of Cincinnati were the first to recruit a Black member. William Haller, a former militant abolitionist, became Cincinnati's "foremost voice of socialist protest in the post-Civil War years," and he sought, through his English-language socialist weekly, *The Emancipator,* to turn the socialist movement in the Queen City from a predominantly German-speaking orientation to one which would appeal to English-speaking workers as well.[14] In 1870, Haller, as a representative of the "Workingmen's Organization," was among the fourteen delegates from Cincinnati at the convention of the National Labor Union. Another delegate from Cincinnati was Peter H. Clark, representing the Colored Teachers' Co-operative Association, an organization which, from all available evidence, appears to have been the first trade union of teachers in American history. Haller and Clark became lifelong friends, and eventually, the Black teacher became convinced that the socialist ideology propounded by Haller offered the best answer to the problems facing the Negro people in the United States.[15]

Peter Humphries Clark was born in Cincinnati in 1829. His grandfather, William Clark, was the "Clark" of the Lewis-Clark expedition sent by Thomas Jefferson in 1804 to explore the continent and find a route to the Pacific. Clark, a Southern White who had close relations with a Black woman and fathered several children by her, feared that he might not return from the expedition and that his family, living as it did in the South, might be enslaved. He therefore moved them to Cincinnati with enough money for their support during his absence. One of his children, Michael Clark, was the father of Peter H. Clark.[16]

In choosing Cincinnati, William Clark selected the gateway to the South, a city that was anything but receptive to Negroes. The Black Laws passed in 1804 required Negroes to secure a $1,500 bond signed by two "approved" White men, who would guarantee both their behavior and support. Twenty-five years later, the city's attempt to rigidly enforce the law brought on an anti-Negro riot in which Black lives and property were lost. As a result, 1,200 Negroes left Cincinnati for Canada. There were other riots in 1836 and 1841.[17]

It is hardly surprising that Cincinnati had no public schools for Blacks until well into the nineteenth century. Peter H. Clark began attending high school in 1844 at the Cincinnati High School, the first of its kind established for the education of the free Black youths of the city and its surrounding area. Many of its graduates went on to Oberlin College or to other colleges where no color line was drawn. Clark left the school in 1848, refusing a job with his father, a barber, "because it would make him move around at the dictates of every class of white men," and apprenticed himself to a liberal artisan, Thomas Varney, to learn stereotyping.[18]

In 1849, Clark became a teacher in the colored public schools that were established in Cincinnati that year. Since the law establishing free schools for colored children authorized Blacks to elect their school directors, the racist school authorities, with the support of Cincinnati's city officials, mounted a challenge against its constitutionality, and refused, meanwhile, to turn over the money that was necessary for the maintenance of the schools. Clark taught without salary for two years until the courts upheld the law's constitutionality and ordered the city to pay the salaries of colored teachers, retroactive to the time the schools were established. However, the suit against the city had been very costly for Cincinnati's Blacks, and when Clark received his back pay of $105, he turned over the entire sum to the fund to defray the cost of the suit.[19]

Still, the prolonged legal battle must have caused Clark to question whether there was actually a place for a Black in American society, for he showed some interest in the colonization movement. John McMicken, son of the founder of the University of Cincinnati, had been urged to do something for colored youth. He responded by purchasing 10,000 acres of land in Africa, between Liberia and Sierra Leone, and naming it "Ohio in Africa," he offered to finance any Blacks who desired to settle there. Clark chose to go as an explorer, but upon reaching New Orleans, he refused to embark in the dirty lumber schooner that had been chartered for him and the 119 others. The others did leave, but because of the unseaworthiness of the vessel, they had to put into Charleston, South Carolina for repairs. There they were all promptly jailed as constituting a potential danger to the slave system. Three months later, they embarked again. Within six months after arriving in Africa, ninety percent of them had died of various diseases.[20]

Upon returning to Cincinnati, Clark continued with his teaching duties, but he quickly ran afoul of the colored school board because of his Unitarian views, and was fired from his job. This gave him time to devote to the struggle against slavery and to the free Black convention movement of the 1850's. He was active in the 1852 Convention of Colored Freemen of Ohio, held in Cincinnati, and a year later, he was appointed secretary of the 1853 National Convention of Colored Men, held in Rochester, New York. Clark played a leading role in the 1856 and 1857 conventions of Colored Men of Ohio, and at the latter meeting, he was appointed secretary of the gathering.[21]

In 1855, Clark launched his own newspaper—the Cincinnati *Herald of Freedom.* Unfortunately, there is no copy of the paper in existence, but it was reportedly "filled with vigorous matter." In any case, the paper did not last out the year, and Clark went to work for William S. Bailey, publisher of a free-soil paper in Newport, Kentucky. The latter had several times been the object of mob action, and in the fall of 1840, a racist mob had thrown his presses into the Ohio River. Clark served as editor of the paper for several months, and during the same period, he served as correspondent of *Frederick Douglass' Paper.* At the 1857 convention of Colored Men of Ohio, he was referred to as the "assistant editor of 'Frederick Douglass' Paper.' "[22]

From the mid-1850's on, Clark was a Republican, but not an uncritical one. In 1858, when the Republicans of Ohio refused to take a firm stand against the state's "black codes" and other aspects of the racial prejudice that pervaded the state, Clark told a convention of Colored Men in Cincinnati that "the rights of the Negro were no safer with the Republicans than with the Democrats," and that Blacks should make it clear that their support was not to be taken for granted.[23]

During the Civil War, Cincinnati came under attack by the Confederate forces. Preparations were made for the defense of the city, but it was made clear that it would be defended only by White man, and that Blacks (that was not the word used) were "to keep out of this." However, with the Confederates at the very gates of the city, the mayor called on Blacks as well as Whites to come to its defense. When some Blacks volunteered, however, they were seized by the police, arrested, and dragged "to the mule pen on Plum street at the point of a bayonet." Finally, the Negroes were allowed to form a Black Brigade and, a thousand strong, they helped defend the city. After Cincinnati was saved, members of the Black Brigade enlisted for service with Massachusetts and Ohio Black regiments. Before the Black Brigade disbanded, they were concerned lest the story of their contribution be forgotten, and they selected Clark to write their history.[24] In 1864, Clark published *The Black Brigade of Cincinnati.* He did not spare the Queen City, writing caustically:

> The city of Cincinnati always has been and still is pro-slavery. Nowhere has the prejudice against colored people been more cruelly manifested than here. Further north or further south the feeling is not so intense; but here it almost denies him the right of existence.

Yet Cincinnati was typically American. "There is an ellipsis universal in American writing or speaking," Clark noted. "When an American writes, 'All men are created free and equal,' he means all white men. When he solicits the patronage of the public for his book, his lecture, his concert, his store, his railroad-car, or steamboat, he means the white public."[25] The contributions of the Black Brigade to the victory of the Union and the story Clark wrote detailing them helped produce a climate favorable to the repeal of Ohio's "black laws."[26]

Clark had returned to his position in the colored school system in 1857, and after the war was over, he began to agitate for a colored high school. The plan was opposed by the school board, but it finally passed by one vote in July, 1866, and that September, Gaines High School opened its doors with Peter H. Clark as its principal. In his work, "The Colored Schools of Cincinnati," L. D. Easton writes:

> For a number of years, Mr. Peter H. Clark labored, after school hours, instructing advanced classes of young people, and preparing teachers to maintain the supply demanded by the colored schools within a large radius of Cincinnati. In fact, it is safe to say that from 1859 to 1895, not a teacher in the colored schools, but had been trained by him. No one realized as he did, the pressing need of a high school for colored youth, and in 1865 he began to advocate its establishment. Always timid and apprehensive of its cost, a majority of the Board opposed the scheme, but in July, 1866, the measure received a majority of one vote, and in September, the school was opened under the title of Gaines' High

School with . . . Peter H. Clark, principal. . . . The following studies comprised the curriculum of the school: Algebra, Geometry, Trigonemetry, Astronomy, Higher Arithmetic, Bookkeeping, Physics, Physiology, Botany, Chemistry, Geology, History, Literature, Rhetoric, Measuration, Latin, German, Drawing and Music. . . .[27]

Even though the colored school system of Cincinnati remained independent of the White school board until 1874, it was always financially dependent upon that board. Nevertheless, Clark, who was superintendent until 1866—when he became a full-time principal—lobbied so militantly and effectively for funds that by 1870, expenditures on the colored school system amounted to 4.9 percent of the total, in spite of the fact that Blacks owned property that was only worth less than one-half percent of the total wealth. In fact, so rapidly did the expenditures for Blacks increase that in 1870, they actually exceeded the amount spent per White pupil—the only situation of its kind in the entire country.[28]

After the Civil War, Clark remained a Republican, but he was moving steadily to the left. As indicated above, he was instrumental in organizing the Black teachers of Cincinnati into the first union of teachers—the Colored Teachers Co-operative Association—and was sent by them to the 1870 convention of the National Labor Union. In 1872, enraged over the failure of the Republicans to protect the citizen rights of his people in the South, and concerned over the growing influence of industrial capitalists in the party, Clark joined the Liberal Republicans. He became disillusioned with that movement when it nominated Horace Greeley for president. At a meeting in Cincinnati on August 15, 1872, Clark rejected Charles Sumner's plea on behalf of Greeley and criticized the long-time editor of the *New York Tribune* for having advised President Lincoln to offer the slaveholders four hundred million dollars for their slaves:

This earnest Abolitionist, whom Mr. Sumner so much admired, and for whom he advises us to vote, was willing to burden the laboring man of the North with a debt of four hundred millions of dollars to pay the masters of the south that sum for releasing their unfounded claims to the bodies and souls of their slaves. Had the proposed donation been to the slaves, there would have been some justice to the demand.

Although he returned to the Republican fold, Clark again made it clear that he considered it unwise for the Negro vote to be "concentrated in one party."[29]

In August, 1875, Clark addressed the convention of Colored Newspaper Men in Cincinnati and called for a militant Black press, both to "express our wants" and to educate Blacks on the vital social and economic issues of the day—issues "which are for the most part unheeded by the press of the country." In November, 1875, he addressed the local Sovereigns of Industry in Cincinnati, an organization concerned mainly with establishing cooperatives for the distribution of the necessities of life among wage earners. He vigorously supported its program of producer and consumer cooperatives, condemned the extremes of wealth and poverty alike as "curses," and urged the regulation of capital. The Republican *Cincinnati Commercial,* describing Clark's speech as "an intelligent review of the relations of capital and labor," summarized his remarks as follows:

> The question most pertinent to the poor man is whether it is better to give him a benevolent loaf of bread, or put him in the way of earning it. He was decidedly in favor of the latter. Any other way of helping the poor man was a delusion and a snare. All methods at mere benevolence crushed the manhood out of him, and degraded and debased him.

But the economic crisis which had begun in 1873 kept growing worse. Production fell precipitously. Mills either were closed or ran only part time, and the number of unemployed in Cincinnati mounted each month. The continued hard times were converting more and more workers to socialism.[30]

Clark, however, still remained a Republican; he attended the 1876 Republican national convention and publicly supported the candidacy of Rutherford B. Hayes. But toward the end of that year, his radicalism began to clearly emerge. On December 10, he addressed the Cincinnati Workingmen's Society on the subject, "Wages' Slavery and the Remedy." In the course of his speech, he condemned the "inordinate concentration of capital" and "large fortunes" as being "contrary to the welfare of society and to the interests of capital itself." He urged the "gradual reformation of the laws of society and of government" as well as "thorough, intelligent, honest, and faithful labor organizations." Capital, he maintained, had to "give up some of its assumed selfish rights and give labor its share."[31]

On March 26, 1877, Peter H. Clark renounced the Republican Party and announced his support for the Workingmen's Party of the United States. The Socialists who were gathered at Robinson's Opera House sensed that they had acquired a significant recruit and an oratorical gem, and "heartily applauded," interrupting his speech with cheers. Clark bitterly denounced the notion that the interests of capital and labor were the same, and argued that the conflict between them had "drenched the streets of Paris with blood, accounted for . . . strikes in England, the eviction of small tenants in Ireland, and the denial to the freedmen of the South of the right to purchase the land they till." He went on:

> Go to the South and see the capitalists banded together over the poor whites. They carefully calculate how much, and no more, it will require to feed the black laborer and keep him alive from one year to another. That much they will give him for his hard labor, on which the aristocracy live, and not a cent more will they give him. Not a foot of land will they sell to the oppressed race who are trying to crowd out the degradation into which capital has plunged them. And here in Ohio nothing but the bayonet of the militia alone has kept the miners of the Southwestern part of the state groveling in the dust. Here in Cincinnati we have the working woman working hour after hour with her needle to eke out a bare existence. The great middle class of society is being crushed out.

The Black educator pointed out that while the middle class was being pushed into the ranks of the working class, the "millionaires" were growing in number. Only a few years earlier, he said, there had been just a few "millionaires" in American society, "but now they jostle each other in the streets while men—the great mass of men—who toiled . . . to make the city what it is, have passed away in poverty and obscurity." He described his own bitter experience: unemployed for months on end, his wife and baby starving, and so desperate that he felt "like throwing himself in the river, and thus ending all his misery." It was then that he first understood what it meant to be unable to find work in the existing society through no fault of his own. Clark insisted that he did not hope for violence, and that reforms would come "one by one." But he went on: "Capital must not rule, but be ruled and regulated. Capital must be taught that man, and not money, is supreme and that legislation must be had for man." Dismissing the argument of the *laissez-faire* school that the less government the better, he maintained that government "is good; it is not an evil" if it were used in the interests of the working people. It was the government's duty "to so organize society that honest labor should not feel such oppression to drive it to desperation" as he had been driven during his months of unemployment. It was a remarkably moving speech, and William Haller, who had recruited Clark as a member of the Party, rejoiced in his paper, *The Emancipator*. It was, he wrote, one of the best speeches he had ever heard, and "decidedly the best of the evening."[32]

Having joined the Workingmen's Party of Cincinnati, Clark began to speak for the cause at street corner meetings and trade union gatherings. But it was not until the great railroad strike of 1877 that his name became widely known in the working-class circles of Cincinnati.

In the hot mid-July of 1877, exactly one year after the celebration of America's one hundredth birthday, with the nation prostrate after three and one-half years of severe depression, a general railroad strike developed into a national conflagration that brought the country closer to a social revolution than at any other time in its century of existence. The strike came after the third ten percent wage cut since the depression began was put into effect by the railroads. On Tuesday, July 16, railroad workers at Martinsburg, West Virginia went out on strike against the wage cut imposed by the Baltimore & Ohio Railroad. As the militia was called out and violence broke out, the strike extended up the B & O line and spread rapidly to other lines. Other workers came to the support of the railroad strikers, and by the weekend, angry crowds of workers were attacking the railroads and fighting with militiamen in the cities of West Virginia, Pennsylvania, and Ohio. The local militia generally sided with the strikers, and, for the first time since Andrew Jackson's administration, federal troops were called in to suppress a strike.

Almost before the public was aware of what was happening, the huge contagion had spread as far as Chicago, St. Louis, and Kansas City, and then on to San Francisco. Within a few days, one hundred thousand men were on strike in the first nationwide labor upheaval in history. All the main railway lines were affected, and even the employees of some Canadian roads joined the strike. Headlines blared out: "The Movement Rapidly Extending in All Directions," and "The People Excited and Agitated From Ocean to Ocean."[33]

The headline in the *Cincinnati Enquirer* of July 23, 1877 read: "THE RED FLAG. IT CASTS ITS UGLY SHADOW OVER OUR QUEENLY CITY."

On the day before, the *Enquirer* had carried the following notice inserted by the Workingmen's Party of Cincinnati:

GREAT MASS-MEETING

THIS AFTERNOON

At 2 o'clock at the Court Street Market Place.
All Good Citizens are Invited to Appear.
Subject:

THE GREAT STRIKE OF THE RAILROAD MEN

At two in the afternoon, many workers fell in behind members of the German, Bohemian, and English-speaking sections of the Workingmen's Party, led by the Eureka Brass Band, headed by a man carrying "the blood-red flag of the Commune." An "immense crowd," estimated in the thousands, filled the market place and was divided into four sections—two for the German-speaking contingent and two for the English. Resolutions were presented and adopted. They charged the Baltimore & Ohio Railroad Company "and similar monopolies" with having reduced the wages of their employees "to a starvation point, and thereby forced them to desperate measures in order to better their condition"; condemned the governors of West Virginia, Pennsylvania, and Maryland and Rutherford B. Hayes for using their military powers "in favor of said monopolies, regardless of the will of the people, and against the people, slaughtering innocent men, women, and children," and concluded by pledging to "use all *lawful* means to support the downtrodden, outraged railroad employees on strike."[34]

Then came the key speech of the afternoon, delivered by Peter H. Clark, Black member of the English-speaking section. He condemned the railroad companies and their political allies, denounced the slaughter of workers by federal troops and state militia, and analyzed at length the causes of the economic crisis and its impact on the working class. "I sympathize in this struggle with the strikers," he declared, "and I feel sure that in this I have the cooperation of nine-tenths of my fellow citizens." But sympathy, he said, was not enough. It was necessary to create a society in which the widespread suffering that provoked the strike would be eliminated. "Every railroad in the land should be owned or controlled by the government. The title of private owners should be extinguished, and the ownership vested in the people." And this was only the beginning. Machinery—indeed all the means of production—had to be appropriated and used for the benefit of the people and not for private gain. There was only one "remedy for the evils of society"—socialism. "Choose ye this day which course ye shall pursue," Clark concluded to thunderous applause.

The *Cincinnati Commercial,* which published Clark's speech under the heading, "Socialism: The Remedy for the Evils of Society," reported that he was "well received." *The Emancipator* found his speech "characterized by that deep pathos of feeling that is to be expected of one who can look back at the time when the wrong and injustice of capital abused his race, which by its labors and sorrows, helped to build the greatness of this nation."[35] Clark's speech to the railroad strikers was probably the first widely publicized proposal for socialism by a Black American, and *The Emancipator's* comment on it was probably the first recognition by an American socialist organ of the contributions of Blacks to the building of American society.

Although the *Cincinnati Commercial* had published Clark's speech, it made it clear that it did not agree with him. "Mr. Peter H. Clark," it noted editorially, "cannot understand why it is that the military are always against the strikers. It ought not to be a great mystery to a man of his analytic powers." According to the newspaper, a worker had the right to leave his employment if he was not satisfied with his wages, but he had no right to take possession of his employer's property and dictate to him what he should or should not do. The employer had a perfect right to appeal for protection, and if the sheriff could not provide it, the governor of the state was perfectly justified in calling out the militia. The worker, having "done an unlawful thing," had "put himself outside the law, defied the civil authority, and has made himself penally liable." That was all there was to it. "It seems to us if Mr. Clark would give his mind to the subject for a few hours he would be able to discover why it is that the military are in such crisis as the present on the side of law and order."[36]

Clark, however, was not persuaded. In "A Plea for the Strikers," he reminded the newspapers that he had experienced enough of what it meant to be poor to understand the meaning of the words in "Ecclesiastics": "I beheld the tear of such as were oppressed and they had no comforter. . . . With this fact imprinted on my memory by many years' sympathy with and service in unpopular causes, I do not marvel when I see the oppression of the poor, and violent perverting of judgment and justice." As for himself, he was "in every fiber and nerve a law-abiding citizen," one, indeed, who deprecated "violent words and violent deeds as much as any one can. I am, sir, emphatically a law-and-order man." But not all the violent deeds and words "are on the part of the strikers and their friends." The advocates of "law and order" boasted openly that they were prepared to "wipe out the strikers and their sympathizers. Thumbs have been drawn significantly across the throats, and law-and-order men have pulled at imaginary ropes to give me an inkling of the throat-cuttings and hangings in reserve." The press, Clark pointed out, had no words of condemnation for such conduct. But the workers could hardly be blamed if they took such threats seriously and also took steps to defend themselves. Nor should the reaction of the workers to what they saw about them on the railroads be considered surprising. They were told that wages must be reduced because the railroads were losing money:

> But when they see high railroad officials receiving the salaries of princes, when they hear of dividends on stock and interest on bonds, they cannot understand why there is no money for the man whose labors earn these vast sums. . . . When they complain, they are told that they are at liberty to quit and take their services elsewhere. This is equivalent to telling them that they are at liberty to go and starve. . . . Hence they make the effort to obtain an increase of wages and to retain their places at the same time. Understanding their motive, and the dire necessity by which they are driven, I pity, but I can not condemn them. . . .
>
> Then too, the door of justice seemed shut in their faces. They have no representation on the Board of Directors. Every State has laws punishing conspiracy, punishing riot and unlawful assemblages, but no State has laws providing for the examination and redress of the grievances of

which these men complain. The whole force of the State and National Governments may be invoked by the railroad managers, but the laborer has nothing.

Clark declared that the right to resist wrong resided in every man, and that no laws could take this right away from him. "Hedged in and despairing, the railroad men have exercised this right," yet as the newspapers could attest, "the strikers themselves, are neither destructive nor men of blood."

Clark concluded by defending the Workingmen's Party against the charge that it had stirred up the strikers to acts of violence. Actually, he maintained, there was probably not a section of that party in any one of the centers of disturbance: "When workingmen understand that there are peaceful influences at work to relieve them of the thraldom of wages slavery, they will be more patient." Clark even proposed that the railroad managers "plant a section of the Workingmen's party at every station. They would guard their property more effectually than the whole United States army can do it."

The Emancipator applauded Clark's advice to the railway management and called it "correct every word of it." Clark, it observed, had put his finger on the real reason for "mob violence"—the refusal of the capitalists to permit the workers to organize and defend themselves against exploitation. "In endeavoring to weaken the power of the working people to protect their rights, by preventing organization, employers have increased the danger to their possessions an hundredfold. Gentlemen, the way to prevent another reign of terror is to help organize the laborers of the country."[37] Both Clark and *The Emancipator* demonstrated genuine sympathy for understanding of the problems of the strikers. However, they also advanced a naive proposal as to how the Workingmen's Party of the United States could contribute to the elimination of the class struggle.

The railroad workers lost the strike, and over one hundred workers lost their lives. But, the strike resulted in a great upsurge in the movement for labor's independent political action. The Workingmen's Party of the United States entered energetically into the political movement.

An interesting feature of the WPUS electoral campaigns in 1877 was the effort to establish Black-White unity. In Maryland, the

Workingmen's Party appealed to all workers and all other citizens, "without regard to race, nationality or political creed," to support its candidates.[38] In Cincinnati, the Party nominated Peter H. Clark for state superintendent of schools. The other candidates on the socialist ticket were a White American, a Bohemian, a German cigar maker, and an Irish stonecutter. But in the Party's official organ, *The Emancipator,* William Haller called for special efforts to amass a big vote for the Black candidate:

> Peter H. Clark, of all the candidates on the ticket, most thoroughly represents the contest between laborers and capitalists, of the proscribed race, whose sorrows made the name of the United States the synonym of robbery and murder throughout the world; his nomination is therefore above all the finest vindication of the claim that the Workingmen's Party is a purely cosmopolitan organization.
>
> But a long time since this man of learning and culture, now the principal of our colored schools, was a youth, on the streets of Cincinnati battling for a living as a newspaper carrier, hated and proscribed because he belonged to a class whose labors had opened every field in the South, and whose woes and miseries had ladened every breeze with appeals to the hearts of the just for the wrong and injustice of slavery, to be lifted off of Africa's outraged sons and daughters. . . .[39]

Clark campaigned enthusiastically for the Workingmen's Party. That summer and fall, he spoke for the socialists in Louisville and in Jeffersonville, Indiana. A Louisville socialist wrote: "Clark for reasoning can't be beat." Clark's "reasoning" consisted of pointing out to working class audiences that the Great Strike had proved the socialist contention that the local, state, and national governments of the United States were controlled by, of, and for the capitalists, and that, just as the capitalists were preparing for future labor conflicts by building up the armed forces, so the workers should prepare by electing socialists to office to guarantee that these forces would not be used to break strikes.[40]

In December, 1877, the Workingmen's Party of the United States changed its name to the Socialist Labor Party. Peter H. Clark was elected to the SLP National Executive Committee, and was listed in the Party's press as one of the best of the "Socialistic Agitators and Lecturers."[41] In the fall of 1878, Clark was nominated for Congress on the SLP ticket in Cincinnati. While he did not win, he did gain a larger vote than in 1877, and it was observed in the Cincinnati press that he obtained considerable support in the city's Black sections.[42] The socialist press credited him with recruiting several Blacks as members of the Party. *The Socialist,* the leading English-language SLO organ, published in Chicago, boasted that not only "has Peter H. Clark for some time past been a member of the organization . . . [and] has now been for the past year a member of the National Executive Committee, but he has been responsible for the fact that other colored men have lately joined the party."[43]

In the summer of 1879, Peter H. Clark announced his departure from the Socialist Labor Party. He made it clear that his decision was not caused by any lessening in his belief in socialism, for he pointed out that he had remained with the SLP in spite of threats that he would lose his job as principal of Gaines High School in Cincinnati if he did not resign and repudiate socialism. The campaign failed, Clark noted proudly, "when the colored people of Cincinnati, who had stood by me all my life-time, came to my rescue just as if I had been a son and brother. They laid aside political prejudices and religious prejudices, and came out as one man and protested my removal."[44]

Still, Clark found the Cincinnati SLP more and more disappointing as a force through which Blacks might redress their grievances. For one thing, William Haller's influence in the Party declined after 1877, and this led to a muting of the Negro question in the Party's press and activities.[45] For another, intense factionalism plagued the Party and more time was spent in personal recriminations than in discussing concrete issues. Clark found the factional strife and the Party's failure to concern itself with the problems of Blacks too much to ignore. In his farewell address as a member of the SLP on July 21, 1879, Clark announced that he was still "a socialist," but would wait for a movement of socialism to arise which would speak in the interests of his people. "The welfare of the Negro is my controlling political motive," he told his White comrades, as he urged them to abandon their factional disputes and begin paying some attention to issues which might make the Party attractive to blacks.[46]

That Clark remained a socialist for some time after he left the SLP is indicated by the moving eulogy he delivered at the funeral services for William Haller, his old friend in the socialist cause, who died on

March 1, 1881. He began by thanking Haller for having introduced him to socialism, and went on to praise him as an agitator for social justice:

> He had dreams of the millenium. Those visions which have inspired the prophets and sages of the past. To him Utopia was not Utopian; he believed that the city might come when the "lion and the lamb" should lie down together, and a little child should lead them. The New Jerusalem of his hope was not in a different life and beyond the sky, but here—here upon earth, and dwelt in by living men.

Clark concluded:

> Dear friend, it was not given thee to realize all thy hopes for humanity; but thy very life is an evidence and prognostication of the happy future for which thou hast hoped and labored. No hope ever conceived in the human breast, which has for its basis the happiness of man, is too bright for realization, and such lives as thine bring forward that happy time when they shall be realities, not dreams.
>
> Every drop of water that is dashed against the rugged cliff, which frowns upon the ocean's side, does its part in wearing its adamantine front, and the time will come when it must fall.
>
> Thus, such lives as thine, beating themselves out in strife with hoaring wrongs, shall not be lived in vain. Those wrongs, though they seem "rock-ribbed and ancient as the sun," shall crumble and fail, and Astrea shall hang her scales in the sky, and a Golden Age dawn upon the earth, brighter even than thy hope.[47]

It is not possible here to deal with Clark's subsequent career[48] and with his gradual disillusionment with American socialism because it failed to concern itself with the problems of Black Americans.[49] But his decisions were always motivated by what he considered best for the future of Black Americans. As William Wells Brown wrote in 1882: "No man has been truer to his oppressed people than Peter H. Clark, and none are more deserving of their unlimited confidence than he."[50] Of Peter H. Clark we can say what he said of the man who introduced him to socialism: ". . . such lives as thine, beating themselves out in strife with hoary wrongs, shall not be lived in vain."

NOTES

1. The Workingmen's Party of the United States was born at a congress held in Philadelphia from July 19–22, 1876. It was the second Marxist party

established in any country, the first having been set up in Germany in 1875. Like the Social Democratic Party of Germany, the Workingmen's Party of the United States was the result of a merger of two Socialist groups—the disciples of Karl Marx and the followers of Ferdinand Lassalle. For the proceedings of the convention at which the Party was organized, see Philip S. Foner, editor, *The Formation of the Workingmen's Party of the United States: Proceedings of the Union Congress Held at Philadelphia, July 19– 22, 1876,* Occasional Paper No. 18, American Institute for Marxist Studies, 1976.

2. *New Harmony Gazette,* October 1, 1825. In my book, *American Socialism and Black Americans: From the Age of Jackson to World War II,* Westport, Conn., 1978, I deal extensively with the relations between antebellum Socialism and Black Americans.

3. *The Liberator,* June 6, 1845.

4. *Working Man's Advocate,* March 16, 1844; *Young America,* January 3, 1846; *New York Tribune,* February 16, 1850.

5. *National Anti-Slavery Standard,* May 8, 1851.

6. Philip S. Foner, *The Life and Writings of Frederick Douglass,* Vol. I, New York, 1950, pp. 45, 48, 51, 53, 55–57, 59, 110–12.

7. Karl Obermann, *Joseph Weydemeyer: Pioneer of American Socialism,* New York, 1947, pp. 11–30; Statuten des Kommunisten-Klubs in New York. Collection, Political Parties, Box 25.

8. Sociale Republick, Vol. I, No. 14, New York, July 24, 1858. Copy in New York Public Library.

9. Herman Schüter, Die Anfange der deutschen Arbeiterbewegung in *Amerika,* Stuttgart, 1907, pp. 160–62.

10. Obermann, op. cit., pp. 50–51; Friedrich Kapp, *Geschichte der Sklaverei in den Vereinigten Staaten von Amerika,* New York, 1860, pp. 177–85; Karl Marx, *Capital,* edited by Frederick Engels, New York, 1939, Vol. I, p. 287.

11. Karl Marx and Frederick Engels, *Letters to Americans, 1848–1895,* New York, 1953, pp. 7, 42, 160–87.

12. *John Swinton's Paper,* February 21, 1886.

13. Karl Marx and Frederick Engels, *Letters to Americans,* pp. 289–90.

14. James M. Morris, "William Haller, 'The Disturbing Element,' "*Cincinnati Historical Society Bulletin,* Vol. XXVIII, Winter 1970, pp. 120–32.

15. *Workingman's Advocate,* August 27, 1870. The National Labor Union, founded at a congress in Baltimore in 1866, was the first national labor federation of the post-Civil War period. James M. Morris, "The Road to Trade Unionism: Organized Labor in Cincinnati, 1800–1893," unpublished Ph.D. thesis, University of Cincinnati, pp. 87–90.

16. Dovie King Clark, "Peter Humphries Clark," *Negro History Bulletin,*

May, 1942, p. 176; *Dictionary of American Biography,* New York, 1946, Vol. IV, p. 143.

17. Carter G. Woodson, "The Negroes of Cincinnati Prior to the Civil War," *Journal of Negro History,* Vol. I, January, 1916, pp. 120–42; Charles B. Galbreath, *History of Ohio,* New York, 1925, Vol. I, pp. 167–202; Philip S. Foner, *History of Black Americans: From Africa to the Emergence of the Cotton Kingdom,* Westport, Conn. 1975, p. 516.

18. Merrill Goozner, "Peter H. Clark of Cincinnati," unpublished seminar paper, Afro-American History, University of Cincinnati, March, 1974, pp. 1–2; William J. Simmons, *Men of Mark: Eminent, Progressive and Rising,* Cleveland, 1890, p. 374. The Cincinnati High School was founded by Hirman S. Gilmore who became its principal. Gilmore was a Utopian Socialist, and his ideas may have "had an influence" on his students (Goozner, op. cit., p. 2). The school's graduates included P. B. S. Pinchback, lieutenant governor (and for a brief period governor) of Louisiana, John M. Langston, Dean of Howard University and a leading champion of civil rights, Thomas C. Ball, artist, and J. Monroe Trotter, active in the twentieth century in the struggle for Black rights.

19. L. D. Easton, "The Colored Schools of Cincinnati," in Isaac M. Martin, editor, *History of the Schools of Cincinnati and Other Educational Institutions, Public and Private,* Cincinnati, Ohio, 1900, pp. 185–89.

20. Easton, op. cit., p. 248; Goozner, op. cit., p. 4. In 1852 Clark joined with H. Ford Douglass of Columbus and the Langstons (John Mercer and Charles) also of Ohio in supporting colonization. But the proposal was rejected by the delegates to the convention of Ohio Blacks. (*Proceedings of the Colored Freedmen of Ohio. Held in Cincinnati, January 14, 15, 16, 17 and 19, 1852.* pp. 5, 9; Jane H. Pease and William H. Pease, *They Who Would be Free: Blacks' Search for Freedom, 1830–1861,* New York, 1974, p. 258.)

21. *Preceedings of the Colored Freemen of Ohio. . . ,* pp. 6, 9; *Proceedings of a Convention of Colored Men of the State of Ohio, 1856,*

22. Simmons, op. cit., p. 377. William Francis Cheek, III, "Forgotten Prophet: The Life of John Mercer Langston," unpublished Ph.D. Thesis, University of Virginia, 1961, pp. 14–15; *Proceedings of a Convention of Colored Men of the State of Ohio, 1857,* p. 6; William Wells Brown, *The Rising Son; or The Antecedents and Advancement of the Colored Race,* Boston, 1882, p. 521.

23. *Proceedings of a Convention of the Colored Men of Ohio Held in the City of Cincinnati on the 23d, 24th, 25th and 26th Days of November, 1958,* Cincinnati 1958, pp. 28–32; Benjamin Quarles, *Black Abolitionists,* New York, 1969, pp. 3–4.

24. Charles H. Wesley, *Ohio Negroes in the Civil War,* Columbus, 1962, pp. 12–22; Edgar A. Toppin, "Humbly They Served, 'The Black Brigade' in the Defense of Cincinnati," *Journal of Negro History,* Vol. XLVIII, April, 1963, pp. 135–42.

25. Peter H. Clark, *The Black Brigade of Cincinnati,* Cincinnati, 1861, reprinted with a preface by Sara Dunlap Jackson, New York, 1965, pp. 4–5.

26. Toppin, op. cit., p. 147.

27. Easton, op. cit., pp. 185–86.

28. Leonard Harding, "The Negro in Cincinnati, 1860–1870, "unpublished M. A. thesis, University of Cincinnati, 1971, pp. 70–71; Goozner, op. cit., p. 9.

29. *Cincinnati Enquirer,* August 16, 1872.

30. Proceedings, *Convention of Colored Newspaper Men,* Cincinnati, *August 4, 1875,* Cincinnati, 1875, pp. 3–4. The Sovereigns of Industry was founded in January, 1874, by Edward Martin Chamberlin (1835–1892), a member of an English-speaking section of the First International in Boston, as a means of abolishing the wage system. Chamberlin outlined his system in his book, *The Sovereigns of Industry,* Boston, 1875. The Sovereigns maintained and operated cooperative stores. The total membership in 1875–76 was said to be 40,000, of whom 75 percent was in New England. The organization was dead by 1878. *Cincinnati Commercial,* November 27, 1875. Samuel Rezneck, "Distress, Relief and Discontent in the United States during the Depression of 1873–1878," *Journal of Political Economy,* Vol. LVIII, April, 1950, pp. 493–95.

31. *Cincinnati Commercial,* June 17, 26, 1876. Ibid., December 11, 1876.

32. Ibid., March 27, 1877; *The Emancipator,* March 31, 1877.

33. For detailed accounts of the railroad strikes of 1877, see J. A. Dacus, *Annals of the Great Strikes,* Chicago, 1877; Robert V. Bruce, *1877: Year of Violence,* Indianapolis, 1959. For a detailed account of the strike in one city, David T. Burbank, *Reign of the Rabble: The St. Louis General Strike of 1877,* New York, 1966. For general accounts of the strikes, see the following: John R. Commons and Associates, *History of Labour in the United States,* New York, 1918, Vol. II, pp. 185–91; Philip S. Foner, *History of the Labor Movement in the United States,* New York, 1947, pp. 464–74; Samuel Yellen, *American Labor Struggles,* New York, 1936, pp. 3–38; Jeremy Brecher, *Strike,* San Francisco, 1972, pp. 1–24; Philip A. Slaner, "The Railroad Strikes of 1877," *Marxist Quarterly,* Vol. I, April–June, 1937, pp. 214–36; Gerald N. Grob, "The Railroad Strikes of 1877," *Midwest Journal,* Vol. VI, Winter, 1954–55, pp. 16–34. For railroad strikes before the 1877 uprising, see Herbert G. Gutman, "Troubles on the Railroads in 1873–1874: Prelude to the 1877 Crisis," Labor History, Vol. II, Spring, 1961, pp. 202–

28. The present writer has published a study on the Great Strike of 1877, entitled *The Great Labor Uprising of 1877,* New York, 1977.

34. *Cincinnati Enquirer,* July 23, 1877. *Cincinnati Commercial,* July 23, 1877.

35. *Cincinnati Commercial,* July 23, 1877; *The Emancipator,* July 28, 1877. The speech is reprinted in Philip S. Foner, editor, *The Voice of Black America: Major Speeches by Blacks in the United States, 1797–1973,* Vol. I, New York, 1975, pp. 481–87. Excerpts from the speech may be found in Herbert G. Gutman, "Peter H. Clark: Pioneer Negro Socialist, 1877," *Journal of Negro Education,* Vol. XXXIV, Fall, 1965, pp. 413–18.

36. *Cincinnati Commercial,* July 24, 1877.

37. Ibid., July 26, 1877; *The Emancipator,* August 4, 1877.

38. *Labor Standard,* August 4, 1877.

39. Ibid., Aug. 12, 19, Oct. 7, 1877. *The Emancipator,* August 18, 1877.

40. *The Emancipator,* July 21, August 4, 11, 18, 1877.

41. *Cincinnati Commercial,* August 25, October 12, 1877; Morris Hillquit, *History of Socialism in the United States,* New York, 1902, p. 203; *The Socialist* (Chicago), January 11, 1879.

42. Ibid., November 23, 1878, May 3, 10, 24, 1870; *Cincinnati Commercial,* November 24, 1878.

43. *The Socialist* (Chicago), January 11, 1879.

44. *Cincinnati Commercial,* July 22, 1879.

45. Morris, "William Haller," op. cit., pp. 128–29.

46. *Cincinnati Enquirer,* July 4, 11, 28, August 11, 15, 1879; *Cincinnati Commercial,* July 22, 1879.

47. *Cincinnati Enquirer,* March, 3, 4, 1881; *Cincinnati Commercial,* March 3, 1881.

48. Clark was to finish his life as an educator. In 1887 he lost his job in the Cincinnati school system and took a temporary position with the Huntsville, Alabama state normal and industrial school. On a leave of absence to protest railway car discrimination, he was again dismissed because of his militancy, and went on to Sumner High School in St. Louis where he remained as a teacher well into the twentieth century. (Goozner, op. cit., p. 10.)

49. After 1881 Clark moved in and out of the Republican Party and in 1885 supported the Democratic Party (*Washington Bee,* March 14, 1885; August Meier, *Negro Thought in America, 1880–1915,* Ann Arbor, 1963, p. 28.) Although Clark was by no means the only leading Black spokesman who felt by 1885 that allegiance to the Republican Party under any and all circumstances was not the correct procedure for Blacks to follow, his

support of the Democratic Party infuriated Blacks in Cincinnati. Clark was forced to move to St. Louis where he lived and taught school until 1926 when at the rige age of 97 he died. There was an unsuccessful attempt by members of the Cincinnati Black community to have his remains brought back to their city. In his *Cincinnati's Colored Citizens,* Wendell P. Dabney observes: "Dead he was no longer dangerous, therefore more desirable." (Cincinnati, 1926, p. 116.)

50. Brown, op. cit., p. 524.

10

Reverend George Washington Woodbey:
Early Twentieth-Century
California Black Socialist*

In the *Ohio Socialist Bulletin* of February, 1909, Reverend Richard Euell, a black minister of Milford, Ohio, published "A Plan to Reach the Negro." The Negro, he wrote, "belongs to the working class and must be taught class consciousness." Blacks could be more rapidly recruited into the party if Socialists would go to them in their churches and point out "the way to freedom and plenty." Most of them had no experience with any organization other than the church and could think of committing themselves to action only in religious terms. The Bible, even motion pictures about the "Passion Play," could be used effectively to imbue religion with radicalism and convince the black working class of the evils of the capitalist system and the virtues of Socialism.[1]

The first black Socialist to conduct the type of work Reverend Euell recommended was Reverend George Woodbey (sometimes spelled Woodby), and he had already been performing this function for the Socialist cause for several years before a "Plan to Reach the Negro" was published.

George Washington Woodbey, the leading Negro Socialist in the first decade of the 20th century, was born a slave in Johnson County, Tennessee, on October 5, 1854, the son of Charles and Rachel (Wagner) Woodbey. Of his early life nothing is known other than that he learned to read after freedom came, was self-educated, except for two terms in a common school, and that his life was one of "hard work and hard study carried on together." A fellow Socialist who

*Reprinted from *The Journal of Negro History,* LXI (April, 1976), 136–157.

knew him wrote: "He has worked in mines, factories, on the streets, and at everything which would supply food, clothing and shelter."

Woodbey was ordained a Baptist minister at Emporia, Kansas, in 1874. He was active in the Republican Party of Missouri and Kansas and was a leader in the Prohibition Party, and when he moved to Nebraska he became a prominent force in the prohibition movement in that state. In 1896 Woodbey ran for lieutenant governor and Congress on the Prohibition ticket in Nebraska.

That same year, he made his first acquaintance with the principles of Socialism when he read Edward Bellamy's *Looking Backwards,* and his interest was further aroused by copies of the *Appeal to Reason* which came into his hands. Although he subscribed to the *Appeal,* he did not join the Socialists. Instead, he joined the Populist Party, and in 1900, he supported William Jennings Bryan, the Democratic and Populist candidate for President. But he also heard Eugene V. Debs speaking during the presidential campaign and was so impressed that when the Democratic Party asked Woodbey to speak for Bryan, he agreed but delivered speeches which were geared more to the ideas advanced by Debs than those by the Democratic candidate. After several such speeches, the Democrats stopped scheduling dates for Woodbey's speeches, and the black minister came to the conclusion that his place was in the Socialist camp. He resigned his pulpit and announced to his friends that henceforth his life "would be consecrated to the Socialist movement." A Nebraska Socialist recalls:

> We remember him in the stirring days of the inception of the Socialist movement in Omaha. Night after night he spoke on the streets and in the parts of that city. Omaha had never had the crowds that attended Woodbey's meetings.[2]

Woodbey visited his mother in San Diego during the spring of 1902, and immediately made an impression on the comrades in Southern California. A dispatch to the *Los Angeles Socialist* on May 31, 1902 expresses this clearly:

> Socialism is on the boom here in this county and city. We have had Rev. G. W. Woodbey, the Colored Socialist orator of Nebraska with us for nearly a month during which time he has delivered 23 addresses and will speak again tonight, and then he will do some work in the country districts where he has been invited to speak. . . .

Comrade Woodbey is great and is a favorite with all classes. He came here unannounced ostensibly to see his mother who resides here but as he says that he is "so anxious to be free," that he feels impressed to work for the cause constantly. He has had very respectable audiences both on the streets and in the halls. He likes to speak on the street and it is the general verdict that he has done more good for the cause than any of our most eloquent speakers who have preceded him. He is full of resources and never repeats his speeches, but gives them something new every time. He requested me to state in my notes to the "Socialist" that he desires to visit Los Angeles later on if you folks can find a place for him. He makes no charges but depends entirely on passing the hat for his support. . . .[3]

Los Angeles did find a place for Woodbey, and he delivered a series of soap-box speeches and lectures in the leading hall. When after one of his speeches, Woodbey was denied admittance to the Southern Hotel and Northern Restaurant because of his color, the Los Angeles Socialist Party organized a successful boycott of the establishments and distributed leaflets reading:

We demand as trade unionists and socialists, that every wage-worker in Los Angeles bear well in mind these two places that depend on public patronage—the Northern Restaurant and the Southern Hotel—keep away from them. They draw the color line.[4]

Woodbey accepted an offer to become minister of the Mount Zion Baptist Church in San Diego and made his home in California for the next two decades. He was elected a member of the state executive board of the Socialist Party, and soon became widely known in the state as "The Great Negro Socialist Orator." In a Los Angeles debate with Archibald Huntley, Ph.D., where Woodbey took the affirmative of the topic, "Resolved that Socialism is the True Interpretation of Economic Conditions and that it is the Solution of the Labor Problem," he was listed as a "well-known Socialist Lecturer."[5]

An announcement that Woodbey would deliver a reply to Booker T. Washington's "Capitalist Argument for the Negro" packed Los Angeles' leading hall on May 1, 1903. He paid tribute to Washington "as a gentleman" and educator, but added: "He has all the ability necessary to make a good servant of capitalism by educating other servants for capitalism." Woodbey charged that whether consciously or not, Tuskeegee Institute fulfilled the role of providing black workers to be pitted against white workers so as to bring about a general lowering of wage scales. What Washington failed to understand was that there was basically no unity between capitalists, white or black, and workers, white or black. "There is no race division industrially, but an ever-growing antagonism between the exploiting capitalists black or white, and the exploited workers, black or white." In this "industrial struggle," the working class was bound to "ultimately triumph."

> And then the men of all races will share in the results of production according to their services in the process of production. This is Socialism and the only solution to the race problem.[6]

A frequent target of the police of San Diego, Los Angeles, San Francisco, and other California communities. Woodbey was in and out of jail several times between 1902 and 1908, and was hospitalized more than once as a result of police brutality. But he gave as well as received. When he was attacked and driven off a street corner in San Diego in July, 1905 by Police Officer George H. Cooley, Woodbey led a group of protestors to the police station to lodge a complaint. There Cooley again attacked the black Socialist, "using at the same time oaths and language too mean and vile to print." Woodbey was literally thrown bodily out of the station house. He immediately brought charges against the police officer for assault and battery and informed his California comrades:

> In the days of chattel slavery the masters had a patrol force to keep the negroes in their place and protect the interests of the masters. Today the capitalists use the police for the same purpose.

But slaves had rebelled despite the patrols, and he was following that tradition by telling the police that they could not get away with their brutality against enemies of the capitalist system.

Although Woodbey's case against the police was prosecuted by the County Attorney, assisted by Job Harriman, California's leading Socialist attorney, and although all witnesses testified that the Negro Socialist's conduct had been "perfectly gentlemanly," and that he had a perfectly lawful right to be at the station house, the jury, composed of conservative property owners, took only fifteen minutes to find the defendent not guilty. Woodbey was furious and published the names of the jury men, calling upon all decent citizens to have nothing to do with them. He followed this up by returning immediately to the soap box in San Diego and held one of the biggest street corner meetings in the city up to this time. As he wrote:

> The case has made more Socialists that I could possibly have made in many speeches. Had I not gone to the court with the matter the public would forever have contended that I was doubtless doing or saying something that I had not right to do or say. And when I complained I would have been told that if I had gone to the courts I would have got justice. Now, as it is, nothing of the kind can be said, and the responsibility is placed where it rightly belongs.

Many non-Socialists in San Diego, Woodbey noted, were learning the truth of the Socialist contention that "the police force are the watch dogs of capitalism."[7]

In more than one California city Woodbey was arrested and hauled off to jail for trying to sell copies of his Socialist booklets.[8] The writings made Woodbey's name known throughout the entire Party in the United States and even internationally.

Describing Woodbey as "the greatest living negro in America," a white Socialist noted that "his style is simple and his logic invincible. He knows the race question, and one of his most popular lectures relates to the settlement of this vexed question under Socialism." Woodbey's ability to explain Socialism in simple terms led to the demand that he "embody some of the things he has said to the thousands who have listened to his talks, in a written form. . . ." The response was the pamphlet *What To Do and How To Do It or Socialism vs. Capitalism*. A copy of a small edition, privately printed, fell into the hands of A. W. Ricker, a Socialist organizer in the West and South. While at the home of Socialist publisher Julius A. Wayland, in Girard, Kansas, he read it aloud to the Wayland family. "At the conclusion," Ricker wrote, "we decided that the book ought to be in the hands of the millions of American wage slaves, and we forthwith wrote to Rev. Mr. Woodbey for the right to bring it out."[9]

It was published as No. 40 of the widely distributed *Wayland's Monthly* in August, 1903. Ricker gave it a send-off in the *Appeal to Reason* writing:

> The book in many respects is the equal of "Merrie England," and in the

matter of its clear teaching of the class struggle, it is superior. It has been read by every negro in Girard, (Kansas), and has made Socialists of those who were susceptible of understanding after every other effort had failed to shake their unreasoning adherence to the republican party. A good supply should be ordered by every local in the land, there is no book in the language that will excel it in propaganda value, and we expect to see it pass through one edition after another, as soon as it is read by the comrades.[10]

Since Robert Blatchford's *Merrie England*, published in England in 1894 and in the United States in 1900, was considered one of the best of the Socialist educational publications, the tribute to Reverend Woodbey's pamphlet was well understood by readers of the *Appeal to Reason.*

Woodbey's forty-four-page booklet carried the touching dedication:

This little book is dedicated to that class of citizens who desire to know what the Socialists want to do and how they propose to do it. By one who was once a chattel slave freed by the proclamation of Lincoln and wishes to be free from the slavery of capitalism.[11]

In his preface Reverend Woodbey acknowledged that there was "nothing original" in his little book, his aim being simply to make the subjects treated "as plain as possible to the reader." It was not directed to those who were already convinced of the superiority of Socialism over Capitalism, but to "meet the demands of that large and increasing class of persons who have not yet accepted Socialism, but would do so if they could see any possible way of putting it into practice." Within this framework, Reverend Woodbey's booklet is an effective piece of Socialist propaganda, and so highly thought of in Socialist circles, that by 1908 it had been translated into three languages and gained for its author an international reputation.[12]

Basically, the booklet consisted of a dialogue between the author and his mother whom he has rejoined after nearly seventeen years of separation. She expresses her astonishment at having learned that her son had become a Socialist. "Have you given up the Bible and the ministry and gone into politics?" she asks. Her son attempts to convince his mother that it is precisely because of his devotion to the principles enunciated in the Bible that he became a Socialist, and that as the years passed, he became more and more convinced of the correctness of his decision. When his mother points out that among his comrades were a few who believed neither in God nor in the Bible, her son readily agrees, but reminds her that he found "a still larger number of unbelievers in the republican party before I left it some twenty years ago," and that other parties had their "equal portion" of nonbelievers. More important, while he believed in the Biblical account of God, the origin of the earth and man, and members of his Party did not, he and they were able to agree that "man is here, and the earth is here, and that it is the present home of the race, at least." They did not, to be sure, see eye-to-eye about the "hereafter." Since Socialism was "a scheme for bettering things here first," he could be a "good Socialist" without surrendering his belief in God or in the Bible. There was room in the Socialist Party for those who were interested only in what it could do for mankind in the present world and for those who, like himself, were "Socialists because they think that mankind is entitled to the best of everything in both this world and the next." Finally, his mother accepts the idea that under Socialism persons would be free to have "their own religion or none, just as they please, as long as they do not interfere with others."[13]

Having laid at rest his mother's anxiety and made her willing to listen to the fundamental principles of a movement which obviously had not destroyed her son's religious convictions, Reverend Woodbey proceeds to explain to her the evils of capitalist society and the way by which Socialism, gaining power through the ballot box, would set out to eliminate these evils. After he takes his mother through such subjects as rent, interest, and profits, all gained from labor's production, and value which is created only by labor but the fruits of which are appropriated entirely by the capitalists, she expresses bewilderment at the meaning of such words. Her son then illustrates what they mean in simple language and in terms of daily experience. Here, for example, is how he explained surplus value:

> Why didn't the slave have wealth at the close of the war? He worked hard.
> "Because his master got it," mother replied.
> "The wage worker's master got what he produced, too."
> "But wasn't he paid for his work?" asked mother.
> Yes, about seventeen cents on every dollar's worth of wealth he created. . . .

Under Socialism, he continues, the capitalist would have to turn over to the State a "large amount of capital created by labor" which he had taken from the worker while the latter, having been deprived of all he produced under capitalism, would have nothing to turn over. The very rich would have no reason to complain "since he and his children, who have done nothing but live off the labor of those who have nothing to turn over, are to be given an equal share of interest with those who have produced it all. So you see we Socialists are not such bad fellows as you thought. We propose to do good unto those who spitefully use us, and to those who curse us, by giving them an equal show with ourselves, provided that they will here-after do their share of the useful work."[14]

But his mother expresses concern that the capitalists will not yield peacefully to having the "land, factories, and means of production" turned over to the cooperative commonwealth by a Socialist Congress elected by the people, and that they would start a war to retain their holdings. Her son concedes that this would quite likely occur just as the slaveholders had refused to abide by Lincoln's electoral victory and precipitated a civil war. But the capitalists would never succeed in the war they would seek to stimulate, for the majority of the people had clearly become convinced that Socialism was the only solution to their problems, or else the Socialists could not have won their electoral victories. Hence, the capitalists would have no one to do the fighting for them:

> The slaveholder did not dare to arm the negro, on his side, without proclaiming emancipation, and to do that was to lose his cause; so with the capitalist, if he dares to offer all to the poor man who must fight his battles, he has lost his cause; and with this condition confronting the capitalist, there is no danger in taking over the entire industrial plant as soon as the Socialists can be elected and pass the necessary laws. And the Socialist party will go into power just as soon as the majority finds that the only way to secure to itself its entire product is to vote that ticket.[15]

Mother has only one question left about the transition from capitalism to Socialism: "Have the people a right to do this?" Her son reminds her of the Declaration of Independence which clearly affirmed the right of the people, when any form of government became destructive of the rights of life, liberty and the pursuit of happiness, "to alter and abolish it and institute a new government" which would be most likely to affect "their safety and happiness." On this the Socialists stand, the son declares firmly. Moreover, it was none other than Abraham Lincoln who, in his speech of January 12, 1840, in the House of Representatives, had said "just what the Socialists now say." He had then declared: "Any people anywhere being inclined and having the power have the right to rise up and shake off the existing government and form a new one that suits them better. . . ."[16]

His mother now fully satisfied, the son proceeds to describe how different departments of government—agriculture, transportation, distribution, intelligence, education, and health—will operate under Socialism providing for the needs of the people rather than under capitalism, for the profits of the capitalist. Occasionally, the mother interrupts the narrative with questions that bring answers that satisfy her. Thus, when she asks whether the workers who would own and operate the factories under Socialism, "would know how to do the work," the answer reassures her:

> Why, the workers are the only ones who do know how to run a factory. The stockholders who own the concern know nothing about doing the work. If the girl who weaves in the factory should be told that Socialism is now established, and that henceforth she is to have shorter hours of labor, a beautiful sanitary place to work in, and an equal share of all the wealth of the nation, to be taken in any kind of thing she wants, do you think she would forget how to work? And if on the other hand, all she produces is to go to the girl who does nothing but own the stocks, then she can work right along. Seems to me, you might see the absurdity of that, mother. "I believe I do see, now," she said, after a moment's hesitation. Then apply that illustration about the girls, to all the workers, and you will get my meaning.[17]

As might be expected, mother asks, "Like all other women, I want to know where we are to come in." Her son assures her that it was to the interest of "the women, more than the men, if possible, to be Socialists because they suffer more from capitalism than anyone else." For one thing, the Socialist platform demands "the absolute equality of the sexes before the law, and the repeal of the law that in any way discriminates against women." Then again, under Socialism each woman would, like each man, have her own independent income, and would become "an equal shareholder in the industries of the nation." Under such liberating conditions, a woman would have no need "to sell herself through a so-called marriage to someone she did not love, in order to get a living," and, for the first time in history, could marry only for love. Under capitalism, the working man was a slave, "and his wife is the slave of a slave." Socialism would liberate both, but since it would give women political equality and economic freedom, it would actually do more for women than ever for men.[18]

By now mother has been converted, and the booklet ends with the comment: "Well, you have convinced me that I am about as much of a slave now as I was in the south, and I am ready to accept any way out of this drudgery, mother remarked as the conversation turned on other subjects."[19]

Here and there *What To Do and How To Do It* reflected Edward Bellamy's influence on Reverend Woodbey, and sections of the 1903 pamphlet are shortened versions of the 1887 *Looking Backward.*[20] In the main, however, the pamphlet revealed that the black minister had broken with Bellamy's utopianism. While Bellamy emphasized "equitable" distribution of wealth under Nationalism, Woodbey was convinced that the solution lay closer to Marx's maxim, "From each according to his abilities, to each according to his needs." Bellamy rejected the label "socialism" as dangerous and un-American.[21] But Woodbey welcomed it and believed its principles were in keeping with the best in the American tradition. Like many in the Socialist Party, Woodbey believed that with the capture of sufficient political offices through the ballot box, socialism could be rapidly achieved. But he was one of the very few in the Party in 1903 who took into account the danger that the capitalists would not sit by and calmly watch their control of society eliminated by legislative enactments, and instead would, like the slave owners in 1860, resort to violence to prevent the people's will from being carried into effect. To be sure, unlike Jack London, who in his great 1908 novel *The Iron Heel,* predicted that the oligarchy of American capitalists would seize power from the Socialists and destroy the democratic process by violence. Woodbey was confident that the capitalists would fail.[22] Nevertheless, by even raising this issue in his pamphlet, Woodbey was in advance of nearly all Christian Socialists.

Early in *What To Do and How To Do It,* Reverend Woodbey

assured his mother that he would at a future date tell her "more about what the Bible teaches on this subject" of Socialism.[23] He fulfilled his promise a year later with *The Bible and Socialism: A Conversation Between Two Preachers,* published in San Diego, California by the author. The 96-page booklet was dedicated to

> . . . the Preachers and Members of the Churches, and all others who are interested in knowing what the Bible teaches on the question at issue between the Socialists and the Capitalists, by one who began preaching twenty-nine years ago, and still continues.[24]

As the sub-title indicates, *The Bible and Socialism* consists of a dialogue between Woodbey and another clergyman. The latter is a local pastor to whom Woodbey's mother has given a copy of the 1903 pamphlet and invited to her home to hear her son convince him that he was wrong in contending that "there is no Socialism in the Bible." When the skeptical pastor questions Woodbey about the Socialist claim that Karl Marx discovered the principles of Scientific Socialism and points out that this was centuries after the Bible was written, Woodbey notes, first, that no new idea is ever entirely new and is in some way based on what went before, and, second, that

> Marx, the greatest philospher of modern times, belonged to the same wonderful Hebrew race that gave to the world Moses, the Lawgiver, the kings and prophets, and Christ the Son of the Highest, with his apostles, who, together, gave us the Bible that, we claim, teaches Socialism. Doubtless Marx, like other young Hebrews, was made acquainted with the economic teachings of Moses, and all the rest of the Old Testament sages and prophets, whatever we find him believing in after life.
>
> If we are able to show that the Bible opposes both rent, interest, and profits, and the exploiting of the poor, then it stands just where the Socialists do.[25]

After agreeing that Marx was not a Christian but noting that this was of no significance since Socialism had nothing to do with a man's religion or lack of it, Reverend Woodbey devotes the rest of his pamphlet to detailed references, quotations, and citations to convince the pastor that since the Bible—both the Old and New Testaments—did actually oppose "rent, interest, and profits, and the exploiting of the poor," it was a Socialist document with close affinity to such classics as *The Communist Manifesto, Capital* and other writings of Marx. As a Jew, Woodbey emphasizes, Marx was able to do "the greatly needed work of reasoning out from the standpoint of the philosopher, what his ancestors, the writers of the Old and New Testaments, had already done from a moral and religious standpoint."[26] This is not to say, he continues, that there is no difference between a Socialism based merely on a "moral and religious standpoint" and Scientific Socialism just as there was a fundamental difference between the Socialism advanced by Utopian reformers prior to Marx and that set forth by the father of Scientific Socialism. For Scientific Socialism was based on the class struggle which had dominated all history and dominated existing relationships in capitalist society. When the pastor asks Woodbey if the class struggle also exists in the church, there is the following discussion in which his mother joins:

> Master and slave, before the war, all belonged to the same church. They met on Sunday and prayed together, and one church member sold the other the next day. So now, in many cases, master and wage slave belong to the same church, meet on Sunday and pray together, and the one turns the other off from even the pittance he allowed him to take out of his earnings as wages or sets him out of house and home for non-payment of rent, or under mortgage, the next day. All that, notwithstanding the Bible says love brother and the stranger as oneself.
>
> It took the abolitionist, in and out of the church, to show the inconsistency of slavery and force a division, as the Socialists are now doing.
>
> "Yes," said mother, "I belonged to one of that kind of churches, myself, before the war."[27]

Just as his mother was converted at the end of the 1903 pamphlet, so, too, the pastor by the close of *The Bible and Socialism*. He confesses he had learned little of economics while in college, and since he joined the ministry, he had been too busy to give more than a casual thought to the Bible's "economic teachings" and whether or not the churches adhered to them. But as a result of the "interesting evening conversations," he was a changed man.

> . . . being convinced that Socialism is but the carrying out of the economic teachings of the Bible, I shall endeavor to study it and lay it before my people to the best of my ability.[28]

There may have been little new for white religiously-inclined Socialists in Woodbey's pamphlet since the Christian Socialists had already published a considerable body of literature demonstrating to their satisfaction that the Bible and Socialism were compatible. But to black church-goers much of what was in the pamphlet was new and certainly must have made an impressive impact. Moreover, while many Christian Socialists preached an emotional propaganda replete with Christian ethics, they tended to ignore the class struggle or to relate their biblical references to the contemporary scene. Not so Woodbey; he was a firm believer in the class struggle, had read Marx, and was not in the least reluctant to couple discussions of the Old and New Testaments with specific evils in twentieth-century American society.

Woodbey's third and last Socialist pamphlet was *The Distribution of Wealth,* published in 1910 at San Diego by the author. The sixty-eight-page booklet consists of a series of letters to J. Jones, a California rancher-friend of the author, in which Woodbey describes how the distribution of wealth created by productive labor would operate "after Socialism has overthrown the capitalist method of production." Pointing out in his preface that there was little in Socialist literature on how the future co-operative commonwealth would function, Woodbey, without the slightest hesitation, declared he would attempt to fill the gap. Affirming his right to do so, he noted:

> If the socialist movement is based upon truth, it cannot be destroyed by the utmost freedom of discussion, nor is the movement or the party necessarily in danger, because your views or mine are not at once adopted even should they be corrected. All I ask of the reader is a fair, honest consideration of what I have written.[29]

What he wrote is an interesting elaboration of how the different institutions under capitalism would operate in the new Socialist society. Some of this had already been set forth in his 1903 *What To Do and How To Do It,* but here he develops it further. In 1903, it will be recalled, Woodbey had conceded that the capitalists would resort to armed resistance to prevent the Socialist society from coming into being. Now, however, he appears to believe that while capitalists would resist the transition to Socialism with "tremendous opposition," it would not necessarily lead to war. Once socialism had proven its superiority over capitalism even the capitalists and their children would acquiesce and decide to live under it. (A clear throwback to *Looking Backward*.) He writes:

> Let us go back, for instance, to the slaveholder, by the way of illustration. He declared that he would go to war before he would permit himself and family to labor like the negro slave and live in poverty, rags and ignorance. He had been taught to believe that that was the necessary outgrowth of labor. And I submit that the condition of labor under chattel slavery was a poor school in which to teach the child of the master a desire to labor. So the capitalist of today and his children look upon the workers as he has them in the sweatshops, mines and factories of the country, putting in long hours for a bare existence, under the most unsanitary conditions, living in the worst of places, and eating of the worst of food; and, like his brother, the slaveholder, he is determined that he and his shall not be reduced to such straits. It has not yet dawned upon him that when the people who work own the industries in place of him, all of these disagreeable conditions will at once disappear. . . . It is my opinion that, notwithstanding the false education of the children of the wealthy, even they in the first generation will have so much of their distaste for labor taken away that we will have little or no trouble with them when the majority have changed conditions.[30]

Woodbey's rancher friend keeps asking whether people would work under socialism once the fear of poverty and unemployment were removed. Woodbey's answer is interesting:

> . . . when chattel slavery prevailed, as we said, men thought that labor must continue to be always what it was then, and that because the slave sought to escape he wouldn't work for wages. So now the capitalist, and those who believe in capitalism, think that labor must continue always to be just what it is now; and as some people won't work under the new and better conditions.
>
> It is a wonder to me that men are so willing to work as they are under the present conditions. The fact is, the mind of the child is such that it accepts what it is taught now, and will do the same then.
>
> The boy that was born a slave thought that it was natural for him to be one, and the young master took it for granted that he was intended to be master. But the boy that is born free, never thinks that any one ought to own him; nor does the youngster born at the same time with him

think that he ought to own him. But instead, they both go to school often in the same class. They at once accept the conditions under which they were born. No, my friend, there is no danger of the children not at once accepting the new conditions under Socialism, and we have proved there will be so little loss through idlers, even in the first generation of old folks, that it will not be found worth bothering about. And as the old and infirm should of necessity be looked after with the best of everything from the very beginning, it will be found when the time comes that the thing to do will be to let every one work and be sure that we have abundance of everything for all, and then let everybody help themselves, wherever they may be, to what we have on hand, as we do with what the public now owns. Indeed, they can be better trusted then than now, with all fear of the future banished forever.[31]

It is perhaps significant that this is the only one of Woodbey's pamphlets which ends without the second party convinced of the truth of the author's arguments and converted to Socialism. Probably Woodbey himself realized that he had tackled a difficult subject, and that his presentation was too tentative to be effective in total conversion. At any rate, he ended his last letter:

Hoping that I have been able to make it clear to you that under Socialism it will be possible to equitably distribute the products of industry and that you and your family will at once join the movement, I will close this somewhat lengthy correspondence by saying that I would be pleased to hear from you soon.

Yours for the cause of the Revolution,
G. W. Woodbey[32]

Reverend Woodbey was a delegate to the Socialist Party conventions of 1904 and 1908; indeed, he was the sole representative of the Negro people at these gatherings. At the 1904 convention Woodbey took the floor twice. On the first occasion, he expressed his opinion on the seating of A. T. Gridely of Indiana who was being challenged because he had accepted a position in the state government after passing a civil service examination. The question at issue was whether A. T. Gridely had violated the Socialist principle of not accepting a position under a capitalist government. Woodbey spoke in favor of seating A. T. Gridely, arguing that in Germany the Socialists boasted of the number of comrades in the army, and noting that certainly such Socialists were doing work for a capitalist government. "We all know," he continued, "that we work for capitalists when we work at all, and we would be pretty poor if we did not work for capitalists at all."[33] On the second occasion, he spoke up in favor of the Party National Secretary receiving a salary of $1,500 a year which he called "not a dollar too much."[34] But the failure of the convention to deal with the Negro question in the Party platform or of the delegates to discuss it once during the entire convention, aroused no comment from the only black delegate.

At the 1908 convention, Woodbey took the floor four times. On one occasion, in a discussion of franchises held by private corporations, he advanced what for the Socialist Party was the bold position that the Socialists declare themselves "in favor as fast as they can get in possession in any locality, of taking everything without a cent, and forcing the issue as to whether there is to be compensation or not. (Applause). I take the ground that you have already paid for these franchises—already paid more than they are worth, and we are simply proposing to take possession of what we have already paid for."[35] On another occasion, Woodbey recommended that the National Committee elect its own executive committee from its own members, and on still another, he opposed a time limit being imposed before a Party member could be nominated for office on the Socialist ticket to ensure that he would not betray the movement. Woodbey argued that the danger of such persons "selling out" was just as great if they were members for years instead of months. "In my judgment, a man who understands its [the Party's] principles is not more liable to do it after he has been in the party six months than five years."[38]

The other occasion in which Woodbey spoke at the 1908 convention marked the only time during the two national gatherings that he commented on an issue related to the race question. That was when he took a firm stand, during the discussion of the immigration resolution, against Oriental exclusion and, indeed, exclusion of any immigrants. His speech, coming as it did from a California delegate, was a remarkable statement and certainly not calculated to win friends among Socialists in his state. But it was in keeping with the tradition of black Americans since the era of Reconstruction: in 1869, the Colored National Labor Union went on record against exclusion of Chinese immigration. Woodbey conceded that it was generally believed that all who lived on the Pacific coast were as "a unit" in opposing Oriental immigration. But he did not, though a delegate from California, share this view:

> I am in favor of throwing the entire world open to the inhabitants of the world. (Applause). There are no foreigners, and cannot be unless some person comes down from Mars, or Jupiter, or some place.
>
> I stand on the declaration of Thomas Paine when he said "The world is my country." (Applause). It would be a curious state of affairs for immigrants or descendants of immigrants from Europe themselves to get control of affairs in this country, and then say to the Oriental immigrants that they should not come here. So far as making this a mere matter of race, I disagree decidedly with the committee, that we need any kind of a committee to decide this matter from a scientific stand-point. We know what we think upon the question of race now as well as we would know two years from now or any other time.[37]

Woodbey scoffed at the idea that the entrance of Oriental immigrants would reduce the existing standard of living, arguing that regardless of immigration or no immigration, it was the "natural tendency of capitalism" to reduce the standard of living of the working class, and that if they could not get Oriental labor to do work more cheaply in the United States, they would export their production to the Oriental countries where goods could be produced more cheaply than in this country.[38] Woodbey's prediction that American capitalists would export production to cheap labor countries of the Orient, was, as American workers today fully realize, to bear fruit.

Continuing, Woodbey spoke eloquently of the contradiction between immigration restriction and the principles of international Socialism. As he saw it, Socialism was based "upon the Brotherhood of Man," and any stand in opposition to immigration would be "opposed to the very spirit of the Brotherhood of Man." Reminding the delegates that Socialists were organized in China and Japan as well as in other countries, he asked:

> Are the Socialists of this country to say to the Socialists of Germany, or the Socialists of Sweden, Norway, Japan, China, or any other country, that they are not to go anywhere on the face of the earth? It seems to me absurd to take that position. Therefore, I hope and move that any sort of restriction of immigration will be stricken out of the committee's resolution. (Applause.)[39]

It is unfortunate that while he had the floor, Woodbey did not attack delegates like Ernest Untermann and Victor Berger for the anti-Negro character of their arguments in favor of Oriental exclusion. Nevertheless, Woodbey's speech on the immigration resolution, ranks high in Socialist literature even though it has been ignored by all students of the subject.[40]

Only once at either the 1904 or 1908 conventions did the delegates take notice of the fact that Woodbey was a black representative. That was when his name was placed in nomination as Debs' running-mate in the presidential election of 1908. Delegate Ellis Jones of Ohio presented his name to the convention in a brief but moving speech. "Comrades . . . the nomination that I want to make for our Vice-President . . . is a man who is well known in the movement for many years. The socialist Party is a party that does not recognize race prejudice and in order that we may attest this to the world, I offer the name of Comrade Woodbey of California."[41] But Woodbey received only one vote—that of Jones.[42] The nomination went to Ben Hanford who had been Debs' running mate in 1904. Possibly had Debs, who did not attend the convention, wired the delegates that Woodbey's nomination would be a major contribution of American Socialism in the struggle against racism, the vote would have been different. But Debs did not believe that the Party should do anything special on the Negro question, and this view was shared by all at the convention except for the one delegate who nominated and voted for Woodbey. Since the fact that Woodbey was even placed in nomination has escaped the attention of every historian of the Socialist Party,[43] it is clear that the significance of the one vote he received has been generally overlooked.

Following the 1908 convention, Woodbey began a tour of Northern cities with fairly large black populations and delivered a series of soap-box speeches in favor of the Socialist ticket.[44] In addition, the National office of the Socialist Party circulated his four-page leaflet, *Why the Negro Should Vote the Socialist Ticket.* The author was described as a member of the State Executive Committee, Socialist Party of California, and formerly Pastor of African Church, in Omaha Nebraska. Typical of Woodbey's propaganda technique, the leaflet consisted mainly of a speech, supposedly delivered by a Reverend Mr. Johnson, Pastor of the African Baptist Church, who had called his congregation together to explain why he had decided "to vote the Socialist ticket at the coming election."

The Socialist movement, he pointed out, sought to bring together all working people into a party of their own, so that through such a party "they may look after the interest of all who work regardless of race or color." Since Negroes were nearly all wage workers, it was clear that only such a party could really represent them. "All other parties have abandoned the negro, and if he wants an equal chance with everyone else, he can get it in no other way than by voting the Socialist ticket." No other party, including the Republicans, stood for eliminating poverty, and just as once, the elimination of slavery was crucial for the Negro, so today was the elimination of poverty. Socialism would create a society without poverty, a society in which the land, mines, factories, shops, railroads, etc., would be owned collectively, and the Negro "being a part of the public, will have an equal ownership in all that the public owns, and this will entitle him to an equal part in all the good things produced by the nation." In this future society, moreover, he would not have to abandon his belief in religion. On the contrary, by providing all with sufficient food to eat and decent places in which to live, Socialism would be fulfilling the fundamental ideas set down in the Bible.

Finally, Woodbey called for unity of white and black workers, urging them to "lay aside their prejudices and get together for their common good. We poor whites and blacks have fought each other long enough, and while we have fought, the capitalists have been taking everything from both of us." The Socialist movement was the embodiment of this unifying principle, for it was

> part of a great world movement which includes all races and both sexes and has for its motto: "Workers of the world unite. You have nothing to lose but your chains; you have a world to win."[45]

Woodbey's first published appeal directly to his people on behalf of the Socialist Party is an excellent illustration of the black minister's great ability to take a complex subject and simplify it so that even a political illiterate could understand it.

Woodbey expanded on several points in his leaflet in articles early in 1909 in the Chicago *Daily Socialist.* In "The New Emancipation," he emphasized the common interests of black and white workers under capitalism, condemned black strikebreaking and the doctrine that Negroes should seek to solve their problems by the accumulation of wealth. Even if a few Negroes could become wealthy, the fact still remained that "their brothers are getting poorer every day." What then was the answer?

Give the negro along with others the full product of his labor by wrenching the industries out of the hands of the capitalist and putting them into the hands of the workers and what is known as the race problem will be settled forever. Socialism is only another one of those great world movements which is coming to bless mankind. The Socialist party is simply the instrument for bringing it about, and the negro and all other races regardless of former conditions, are invited into its folds.[46]

In another article, "Socialist Agitation," Woodbey called for the use of all forms of educational-techniques to reach the black masses, "the press, the pulpit, the rostrum and private conversation." Socialist agitators must understand that they would face imprisonment and other forms of maltreatment, but this was to be expected when one sought to overthrow an evil system. "For attempting to overthrow the slave system, Lincoln and Lovejoy were shot, John Brown was hung, while Garrison, Phillips and Fred Douglass were mobbed." Naturally, Socialist agitators "are equally hated and despised," and they faced constant distortion of what they stood for.

Because the Socialists recognize the existence of a class struggle they are some times accused of stirring up class hatred. But, instead, they simply recognize the fact that capitalism, by its unequal distribution of wealth, has forced on us a class struggle, which the Socialists are organizing to put down and bring on the long talked of period of universal brotherhood.[17]

When Woodbey advised Socialist agitators to expect to be persecuted, he spoke from personal experience. At the time he was a delegate to the 1908 Socialist convention, he was out on bail, having been arrested in San Francisco early in the year with thirty other Socialist speakers for defying a ban against street-corner meetings. This was in the midst of the economic crisis following the Panic of 1907, and the Socialists were holding meetings to demand relief for the unemployed.

Even before the Wobblies made free-speech fights famous, Socialists had engaged in such battles and had used specific aspects of the strategy followed by the I.W.W. in their spectacular free-speech fights.[48] In the case of the 1908 San Francisco free-speech fight, the Socialists deliberately violated a city ordinance forbidding street meetings without police permits for all organizations except religious groups. When a speaker was arrested for speaking without a permit, his place was speedily filled on the soap-box. Speaker after speaker, men and women, black and white, mounted the soapbox, were arrested, and dragged off to the jail. Woodbey was one of the first to be dragged off and jailed. Along with his comrades he was released on bail.[49]

"The police can't stop us," Woodbey told a reporter during the 1908 convention. "They can and do arrest us when we speak, but they can't stem the tide that has been started no more than they can the ocean. The more they ill treat us, the more Socialists there are." Despite police opposition, the Socialists were determined to obtain relief for "the hordes of honest working men [in San Francisco] who are starving because they can't get the work they so earnestly desire."[50]

With the aid of liberals and labor groups, the Socialists were able to force the City Council of San Francisco to repeal the objectionable ordinance, and charges against Woodbey were dropped.[51] He continued to participate in free-speech fights, and in 1912 was a key figure in what was probably the most famous free-speech fight in American history—the free-speech fight in San Diego, California. San Diego was, of course, Woodbey's home town, and the place where he was the pastor of the Mt. Zion Church for several years until he was removed because, as one who knew him, wrote, he "loosened up his flock with the Bible, then finished his sermon with an oration on Socialism."[52]

On January 8, 1912, the San Diego City Council passed an ordinance creating a "restricted" district, forty nine blocks in the center of town, in which street-corner meetings might not be held. Unlike ordinances in other cities banning street-speaking, that in San Diego made no exception for religious utterances. All street-speaking was banned in the so-called "congested district." The reason given was that the meetings blocked traffic, but it was clear that the real purpose was to suppress the I.W.W.'s effort "to educate the floating and out-of-work population to a true understanding of the interests of labor as a whole," as well as their determination to organize the workers in San Diego who were neglectd by the A.F. of L. Among these neglected workers were the mill and lumber and laundry workers and streetcar conductors and motormen. This determination had infuriated John D. Spreckels, the millionaire sugar capitalist and owner of the streetcar franchise, and he and other employers had applied pressure on the Council to pass the ordinance. Certainly, San Diego had plenty of room for her traffic, and no one believed that this little town in Southern California would suffer a transportation crisis if street corner meetings continued.[53]

Two days before the ordinance was supposed to go into effect, the I.W.W. and the Socialists held a meeting in the center of the restricted district at which Woodbey was a leading speaker. The police broke up the meeting but did not intimidate the fighters for free speech. On January 8, 1912, the *San Diego Union* carried the following on its front page:

SOCIALISTS PROPOSE FIGHT TO FINISH FOR FREE SPEECH

Following a near-riot Saturday night during a clash between the police department, on the one hand, and Socialists, Industrial Workers of the World on the other, the Socialists and I.W.W. members held a running street meeting last night at Fifth and H streets, but the meeting was orderly, and there was not any semblance of trouble.

During the meeting members of the organizations policed the sidewalks and kept them clear, so that the city police would have no objection to make. Among the speakers were Mrs. Laura Emerson, Messrs. Hubbard and Gordon for the Industrial Workers of the World, and George Washington Woodbey, Kaspar Bauer and Attorney E. F. Kirk for the Socialists.

The part played by the police in the affair of Saturday evening was denounced, but none of the speakers grew radical. It was announced that the fight for free speech will be waged with vigor, but in a dignified manner.

The police, aided by vigilantes, responded with more than vigor and in anything but a dignified manner. The brutality against the free-speech fighters in San Diego was so horrendous that after an investigation ordered by Governor Hiram Johnson, Colonel Harris Weinstock reported: "Your commissioner has visited Russia and while there, has heard many horrible tales of high-handed proceedings and outrageous treatment of innocent people at the hands of despotic and tyrannic Russian authorities. Your commissioner is frank to confess that when he became satisfied of the truth of the stories, as related by these unfortunate men (victims of police and vigilante brutality in San Diego), it was hard for him to believe that he was not still sojourning in Russia, conducting his investigation there, instead of in this alleged 'land of the free and home of the brave'."[54]

Woodbey was several times the victim of brutal police assaults as he insisted on exercising his right-of-free speech, and he filed charges of "Malicious and unofficial" conduct against the chief of police, captain of the detectives, and several policemen whom he accused of brutality.[55] As a leading figure in the Free Speech League, the organization which coordinated the free-speech fight, Woodbey was frequently threatened by vigilantes, and on one occasion, he barely escaped death. *The Citizen*, official organ of the Labor Unions of Southern California, reported in mid-April, 1912:

> Rev. Woodbey, a negro preacher, has been threatened for his activity. A few nights ago he was taken to his home by a committee from the Free Speech League. As the party left the car at a corner near Woodbey's home an automobile was noticed in front of the house. Upon examination it was found to contain two armed men. Across the street another vigilante was stationed, and in the alley two more armed men were found. The strength of the committee with Woodbey probably saved his life, as members of the League challenged the vigilantes to do their dirty work. The preacher's house was patrolled by armed men from the League all night.[56]

The free-speech fight in "Barbarous San Diego" was still in full swing in late April, 1912 when Woodbey left to attend the Socialist Party national convention in Chicago as a delegate from California. By the time he returned home, the struggle was still continuing and he did what he could to help the cause, faced with defeat as a result of the power of the police, vigilantes, and the state government. Wobblies continued to be clubbed and arrested, and there was little that could be done to prevent the wholesale violation of their civil rights. "They have the courts, the mails and funds," Laura Payne Emerson lamented.[57] It was not until 1914 that the right of the I.W.W. to hold street meetings was established. Although the ordinance still remained on the statute books, the police no longer interfered when Wobblies spoke at street corners in the forbidden district. On the invitation of the I.W.W., Reverend Woodbey was one of the regular speakers at such meetings.[58]

Woodbey's associations with the I.W.W. may not have pleased some California Socialists and his role in the free-speech fights probably disturbed members of his congregation. But he was candidate for state treasurer on the Socialist ticket in 1914 and was still listed as Pastor of Mt. Zion Church in San Diego and member of the state executive board of the Socialist Party in *The Christian Socialist* of February, 1915 which published two articles by the militant black Socialist minister. These, the last known writings of Reverend Woodbey on Socialism, were "What the Socialists Want" and "Why the Socialists Must Reach the Churches with Their Message." The first was in the form of a dialogue, a familiar Woodbey technique, between the minister (here called Parker) and George Stephenson, a black mail carrier. Stephenson asks to be told "in short, and the simplest way possible, just what it is you Socialists are trying to get any way," and Woodbey proceeds to enlighten him, pointing out the features of the Socialist society which he had presented in greater detail in his previous pamphlets. When the mail carrier leaves convinced that there was no way to answer the arguments in favor of Socialism, his teacher shouts after him: "Hold on a minute, we would solve the race problem of this and all other countries, by establishing the brotherhood of man which Christ taught."

In the second piece, Woodbey insisted that the Socialists would never succeed unless they won over "the millions of working people who belong to the various churches of the country," and proceeded to indicate how he did his part in this endeavor. His chief weapon was to play up the point that "the economic teaching of the Bible and of Socialism is the same, and that for that reason he (the church member) must accept Socialism in order to stand consistently by the teaching of his own religion." After having shown the church member that the Bible, "in every line of it," was "with the poor and against their oppressors," it was necessary to convince him that the solution for the ills of society was not charity which was at best "only a temporary relief," but the collective ownership and operation of the industries. The last point had to be reached slowly and step by step, but if the Socialist agitator keeps using the Bible as his authority, he will carry the church member along to that conclusion. The danger was that too many Socialists antagonized church members by linking anti-religion with Socialism. Hence, he advised against using agitators "who do not understand the Christian people, to carry this message, for the reason that they are sure to say something that will spoil the whole thing."

We know nothing of Reverend Woodbey after 1915. But we leave him at this point in his career still as confirmed a Socialist as ever. "I would not vote for my own wife on a platform which did not have the Socialist message in it," he told an audience in December, 1914.[59]

Just how many blacks Woodbey converted by the method he outlined in his last Socialist writing is impossible to determine. But Hubert H. Harrison, a militant black Socialist in New York, said of Woodbey's work as a national Party organizer: "He has been very effective."[60] At least one prominent black Socialist attributed his conversion to Socialism to Reverend Woodbey. In the Chicago *Daily Socialist* of September 29, 1908, Reverend George W. Slater, Jr., Pastor of the Zion Tabernacle in the Windy City, wrote:

> For years I have felt that there was something wrong with our government. A few weeks ago I heard Comrade Woodbey, a colored national organizer of the Socialist party, speaking on the streets in Chicago. He showed me plainly the trouble and the remedy. From that time on I have been an ardent supporter of the Socialist cause.

NOTES

1. *Ohio Socialist Bulletin,* February 1909.

2. *Chicago Daily Socialist,* May 11, 1908; John Mather, *Who's Who of the Colored Race,* Chicago, 1921; A. W. Ricker in *Appeal to Reason,* October 31, 1903.

3. Reverend George W. Woodbey, *What To Do And How To Do It or Socialism vs. Capitalism, Wayland's Monthly,* No. 40, August, 1903, p. 4; A. W. Ricker in *Appeal to Reason,* Oct. 31, 1903.

Correspondence with the Omaha Public Library, the University of Nebraska Library, the Nebraska State Historical Society, and the United

Methodist Historical Society at Nebraska Wesleyan University has failed to turn up any information on Reverend Woodbey in their files and his role as a Populist and Socialist in Nebraska.

4. *Los Angeles Socialist*, July 12, 1902.

5. *Ibid.*, Dec. 17, 1904; *Common Sense*, Los Angeles, Oct. 27, 1906.

6. *Los Angeles Socialist*, May 2, 1903.

7. *Common Sense*, Los Angeles, August, 1905.

8. *Ibid.*, Oct. 8, 1904, March 7, April 11, 1908.

9. A. W. Ricker *Appeal to Reason*, October 31, 1903.

10. *Ibid.* Robert Blatchford's *Merrie England*, published in London in 1894, was a book of 26 chapters and 210 pages in which the superiority of Socialism over Capitalism is brilliantly set forth in clear, plain language.

11. Woodbey, *op. cit.*, p. 3.

12. *Chicago Daily Socialist*, May 11, 1908.

13. Woodbey, *op. cit.*, pp. 5–7.

14. *Ibid.*, pp. 15–19.

15. *Ibid.*, p. 20.

16. *Ibid.*, pp., 20–21.

17. *Ibid.*, p. 24.

18. *Ibid.*, pp. 37–38.

19. *Ibid.*, p. 44.

20. Compare, for example, Woodbey's discussion of an international credit system under Socialism (pp. 36–37) with Bellamy's discussion of the same system in Chapter 8 of *Looking Backward*.

21. In a letter to William Dean Howells a few months after the publication of *Looking Backward*, Bellamy wrote that "the word socialist is one I could never well stomach. In the first place it is a foreign word in itself, and equal foreign in all its suggestions. . . . Whatever German and French reformers may choose to call themselves, socialist is not a good name for a party to succeed with in America. No such party can or ought to succeed which is not wholly and enthusiastically American and patriotic in spirit and suggestions." (Quoted in Arthur E. Morgan, *Edward Bellamy*, New York, 1941, p. 374.)

22. For a discussion of *The Iron Heel*, see Philip S. Foner, *Jack London: American Rebel*, New York, 1964, pp. 87–97.

23. Woodbey, *op. cit.*, p. 7.

24. G. W. Woodbey, *The Bible and Socialism: A Conversation Between Two Preachers*, San Diego, 1904, Preface.

25. *Ibid.*, p. 7.

26. *Ibid.*, pp. 69, 83, 90.

27. *Ibid.*, p. 69.

28. *Ibid.*, p. 96.

29. G. W. Woodbey, *The Distribution of Wealth,* San Diego, California, 1910, p. 7.

30. *Ibid.,* pp. 41, 44–45.

31. *Ibid.,* pp. 54–55.

32. *Ibid.,* p. 68. Woodbey's fellow-California Socialist closed his letters, "Yours for the Revolution, Jack London."

33. *Proceeding of the National Convention of the Socialist Party Held at Chicago, Illinois, May 1 to 6, 1904,* Chicago, 1904, pp. 47–48.

34. *Ibid.,* p. 182.

35. *Prodeedings, National Convention of the Socialist Party, Held at Chicago, Illinois, May 10 to 17, 1908,* pp. 208–9.

36. *Ibid.,* pp. 290–91.

37. *Ibid.,* p. 106.

38. *Ibid.,* pp. 106–7.

39. *Ibid.,* pp. 107–8.

40. The most detailed discussion of the 1908 convention in relation to the immigration issue is Charles Leinenweber, "The American Socialist Party and 'New' Immigrants," *Science & Society,* Vol. XXXXII, Winter, 1968 pp. 6–12. It does not even mention Woodbey's speech in opposition to the resolution calling for a study of the necessity for immigration restriction.

41. *Proceedings, National Convention. . . , 1908,* p.163.

42. *Ibid.,* p. 164.

43. Neither Ira Kipnis nor Ray Ginger mention Woodbey's nomination in their discussion of the 1908 Convention.

44. New York *Evening Call,* Nov. 2, 1908.

45. Reverend G. W. Woodbey, "Why the Negro Should Vote the Socialist Ticket," four-page leaflet undated, copy in Socialist Party Papers, Duke University Library.

46. G. W. Woodbey, "The New Emancipation," *Chicago Daily Socialist,* Jan. 18, 1909.

47. G. W. Woodbey, "Socialist Agitation," *Ibid.,* Jan. 4, 1909.

48. Philip S. Foner, *History of the Labor Movement in the United States,* Vol. IV, New York, 1965, p. 173.

49. *San Francisco Call, San Francisco Chronicle,* Feb. 1–8, 1908.

50. Chicago *Daily Socialist,* May 11, 1908.

51. San Francisco *Call,* June 12, 1908.

52. In a letter to the author, Harland B. Adams of San Diego summarized a conversation he had with Dennis V. Allen, a black San Diegan who in the years 1912 to 1916, as a postal clerk, delivered mail to the home of Reverend Woodbey. According to Mr. Allen, Reverend Woodbey lived at 12 Twenty Ninth Street, San Diego. He described Woodbey as "a rather dark Negro, slender and about 5 feet 11 inches. Mrs. Woodbey was extremely stout,

almost to the point that with her age and weight, it was difficult for her to get about. She was known by nearly everyone in the small Negro population of San Diego at that time, as Mother Mary or Mother Woodbey. She was a devout Baptist Christian and regularly attended the Baptist Church at 29th and Clay, which still exists." The Woodbeys, Mr. Allen continued, owned the property where he lived, as well as the house next door which he rented to a Negro who was a veteran of the Civil War.

According to Mr. Allen, he was in a group that drafted Reverend Woodbey as the pastor for the Mt. Zion Baptist Church, and was also part of the group which had him removed. Although extremely popular, and though he drew large crowds to his sermons, his dismissal, "was a direct result of mixing too much Socialism with his Bible, and this the members of his church resented."

Dennis V. Allen organized the San Diego Race Relations Society in 1924, and held the post of president for thirty-six years.

53. Foner, *op. cit.*, Vol. IV, pp. 194–95.

54. *Ibid.*, pp. 199–200.

55. San Diego *Union*, Feb. 22, 1912. The charges were ignored by the authorities.

56. *The Citizen* reprinted in *St. Louis Labor*, April 27, 1912. In her study, "The I.W.W. Free Speech Movement San Diego, 1912" (*Journal of San Diego History*, Winter, 1973, pp. 25–33), Rosalie Shank does not once mention Reverend Woodbey.

57. *Industrial Worker*, Oct. 17, 1912.

58. *The Wooden Shoe* (Los Angeles), Jan. 22, 1914.

59. *California Social Democrat*, Dec. 12, 1914.

60. New York *Call*, Dec. 16, 1911.

11

The IWW and
the Black Worker*

In 1913 Mary White Ovington, one of the founders of the NAACP, wrote in her article, "The Status of the Negro in the United States": "There are two organizations in this country that have shown they do care about full rights for the Negro. The first is the National Association for the Advancement of Colored People. . . . The second organization that attacks Negro segregation is the Industrial Workers of the World. . . . The I.W.W. has stood with the Negro."[1] The second organization to which Miss Ovington referred, popularly known as "The Wobblies," was founded in the summer of 1905 by progressive-minded elements in the American labor and Socialist movements, headed by Eugene V. Debs, Daniel De Leon, and William D. (Big Bill) Haywood, who were convinced of three basic principles: (1) the superiority of industrial unionism over craft unionism in the struggle against the monopolistic, highly integrated organizations of employers; (2) the impossibility of converting the conservative American Federation of Labor into a type of organization which would achieve real benefits for the majority of working men and women; and (3) the ineffectiveness of the existing organization of the industrial and radical type to build a movement which would organize and unite the entire working class, regardless of skill, color, sex, or national origin. Clearly, in the eyes of these elements, a new organization of labor was necessary, one that "would correspond to modern industrial conditions, and through which the working people might finally secure complete emancipation from

*Reprinted from *The Journal of Negro History,* LV (1970), 45–64.

wage slavery for all wage workers." It was this conviction that led to the formation of the Industrial Workers of the World.[2]

At 9 A.M. on June 27, 1955, in Chicago's Brand Hall, "Big Bill" Haywood, militant secretary-treasurer of the Western Federation of Miners, called the 200 delegates representing 43 organizations to order and declared: "This is the Continental Congress of the Working Class." Immediately thereafter he made it clear that the new organization of labor about to come into being would take a definite stand against any and all discrimination based upon race or color. In his indictment of the A.F. of L., which he declared contemptuously "does not represent the working class," he cited specifically the well-known fact that "there are organizations that are affiliated with the A.F. of L., which in their constitution and by-laws prohibit the initiation of or conferring the obligation on a colored man." Haywood pledged that such anti-working-class, racist practices, along with other restrictions on the right of black workers to join the labor movement, would be swept into oblivion by the newly-organized industrial union.[3]

At a later session, the delegates adopted the Constitution and by-laws of the Industrial Workers of the World, with the motto. "An Injury to One is the Concern of All" (a modification of the old Knights of Labor motto). The first section of the by-laws stated that "no working man or woman shall be excluded from membership because of creed or color." Haywood in an interview with the press told reporters that though unions affiliated with the A.F. of L., discriminated against a worker who was a Negro, to the I.W.W. it "did not make a bit of difference whether he is a Negro or a white man."[4]

Despite its pledge, the I.W.W. appears to have accomplished little in the way of organizing Negro workers in the first four years of its existence. Torn apart by internal ideological dissensions, and by repeated resignations and expulsions, seriously weakened by the impact of the depression following the Panic of 1907, the I.W.W. hardly organized any workers at all.[5] In 1909 its membership was down to 3,700 in contrast to the 1,488,872 who were affiliated in that year to the A.F. of L. (A negligible number of these members were Negroes.)[6] Yet, though it was written off by Samuel Gompers and other A.F. of L. leaders, the I.W.W. was far from dead. In the next few years, organizers of the I.W.W. would make the Wobblies known throughout the nation for their famous free speech fights, and their unionizing drives in the steel and textile industries of the East, the lumber camps of the Northwest and Southeast, the farm lands of the Pacific Coast, and the great Midwest, and the maritime and shipping industries throughout the country. The spectacular rise of the I.W.W. after 1909 would bring the principle of industrial unionism, under which all workers in an industry were organized into one big union, and the principle of labor solidarity, which the I.W.W. preached day in and day out, to the attention of hundreds of thousands of unorganized American workers, including the most unorganized of all—the black workers.

Beginning in 1910, the I.W.W. made a determined effort to recruit Negro membership. Leaflets and pamphlets were distributed in the thousands to convince the black workers that the only hope for remedying the miserable status they faced in American society was through the Industrial Workers of the World. "The Negro has no chance in the old-line trade unions," an I.W.W. leaflet argued. "They do not want him. They admit him only under compulsion and treat him with contempt. There is only *one* labor organization in the United States that admits the colored worker on a footing of absolute equality with the white—the Industrial Workers of the World. . . . In the I.W.W. the colored worker, man or woman, is on an equal footing with every other worker. He has the same voice in determining the policies of the organization, and his interests are protected as zealously as those of any other member."[7] The Negro, I.W.W. literature emphasized, was subject to discrimination, first because of his color, and second because "for the most part the Negro still belongs in the category of the 'unskilled'." This state of affairs could not be wiped out by appeals to sentiment alone. It could only be altered by the organization of the Negro in a union which educated its members to recognize all workers as equal regardless of color, and which organized the unskilled by the only method through which they could be organized—industrial unionism. Such a union was the I.W.W.[8]

All I.W.W. journals participated actively in this educational campaign, including *The Voice of the People,* the Southern organ of the I.W.W. published at New Orleans. The paper was edited by Covington Hall, born in Woodville, Mississippi, in 1871, an Adjutant General of the United Sons of Confederate Veterans, who became a radical, a Socialist, an active organizer for the I.W.W., especially among Negroes in the South.[9] Covington Hall regularly featured appeals in *The Voice of the People* urging white workers in the South to remember how racism had always been used by the ruling class to divide black and white to injury of both, and predicting that no real improvement could come to the conditions of either black or white unless they united to destroy the chief weapon of a class that profited by keeping both separated. In an article entitled, "Down with Race Prejudice," published in December, 1912, Phineas Eastman asked his "fellow workers of the South if they wish real good feeling to exist between the two races (and each is necessary to the other's success), to please stop calling the colored man 'Nigger'—the tone some use is an insult, much less the word. Call him Negro if you must refer to his race, but 'fellow worker' is the only form of salutation a rebel should use."[10]

Members of the I.W.W. were constantly reminded that the organization of the Negro was an "economic bread and butter" issue. "Leaving the Negro outside of your union makes him a potential, if not an actual scab, dangerous to the organized worker, to say nothing of his own interests as a worker." Race prejudice on the job could only have one result—"keeping the workers fighting each other, while the boss gets the benefits." The idea fostered by the capitalists that the white worker was "superior" was part of the same game. "Actually he is only 'superior' if he shows that he can produce more wealth for the boss than his colored brother can."[11] In an appeal directed especially to Southern workers, the I.W.W. asked:

> If one of you were to fall in a river and could not swim, and a Negro came along who could swim, would you drown rather than accept his offer of aid? Hardly!
> That is the I.W.W. position. Labor organized on race lines will drown. Only organized on *class* lines will it swim. . . .
> Don't let them sidetrack you from the main line which is, Shall we be freemen or slaves?[12]

The I.W.W. condemned all manifestations of Jim Crowism. It denounced the lynching of Negroes as "savagery," pointing out that it was usually resorted to when Negroes "are demanding more of their product."[13]

In a pamphlet entitled, "Justice for the Negro: How Can He Get It," the I.W.W. pointed out:

Two lynchings in a week—one every three or four days—that is the rate at which the people in this "land of the free and home of the brave" have been killing colored men and women for the past thirty years . . . put to death with every kind of torture that human fiends can invent.

The pamphlet made it clear that "The wrongs of the Negro in the United States" were not confined to lynchings. "When allowed to live and work for the community, he is subjected to constant humiliation, injustice and discrimination. In the cities he is forced to live in the meanest districts, where his rent is doubled and tripled, while conditions of health and safety are neglected in favor of the white sections. In many states he is obliged to ride in special 'Jim Crow' cars, hardly fit for cattle. Almost everywhere all semblance of political rights is denied him.

"When the Negro goes to ask for work he meets with the same systematic discrimination. Thousands of jobs are closed to him solely on account of his color. He is considered only fit for the most menial occupation. In many cases he is forced to accept a lower wage than is paid to white men for the same work. *Everywhere the odds are against him in the struggle for existence.*

"Throughout this land of liberty, so-called, the Negro worker is treated as an inferior; he is cursed and spat upon; in short, he is treated not as a human being, but as an animal, a beast of burden for the ruling class. When he tries to improve his condition, he is shoved back into the mire of degradation and poverty and told to 'keep his place'."[14]

In a leaflet entitled, "To Colored Workingmen and Women," the I.W.W. pointed out: "If you are a wage worker you are welcome in the I.W.W. halls, no matter what your color. By this you may see that the I.W.W. is not a white man's union, not a black man's union, not a red man's union, but a working man's union. All of the working class in one big union."[15] On September 19, 1912, the *Industrial Worker* carried the following news report and comment:

Fearing that the I.W.W. will organize the steel mills in the Pittsburgh district the Carnegie Steel Company is importing Negroes so as to create racial hatred and prevent solidarity. It won't work. The I.W.W. organizes without regard to color. The only Negro we fight is he who employs labor. There is no color line in the furnace hells of the steel trust and there will be none in the *One Big Union.* White, black or yellow, the workers of the world must unite!

The I.W.W., unlike most unions of the time and since, practiced what it preached, even in the deepest South where it raised the banner of "No Race, No Creed, No Color," and united black and white workers in a common struggle. This slogan was proclaimed on an international scale. In 1910-11, the Industrial Workers' Union of South Africa, a branch of the I.W.W. founded by Wobbly seamen from the United States, conducted a vigorous campaign to convince the rank and file of the white workers of South Africa "That their real enemy is not the colored laborer, and that it is only by combining and co-operating irrespective of color that the standard of life of the whites can be maintained and improved." The union led the strike of trainwaymen of Johannesburg in which Negro and white workers for the first time united in struggle. The *Voice of Labor,* the I.W.W.'s South African organ, asserted that while the strike was not successful, it had taught "the white and black workers of South Africa some much needed lessons."[16]

It is clear that with the exception of the United Mine Workers,[17] which was affiliated to the A.F. of L., the I.W.W. was the *only* labor organization in the second decade of the twentieth century which stood squarely for the organization of Negro workers on the basis of complete equality. The *Industrial Worker,* official organ of the I.W.W. summed up the I.W.W.'s attitude:

> In this country every tenth person is of acknowledged Negro descent and a large percentage of these ten million are wage workers. There may be for the whole society of America a Negro problem but with the entrance of the Industrial Workers of the World into the industrial arena there was no further need for the labor problem to be complicated by a racial problem. The I.W.W. accepts the Negro wage worker, asking of him the same initiation fees and dues as his white brother, and giving him the same membership privileges as are the common property of all who join. The fight of the Negro wage slave is the fight of the white wage slave; and the two must rise or fall together. Their economic interests are identical and an injury to one is an injury to the other. . . .
> To the I.W.W. there was "no race problem. There is only a class

problem. . . . The economic interests of all workers, be they white, black, brown or yellow, are identical, and all are included in the program of the I.W.W. It has one program for the entire working class—the abolition of the wage system.' "[18]

Yet it is also clear that the I.W.W.'s answer to the special problems of the Negro people facing discrimination, segregation, deprivation of civil and political rights and violence, was weakened by a failure to understand that for the blacks there was a "race problem," and it was no answer to tell Negroes that in "the abolition of the wage system" lay their salvation. Despite its advanced position against race prejudice and its opposition to segregation in the labor movement, the failure of the I.W.W. to understand the special aspect of the Negro problem restricted its appeal to the black masses.

"How can the Negro combat this widespread injustice?" asked the I.W.W. "How can he, not only put a stop to lynchings, but force the white race to grant him equal treatment? How can he get his rights as a human being?" Protests, petitions, resolutions, all sorts of political movements would, in the eyes of the I.W.W., never accomplish anything. They were a waste of time and money. "The government is in the hands of the ruling class of white men and will do as they wish. No appeal to the political powers will ever secure justice to the Negro." The Negro had only one power to use: "the power to fold his arms and refuse to work for the community until he is guaranteed fair treatment. . . . The only power of the Negro is his power as a worker; his one weapon is the strike. . . . When they are in a position to say to any community, 'If you do not stop discrimination against the colored race, we will stop working for you,' the hidden forces behind the government will see to it that lynchings cease and discrimination comes to an end."[19] This sounded extremely militant, of course, and it was in keeping with the I.W.W. belief in syndicalism and the general strike as the real answer to the basic problems of all workers. But what were the Negroes to do to meet the day-to-day problems that faced them until they had achieved the power to force the master class to alter the pattern of discrimination and exploitation overnight? To this question, unfortunately, the I.W.W. had no real answer.

The failure of the I.W.W. to recognize the Negro question as a special question and its lumping of the problems of Negro workers with those of all workers was quite in keeping with the trend in radical circles of this period. The American Socialist Party, like the entire Second International, also had a very simplistic view of the Negro question. The Socialist Party never really recognized the Negro question as a special question. To the Socialist Party the class question was not only primary but it was exclusive—there was no other social question. All questions, the Socialists thought, would be solved as a by-product of the class question and the class revolution. Just so the I.W.W. thought that all questions would be solved through the general strike. The black question as assumed loftily by the Socialists, would be solved as a *by-product* of the class struggle, without any particular or specific attention to each question in its own terms in its own needs.[26] That you might not be able to achieve a Socialist revolution without proper and specific attention to something as vital, as central, in our country as the Negro question, was not perceived either by the Socialist Party or the Socialist Labor Party. That a simplistic class approach might even hinder the efforts to organize the Negro workers was overlooked.

However, there is a fundamental difference between the approach of the Socialist Party and the I.W.W. on the Negro question, even though quite a few Wobblies were members of the S.P.—that is until 1912 when they were expelled presumably for advocating sabotage and "opposing political action." The Socialist Party made no real effort to organize the Negro, and in the South even regarded Negro membership as a drawback inasmuch as it would alienate potential white members. Since the Negro in the South could not vote and the Socialist Party believed that Socialism would come only through the ballot box, it was regarded a waste of time to recruit black members into the Party thereby driving out white members who alone could vote for Socialist candidates.[21] To the limited degree that the Socialist Party recruited black members in the South, where the vast majority of the Negroes lived prior to World War I, it organized them in segregated, Jim Crow branches. To its credit, the I.W.W. would have none of this. For one thing, as a syndicalist organization, it opposed political action at the ballot box as a waste of energy, and put its faith primarily in industrial organization and the general strike. Thus the fact that the Negro was disenfranchised in the South was no problem for the I.W.W. in its plans for building unity of black and white workers. Then again, at no time in its history did the I.W.W., even in the deepest South, ever establish segregated locals for black workers. Wherever it organized, members were brought together in locals regardless of race or color.[22] In fact, the Industrial Workers of the World is the *only* labor federation in the history of the American labor movement which never established a single segregated local. Even the Knights of Labor which brought large numbers of skilled and unskilled Negro workers into the predominantly white labor movement of the 1880's—it is estimated that in 1886, when the membership of the Knights exceeded 700,000, there were no less than 60,000 Negro members—segregated its Negro membership. In 1887 there were 400 all-Negro locals in the Knights of Labor, the bulk of them in the South where Negro workers were mainly concentrated. While the Knights did much in breaking down the walls of prejudice, the color line was never really breached and the Order never succeeded in eliminating the barriers between white and black.[23] The I.W.W. did achieve this goal within its ranks.

No statistics are available which indicate Negro membership in the I.W.W. Sterling D. Spero and Abram L. Harris in *The Black Worker* estimate that of the "one million membership cards" issued by the I.W.W. "during the active part of its life" that is between 1909 and 1924, "100,000 cards were issued to Negroes."[24] Actually, no I.W.W. publication ever made such a claim, and it is likely that the Wobblies never succeeded in recruiting a very large Negro membership.

Partly this was due to the fact that many of the great organizing drives of the I.W.W. were in the steel and textile industries of the North, in Pittsburgh, Lawrence and Fall River, Massachussets, and Paterson and Passaic, New Jersey, and in these industries prior to World War I, few black workers were employed. (A common employer justification for not hiring Negroes in the textile industry was that "the negro could not work in a cotton-mill, because the hum of the looms put him to sleep.")[25] Then again, not many Negroes were employed in the lumber camps of the west or in the western agricultural fields where the I.W.W. also made significant headway. The black migratory workers in these industries found a haven in the I.W.W. In *The Messenger* of July, 1923, George S. Schuyler recalled the racial contacts among migratory workers who belonged to the I.W.W. "There was no discrimination in the 'jungles' of the I.W.W.," he noted. "The writer has seen a white hobo, despised by society, share his last loaf with a black fellow-hobo."

The two main areas where the I.W.W. did recruit Negro membership were among the longshoremen and lumber workers in the South. The Philadelphia longshoremen, with Benjamin Harrison Fletcher as their leader, constituting one of the most effective I.W.W. units when it was first organized in 1913, was made up primarily but not entirely of Negroes. For years prior to 1913, organization on the docks of Philadelphia had been frustrated by the employers' policy of pitting Negroes and whites against each other, threatening that if one group complained about conditions, their jobs would be given to the other. The I.W.W. entered the picture with the appeal that whether white and Negro liked each other or not, their only hope was to organize into one union. Within a few months the Marine Transport Workers Local 3 had been organized, the majority of its members Negroes, and struck for recognition on May 13, 1913. The strike was supported by ministers of the African Methodist Episcopal Church in Philadelphia who told the *Public Ledger* that the church "liked the I.W.W. because it believed in the colored man." After a strike of two weeks, the dock workers won recognition of their union and the right to bargain collectively. The union's membership by the end of 1913 was close to 3,000 and strikes in 1915 and 1916 completed its control of the docks. By 1916 the union had raised wages for black and white longshoremen from $1.25 to $4 a day, time-and-a-half for overtime and double time for Sundays. In keeping with its belief in equality of Negro and white, the local had a rotating system of chairmen. One month a Negro was chairman; the next month, a white member.[26]

Other locals of the Marine Transport Workers, composed largely of Negro longshoremen, were established in Baltimore, Galveston, and New Orleans, though none were as strongly organized as the Philadelphia local. But all maintained the principle of full equality of Negro and white members.

In New Orleans the A.F.of L. Central Labor Council was a lily-white organization, refusing to admit delegates from the black unions of waterfront workers. In 1910 the I.W.W., under the leadership of Covington Hall and backed by the Dock and Cotton Council, established the United Labor Council. Into this Council were admitted delegates from both white and black waterfront unions, and soon the Council was an important force in the New Orleans scene. As in Philadelphia, the meetings of the Council were chaired one week by a black and the next by a white waterfront worker.[27]

One of the most inspiring chapters of the I.W.W.'s organizing activity relates to the lumber industry of the South. The labor force of the Southern lumber industry was made up of both white and Negro workers; indeed, in 1910, over half of the 262,000 workers was composed of Negroes. In the main, the blacks were unskilled workers in the lowest-paid jobs. They did most of the heavy manual work in the saw-mills, on railroads, in the turpentine camps, at skidways, and in the swamps. In 1910, of 7,958 Negroes in the sawmills and planning mills of Texas, 7,216 were laborers; there was not a single Negro sawyer. The St. Louis *Lumberman,* the employers' organ, justified this situation on the ground that "there is a limit to the amount of wages that can be paid with safety to colored laborers around sawmills and wood camps. Too much pay causes discontent and idleness among them." To the Negro lumber workers, notes a student of the Mississippi lumber industry, "emancipation from slavery had not brought the fruits of freedom. He simply had exchanged his lot for a different system of economic bondage."[28]

Having stolen the magnificent forests of Florida, Alabama, Louisiana, Mississippi, East Texas, and South Georgia from the public domain, the lumber companies proceeded to operate them as feudal domains, filling the towns with gunmen whom the authorities commissioned as deputy sheriffs, and jailing anyone who questioned their rule. The jails also provided the companies with a cheap supply of labor. Men were seized on the railroads for "beating their way" and sentenced to 90 days in jail. Then these unfortunate workers were forced to toil for the period of their sentence in the turpentine camps. Negro and white laborers were frequently arrested, fined, and imprisoned for no offense at all, or simply for being out of a job and forced to work out their sentence in the lumber camps. Often an employer would arrange to pay the fine on condition that the debt was worked out. In 1904 the Supreme Court upheld laws enacted at the close of the century eliminating peonage, but in the isolated camps in the Southern woods these laws and the Supreme Court decision cut little ice. To be sure, individuals found guilty of establishing peonage could be prosecuted and convicted, but few workers in Southern lumbering, particularly Negro workers, dared to protest to the authorities, knowing that the company-dominated local courts would never convict the guilty parties. "The timber and lumber workers," read a complaint in 1912, "in many places are being practically held as peons within barbed wire enclosures; where there is no law except the will of the Lumber Trust's imported thugs and gunmen."[29]

For wages as low as $1.25 a day or average weekly wages of from $7 to $9, men were forced to labor ten to twelve hours a day. With a few exceptions, wages were paid monthly, and usually either entirely, or in large part, in scrip or time checks. "Scrip" was simply some substitute for legal money—paper, chits, cardboard coin, metal tags, etc.—which ordinarily bore the name of the issuing company, a valuation and the statement "good for merchandise only." If spent in the company store, it passed at face value; but it could be converted to cash only at a customary discount of five to 30 percent. Since prices in the company stores ranged from one-third to 50 per cent above prices in surrounding communities, the face value of the wages used for merchandise was always considerably reduced.

The time check bore the condition that it was to be cashed at some future specified date. If the bearer, for whatever reason, cashed it prior to the specified date, he was generally forced to take a discount of from five to ten per cent. Some workers, to obtain legal currency, were forced to borrow from the employer at usurious rates of interest. In other words, these workers were actually paying interest on their wages being withheld from them.[30]

The great majority of the lumber workers lived and died in communities owned and operated by the mill companies. They were charged outrageous rents for primitive huts heated with open fires. They were forced to pay a compulsory medical-insurance fee, usually $1.00 to $1.50 a month, for doctors in whose selection they had no voice and who knew little or nothing of medicine. They were forced to pay from 75 cents to $1 per month for "accident insurance," which was bought by the lumber company at from 50 to 60 cents per man.[31]

A comprehensive study of conditions in the lumber industry in Louisiana by the State Bureau of Statistics of Labor pointed out: "We found . . . every labor law on the statutes being violated." Following a similar study in Texas, the Commission on Industrial

Relations found "that in such communities, political liberty does not exist and its forms are hollow mockery. . . . Free speech, free assembly, and a free press may be denied as they have been denied time and again, and the employer's agent may be placed in public office to do his bidding."[32]

Since the A.F. of L. showed no interest in organizing the oppressed workers of the Southern lumber industry, they were required to unionize by themselves. On December 3, 1910, Arthur L. Emerson and Jay Smith and a group of lumber workers in the De Ridder area of Louisiana, most of them sympathetic to the I.W.W. and to the Socialist Party, set up a local union. Emerson, Smith and a few others, who were Wobblies, then traveled in the guise of book agents, insurance solicitors, evangelists, even card sharps, to avoid company gunmen, going from camp to camp, mill to mill, bringing the message of unionism to the lumber workers. By June 1911, enough locals had been organized to setup the Brotherhood of Timber Workers (or B. of T.W. as it was popularly known) as a national union with Emerson as President and Smith as general secretary.

Since Negroes comprised so large a portion of the labor force, the leaders of the Brotherhood knew that no union could be effective in the yellow pine region unless it opened its doors to Negroes as well as whites. The Constitution of the organization allowed Negroes to join, but the Southern tradition of segregation was retained by providing for "colored lodges" which were forbidden to retain their initiation fees and dues but were required to deliver all such funds for safe-keeping to the nearest white local.[33]

The B. of T.W. spread rapidly over Texas, Louisiana, and Arkansas, recruiting Negro and white lumberjacks, mill workers, tenant and small farmers who worked in the lumber industry for parts of the year, and town craftsmen. But the employers quickly struck back. During the summer and fall of 1911 between 5,000 and 7,000 of the most active members of the Brotherhood, white and Negro, were blacklisted. At the same time, the companies shut down their plants, and announced that they would not reopen them until the Brotherhood had gone out of existence. But, though the lumber workers suffered severe privation, neither the lockout nor the blacklisting destroyed the union. The Southern Lumber Operators' Association then decided to reopen the plants, invite Negro members of the

Brotherhood to go back to work at higher wages, and recruit Negro scabs from all parts of Louisiana and Texas to keep the mills operating.[34]

Neither of these two plans succeeded. No Negro members of the Brotherhood went back to work, and few black scabs were recruited. When the mills reopened in the winter of 1912—the lockout was officially ended by February—it was not with scab labor. By May, 1912, the Brotherhood had a membership of between 20,000 to 25,000 workers, about half of whom were Negroes.[35]

The experience in the battle against the lockout, the refusal of the Negro members to desert the union and of blacks to scab, had imbued the Brotherhood with a clearer understanding of what it called the "Negro question." In *An Appeal to Timber and Lumber Workers,* the union declared: "As far as the 'Negro question' goes, it means simply this: Either the whites organize with the Negroes, or the bosses will organize the Negroes against the whites, in which last case it is hardly up to the white to damn the 'niggers.' Southern workers ought to realize that while there are two colors among the workers in the South there is actually only one class. It is the object of this organization . . . to teach that the only hope of the workers is through industrial organization, that while the colors in question are two, the class in question is only one; that the first thing for a real workingman to do is to learn by a little study that he belongs to the working class, line up with the Brotherhood of Timber Workers or the Industrial Workers of the World, and make a start for industrial freedom."[36]

Up to this point, the Brotherhood, though friendly to the Wobblies, had not affiliated to the I.W.W. But with the A.F. of L. still showing no interest in a movement of which Negroes were a substantial number, the Brotherhood turned to the I.W.W. for assistance, and proposed affiliation. When the proposed affiliation was agreed to by the leaders of the B. of T.W. and I.W.W., the latter organization sent Bill Haywood and Covington Hall, editor of *The Voice of the People*, to the Brotherhood's convention at Alexandria, Louisiana, May 1912, to present the case for affiliation to the delegates.

Arriving at the convention, Haywood expressed surprise that no Negroes were present. He was informed that the Negro workers were meeting separately in another hall because it was against the law in Louisiana for white and Negroes to meet together. Haywood brushed this explanation aside, declaring:

"You work in the same mills together. Sometimes a black man and a white man chop down the same tree together. You are meeting in convention now to discuss the conditions under which you labor. This can't be done intelligently by passing resolutions here and then sending them out to another room for the black man to act upon. Why not be sensible about this and call the Negroes into this convention? If it is against the law, this is one time when the law should be broken."

Haywood was followed by Covington Hall, who told the delegates that he was not only a Southerner, "bawn and raised," but also Past-Adjutant General (National Secretary) of the United Sons of Confederate Veterans, and that he supported Haywood's suggestion completely. "Let the Negroes come together with us, and if any arrests are made, all of us will go to jail, white and colored together."[37]

The advice was followed, and the Negroes were called into the session. The mixed gathering adopted the proposal of affiliation with the I.W.W. and elected Negro and white delegates to the September convention of the I.W.W. in Chicago, where the merger was to be formally effected.

Haywood and Covington also addressed a mass meeting at the Alexandria Opera House under the Brotherhood's sponsorship. Here, too, there was no segregation, and for the first time in the city's history, Negro and white sat together in all parts of the hall at a public meeting. (Not even the Socialist Party in Louisiana allowed Negroes and whites to meet together.[38]) "There was no interference by the management or the police," Haywood reported, "and the meeting had a tremendous effect on the workers who discovered that they could mingle in meetings as they mingled at work." The *Industrial Worker* carried the news from Alexandria under the heading: "Miracle of the New South."[39]

In July, the convention's vote to affiliate with the I.W.W. was overwhelmingly confirmed by the Brotherhood's rank and file membership in a general referendum. At the September convention of the I.W.W., with black and white delegates from the South present, the merger was consummated, and the Brotherhood of Timber Workers became the Southern District of the National Industrial Union of Forest and Lumber Workers.[40] Space does not permit a full account of the moving history of the Southern lumber workers after the decision to affiliate with the I.W.W. Suffice it to say that it is a history filled with intensive efforts of the feudal-minded lumber barons to destroy the unity of black and white workers and smash the union. In this drive they resorted to every weapon in the arsenal of anti-unionism: blacklisting of union members; arrests and trial of the president and 64 leading members, Negro and white; eviction of union members from company houses; and spreading the charge throughout the South that the union was a revolutionary organization which sought to carry out the I.W.W.'s policy of equality for black and white, which if not checked, would undermine the entire fabric of Southern society. Yet none of these measures succeeded. The men brought to trial were acquitted, after having been held in jail for four months.[41] On November 11, 1913, nine days after the close of the trial in Grabow, Louisiana, 1,300 union men, whites, Indians, and Negroes went on strike at the American Lumber Company in Merryville, Louisiana. This was to be the biggest strike in the Brotherhood's history. Soon after the strike began, the company erected enclosures about the workers' shacks and the mills and began shipping in non-union crews, especially Negroes, from other parts of Louisiana and Texas—men who knew nothing of what had taken place in the mill. The Negro quarters were surrounded with a high barbed-wire fence which was charged with electricity to keep the strikers from talking to the scabs. But the strikers did get to them nevertheless. The railroad track was lined with pickets four miles on each side of town, and as the trains carrying the scabs slowed down to enter Merryville, leaflets were thrown through the windows or on the platforms, pointing out that a strike was taking place, and appealing "to you colored wage workers of Louisiana and Texas to do your duty by the lumberjacks of Merryville, white, Indian and Negro."

The appeal brought results. Many Negroes refused to enter the mill, and quite a few joined the strikers, living with the families of Negro strikers. Foreign-born workers and Mexicans who were brought in as scabs also showed their solidarity with the strikers. As the union pointed out in a statement that was widely published:

"It is a glorious thing to see, the miracle that has happened here in

Dixie. This is coming true of the 'impossible'—this union of workers regardless of color, creed or nationality. To hear the Americans saying 'You can starve us, but you cannot whip us'; the Negroes saying, 'You can fence us in, but you cannot make us scab'; the Mexicans shouting vivas for the union. Never did the Southern Lumber Operators' Association and the American Lumber Company expect to see such complete and defiant solidarity."[42]

The unity of Negro and white workers during the strike was so firm that one of the I.W.W. organizers in the area cited it as a lesson for the entire working class which "may feel proud of the solidarity displayed by these fighting timbermen and their wives and daughters . . . For be it known, that the many colored men belonging to the union, are standing pat with their white fellow slaves; and also be it known that the writer has known for years that all the colored workers needed was for the white workers 'to meet them halfway,' and they will always respond, eager and anxious to fight to better their conditions." He pointed out that Negro strikers were arrested and jailed on the charge of "unlawfully meeting in the same hall with white men," but "they laughingly line up and marched to jail, singing the rebel songs thay had learned at the daily mass meetings in the Union Hall, and despite threats, after their release, they appeared in greater numbers the next day to hear speakers, and sing more songs to fan the flames of discontent."[43]

When one worker told a meeting that even though he had nine children, he was willing to strike "if the Union can guarantee food for my children," the following dramatic episode occurred:

> When he made his plea for his family every farmer in the audience rose and confirmed the pledge of the one Negro present, who said, 'We farmers and workers will have to stick together in the Union and win this fight, or all of us, white and colored, are going back to slavery. I have so many pigs in my pen, so many heads of cattle in the woods, so many chickens in the yard, and so many bushels of corn and sweet potatoes, and so many gallons of syrup in my barn, and I pledge myself that so long as I have a pound of meat, or a peck of corn, no man, white or colored, who goes out in this strike will starve, nor will his children; and I believe all the white farmers here are ready to pledge the same.'

"They did to a man," quotes Covington Hall in his account of the incident.[44]

Failing to break the strike, the company recruited a gang of thugs and criminals and had them sworn in as deputy sheriffs. The deputies proceeded to move about the town, molesting Negro strikers and ransacking their homes. On January 9, Robert Allen, a Negro striker, who had been one of the most faithful pickets, was arrested at a union meeting and taken away to jail. No warrant was served nor was any reason given for the arrest. The same evening, Allen was placed in an automobile and deported from Merryville, leaving behind his wife and five children.

The arrests and deportations reached a climax in mid-February when deputy sheriffs, mobs of businessmen and company officials destroyed the union headquarters, and deported all union members from Merryville under penalty of death if they returned. Anyone found with a union leaflet or circular on him was arrested and deported. The town of Merryville was now completely in the hands of the mob as company gunmen, many deputized as sheriffs, armed with rifles, marched through the streets, seizing Negro and white union members and shipping them out of town. The union tried to get Governor Hall to do something to halt the reign of terror, pointing out that under the civil rights bill, the town was liable for expulsion of even strangers without due process of law. But the Governor, charging that the union, by allowing Negroes to meet together with whites in the same union halls, was seeking to destroy the Southern way of life, refused to act.[45]

The four-day wave of mob violence broke the back of the strike. Most of the Negro and white strikers were refused reemployment and blacklisted throughout the entire Southern lumber industry. Everywhere in the South the union met with the same experience: mob violence, attacks by gunmen, arrests and deportation of union members. Appeals to Governors, even to the President of the United States for interference in the illegal company persecution brought only silence. By the spring of 1914, the Brotherhood of Timber Workers had been effectively destroyed. Yet it left behind a noble tradition of militant struggle and labor solidarity, uniting Negro and white workers as never before in a Southern industry. Clearly Selig Perlman and Philip Taft were incorrect when they wrote in 1935 that "The I.W.W. was acutely aware of the danger of raising or even appearing to raise the issue of race equality in a Southern community where even the workers for whom it was leading this fight might have been completely alienated by that issue."[46] The I.W.W. did raise the issue of race equality in the lumber communities of the South, but it was the lumber companies and their allies, not the workers, who were "completely alienated by that issue."

Beginning in 1916 the I.W.W. launched determined campaigns to organize a number of industries and achieved a large measure of success in the western lumber areas and among the agricultural workers of the Middle and Far West. In 1917–18, it initiated an organizing drive to recruit members in the factories and mills of the East. This drive took place at a time when the "Great Migration" of Negroes from the South to the North was fully under way, and the I.W.W. looked forward to the prospects of bringing large numbers of the black workers newly-entered into northern industry into its ranks.

The I.W.W.'s plans for recruiting Negro workers received a great impetus when it obtained the endorsement of *The Messenger*, a black radical, pro-Socialist monthly published by A. Phillip Randolph and Chandler Owens in New York City. Strongly critical of the A.F. of L. for its discriminatory policies and refusal to take a stand against affiliated unions which barred Negroes as members, *The Messenger* came out strongly in support of the I.W.W. In its issue of August, 1919, it declared:

> The Industrial Workers of the World commonly termed the I.W.W. draws no race, creed, color or sex lines in their organization. They are making a desperate effort to get the colored men into the One Big Union. The Negroes are at least giving them an ear, and the prospects point to their soon giving them a hand. With the Industrial Workers Organization already numbering 800,000, to augment it with a million and a half or two million Negroes, would make it fairly rival the American Federation of Labor. This may still be done anyhow and the reactionaries of this country, together with Samuel Gompers, the reactionary President of the American Federation of Labor, desire to hold back this trend of Negro labor radicalism.[47]

To hold back this trend, an alliance of big business, government and conservative labor officials, set out to take advantage of wartime hysteria to overwhelm and destroy the I.W.W. Denouncing the Wobblies as "traitors," state legislatures passed criminal syndicalist laws which, together with the federal Espionage Act, were to be used to round up and imprison most of the I.W.W.'s active leaders, hundreds of organizers and rank and file members. In 1918 and 1919 the United States government brought 184 members of the I.W.W. to trial on charges of interfering with the war effort and encouraging resistance to the Selective Service Act. Their real "crime" was that they were actively engaged in organizing the most exploited sections of the American working class, including Negro workers, those who were traditionally neglected by nearly all unions affiliated with the A.F. of L. Among the I.W.W. leaders brought to trial was Ben Fletcher, black leader of the Philadelphia branch of the Marine Transport Workers, an organization hated by the employers for its effectiveness in nullifying the traditional practice of playing negro and white workers against each other for the benefit of the companies.

The defendants were tried in three separate groups in Chicago, Sacramento and Wichita. In Chicago, 101 were convicted and 12 were released during the course of the trial; 46 accused were convicted in Sacramento and 26 in Wichita. Many of the convicted received sentences of up to 20 years in prison. Fletcher was tried in Chicago, sentenced to 10 years in Federal penitentiary in Leavenworth, Kansas, and fined $30,000.[48]

Condemning the trials of the I.W.W. leaders as a deliberate effort to stem the drive to organize the unorganized, especially the Negro workers, *The Messenger* launched a campaign to bring about Ben Fletcher's release from prison. Though critical of the I.W.W.'s syndicalist position, W. E. B. DuBois supported *The Messenger's* campaign for Ben Fletcher. "We respect the Industrial Workers of the World," DuBois wrote in *The Crisis* of June, 1919, "as one of the social and political movements in modern times that draws no color line." In August, 1919, A. Phillip Randolph wrote in his militant journal:

> Negro newspapers seldom publish anything about men who are useful to the race. Some parasite, ecclesiastical poltroon, sacredotal tax gatherer, political faker or business exploiter will have his name in the papers, weekly or daily. But when it comes to one of those who fights for the great masses to lessen their hours of work, to increase their wages, to decrease their high cost of living, to make life more livable for the toiling black workers—that man is not respectable for the average Negro sheet.

Such a man is Ben Fletcher. He is one of the leading organizers of the Industrial Workers of the World, commonly known as I.W.W. He is in Leavenworth Penitentiary, Kansas, where he was sent for trying to secure better working conditions for colored men and women in the United States. He has a vision far beyond that of almost any Negro leader whom we know. He threw in his lot with his fellow white workers, who work side by side with black men and black women to raise their standard of living. . . . Ben Fletcher is in Leavenworth for principles— a principle which, when adopted, will put all the Negro leaders out of their parasitical jobs. That principle is that to the workers belong the world, but useful work is not done by Negro leaders.

We want to advocate and urge that Negro societies, lodges, churches, NAACP branches and, of course, their labor organizations begin to protest against the imprisonment of Ben Fletcher and to demand his release. He has been of more service to the masses of the plain Negro people than all the wind-jamming Negro leaders in the United States.[49]

At first the response to this appeal was not encouraging. This was the period of the great "Red Scare" and the Palmer Raids, and few Negro organizations were willing to speak up for a militant black labor leader convicted of "Conspiracy and violating the Espionage Act." But slowly the defense campaign for Fletcher mounted, and petitions and letters from black and white Americans urged President Harding to pardon the black Wobbly leader and release him from the federal penitentiary. In December, 1921, the Department of Justice in a "Report on all War Time Offenders Confined in Federal or State Penitentiaries," advised the Attorney General against recommending Executive Clemency for Ben Fletcher. The reason is stated quite bluntly:

He was a negro who had great influence with the colored stevedores, dock workers, firemen, and sailors, and materially assisted in building up the Marine Transport Workers Union which at the time of the indictment had become so strong that it practically controlled all shipping on the Atlantic Coast.[50]

Ben Fletcher's sentence was commuted in 1923 by President Harding and he was released from prison. (In 1933 President Franklin D. Roosevelt granted him a full pardon.) After his release, Fletcher remained in the I.W.W. and continued to speak and write on industrial unionism and the need for labor solidarity. "No genuine attempt by Organized Labor," he wrote prophetically in July, 1923, "to wrest any worthwhile and lasting concessions from the employing Class can succeed as long as Organized Labor for the most part is indifferent and in opposition to the fate of Negro Labor."[51] Fletcher was reported delivering a street corner speech for the Wobblies as late as August, 1931[52] but by that time the I.W.W. had long been only a shell of an organization. War-time repression had all but destroyed the Wobblies, and what was left when the war was over was further weakened by a split in the ranks over attitudes toward the Soviet Union and the Communist International, with one group supporting the first Socialist state and another refusing its support because it was not based on the principles of syndicalism which the I.W.W. favored.[53] Today the I.W.W. still maintains headquarters in Chicago and occasionally issues the *Industrial Worker*, but essentially it has long ceased to exist.

At no time in its history did the I.W.W. achieve a membership rivaling that of the A.F. of L., and it never succeeded in recruiting the great mass of black workers even though it would have welcomed them into its ranks. When it was at the height of its influence and power, the vast majority of Negroes lived in the South, were mainly tenant farmers and sharecroppers, and resided in communities where even the attempt to unionize—as the Elaine, Arkansas, massacres of 1919 revealed—would have brought wholesale arrests, imprisonments and lynchings. By the time the Negroes began entering Northern industries in considerable numbers, the I.W.W. was in the process of being destroyed by the government's savage repression.

Yet despite its rapid demise after its rapid rise, despite the fact that it never succeeded in retaining most of the members it organized, the I.W.W. wrote some of the most important chapters in the history of the American labor movement. To many, the letters "I.W.W." still conjure up the picture of a sinister internal enemy of American society, an organization of "bomb-throwing" hoboes, who preached and practiced violence for no reason but to make trouble. The truth is, however, that the I.W.W. made valuable contributions in the campaigns to organize the unorganized (particularly the unskilled, the foreign-born, women and Negro workers), spearheaded the fight for free speech and pioneered the battle for industrial unionism. It united black and white workers as never before in our history, and consistently maintained a tradition of solidarity and equality in the labor movement regardless of race or color that is yet to be equalled by most labor organizations today. The spirit of the Wobblies fortunately is not entirely dead. It was present in the spring and summer of 1968 in Charleston, South Carolina, when the union-civil rights coalition conducted the successful four-month strike of Negro hospital workers and which ever since has been moving toward higher pay and union recognition for black hospital employees in other cities, North and South. "Union Power Plus Soul Power Equals Victory," is the rallying cry.

The Wobblies were never much for religion, but they called Jesus "Fellow Worker Christ," and they welcomed clergymen who came to their support in their free speech fights and organizing campaigns. They would have appreciated the role that the Southern Christian Leadership Conference, led by Reverend Ralph Abernathy and Mrs. Martin Luther King, Jr., played together with Local 1199, Drug and Hospital Workers of New York in organizing the Negro hospital workers in Charleston.

NOTES

1. *The New Review,* September, 1913, pp. 747–48.
2. Philip S. Foner, *History of the Labor Movement in the United States,* vol. IV New York, 1965, p. 13; *Proceedings of the First Convention of the Industrial Workers of the World,* New York, 1905, p. 82. (Hereinafter cited as *Proceedings, First Convention, I.W.W.*)
3. *Proceedings, First Convention, I.W.W.,* p. 18.
4. *Ibid.,* pp. 154, 298–99.
5. Foner, *op. cit.,* vol. IV, pp. 60–95.
6. *Ibid.,* p. 13; Frank E. Wolfe, *Admission to American Trade Unions,* Baltimore, 1912, pp. 12224.
7. "Justice for the Negro—How Can He Get It" four-page leaflet, Wisconsin State Historical Society, Elizabeth Gurley Flynn Collection, (Hereinafter cited as WSHS.)
8. *Solidarity,* June 24, 1911, June 6, 1914; "To Colored Workingmen and Workingwomen," I.W.W. leaflet, Elizabeth Gurley Flynn Collection, WSHS.
9. Covington Hall, *Battle Hymns of Toil,* Oklahoma City, n.d., pp. 1–2. (Copy in New Orleans Public Library.)

10. *Voice of the People,* Dec. 14, 1912; *Industrial Worker,* Dec. 26, 1912.

11. *Industrial Worker,* Aug. 1, 1914.

12. *Ibid.,* Aug. 15, 1914.

13. *Ibid.,* June 4, 1910; *Solidarity,* June 8, 1912.

14. "Justice for the Negro—How Can He Get It," *op. cit.*

15. "To Colored Workingmen and Workingwomen," *op. cit.*

16. *Voice of Labor,* reprinted in *Solidarity,* June 24, 1911.

17. In 1910–12, the United Mine Workers with 40,000 Negro members had the largest Negro membership of any A.F. of L. union. See Herbert G. Gutman, "The Negro and the United Mine Workers of America," in Julius Jacobson, editor, *The Negro and the American Labor Movement,* New York, 1968, pp. 49–127. For evidence of discrimination against Negro workers in the U.M.W., see Herbert Northup, "The Negro and the United Mine Workers of America," *Southern Economic Journal,* April, 1943, p. 322.

18. *Industrial Workers,* Feb. 3, 1917; Sept. 19, 1919.

19. "Justice for the Negro—How Can He Get It," *op. cit.*

20. Ira Kipnis, *The American Socialist Movement,* 1897, 1912, New York, 1952, pp. 130–35, 260, 282–83; Philip S. Foner *History of the Labor Movement in the United States,* Vol. III, New York, 1964, pp. 381–82.

21. *The Worker,* Nov. 6, 1903; *Social Democratic Herald,* Nov. 21, 1903; Grace McWhiney, "Louisiana Socialists in the Early Twentieth Century: A Study in Rustic Radicalism," *Journal of Southern History,* Vol. XXX, Aug. 1945, pp. 333–35.

22. *International Socialist Review,* Vol. XIV, Nov. 1913, p. 275; Herbert Hill *The Racial Practices of Organized Labor – In the Age of Gompers and After,* pamphlet, New York, n.d., p. 4.

23. Sidney H. Kessler, "The Negro in the Knights of Labor," unpublished M.A. thesis, Columbia University, 1950, pp. 50–67; Philip S. Foner, *History of the Labor Movement in the United States,* Vol. II, New York, 1955, pp. 69–76; Philip S. Foner, "The Knights of Labor," *Journal of Negro History,* Vol. LIII, Jan., 1968, pp. 70–75.

24. Sterling D. Spero and Abram L. Harris, *The Black Worker: The Negro and the Labor Movement,* New York, 1931, p. 331; Donald M. Barnes, "The Ideology of the Industrial Workers of the World," unpublished Ph.D. thesis, Washington State University, 1962, p. 21.

25. Jerome Dowd, "Textile War between the North and South," *The Forum,* June, 1898, p. 443.

26. Philadelphia *North American,* May 14–30, 1913; Philadelphia *Public Ledger,* June 19, 1913; *Industrial Worker,* Feb. 3–24, 1917, July 28, 1945. Information on Benjamin Fletcher prior to his joining the I.W.W. is

extremely sparse. We do know that he was born in Philadelphia on April 13, 1890, and that some of his ancestors were American Indians. (*Industrial Worker,* July 22, 1949.)

27. Covington Hall in *Industrial Worker,* July 7, 1945.

28. Ruth A. Allen, *East Texas Lumber Workers; An Economic and Social Picture,* 1870–1950, Austin, Texas, 1961, pp. 54, 58; Hollie Hickman, *Mississippi Harvest: Lumbering in the Longleaf Pine Belt,* 1840–1915, University of Mississippi, 1962, pp. 142–43.

29. Marcy C. Terrell, "Bondage in the United States," *Nineteenth Century and After,* Vol. LXII, 1907, pp. 202–05.

30. G. T. Starnes and F. T. De Vyver, *Labor in the Industrial South,* Charlottesville, Va., 1930, pp. 45, 51; New Orleans *Times Democrat,* July 28, 1912.

31. Allen, *op. cit.,* pp. 116–17; *Solidarity,* Aug. 17, 1912. Melvyn Dubofsky, *We Shall Be All: A History of the Industrial Workers of the World,* Chicago, 1969, pp. 210–11.

32. *Ninth Biennial Report of the Bureau of Statistics of Labor of the State of Louisiana,* 1916–18, pp. 96, 124–34.

33. Charles H. McCord, "A Brief History of the Brotherhood of Timber Workers," unpublished M.A. thesis, University of Texas, 1959, pp. 19–20, 27; H. C. Creel in *National Rip-Saw,* Nov. 1912.

34. Covington Hall, "Louisiana Lumber War," *Industrial Worker,* July 14, 21, 1945; New Orleans *Times Democrat,* July 20, Aug. 8, 1911; George T. Morgan, Jr., "No Compromise—No Recognition: John Henry Kirby, the Southern Lumber Operators' Association, and Unionism in the Pine Woods," *Labor History,* Vol. X, Spring, 1969, pp. 197–200.

35. McCord, *op. cit.,* p. 36.

36. *Voice of the People,* Dec. 25, 1913.

37. *Bill Haywood's Book,* New York, 1929, pp. 241–42; *Solidarity,* May 25, Sept. 28, 1912; Covington Hall, "Labor Struggles in the Deep South," unpublished manuscript, Howard-Tilton Library, Tulane University, p. 138.

F. Ray Marshall (*Labor in the South,* Cambridge, Mass., 1967, p. 97) cites Covington Hall's unpublished manuscript, "Labor Struggles in the Deep South" (pp. 136–38) as evidence of the fact that "Negroes were segregated at the convention." This was true only until Haywood and Hall urged that white and Negroes meet in the same hall. Hall notes in his manuscript: "The colored delegates came to the hall that afternoon, and no arrests or trouble occurred during the remaining days of the convention." (Hall, *op. cit.,* p. 138.)

38. McWhiney, *op. cit.,* p. 332.

39. *Industrial Worker,* May 30, 1912.

40. Chicago *World,* Sept. 23, 1912; *Solidarity,* Sept. 28, 1912.

41. New Orleans *Times-Democrat,* July 24, Oct. 6, 1912; New Orleans *Daily Picayune,* Aug. 12, 1912; *The Rebel,* July 20, Aug. 17, 1912.

42. *Industrial Worker,* Nov. 28, Dec. 26, 1912; *The Rebel,* Nov. 16, 1912; *The Crisis,* Feb., 1913, p. 164.

I.W.W. speakers and newspapers always referred to black strike-breakers as "niggers" and to black union men as "Negro Fellow Workers." (See *Lumberjack,* Feb. 27, 1913.) However, Negroes who acted as strikebreakers in strikes involving craft unions were viewed differently than those who scabbed against an industrial union like the I.W.W. "The whole trend of the white craft labor organizations is to discriminate against the Negro; and to refuse to accord him equal economic rights," declared *Solidarity* on March 18, 1911. "When, as a consequence, the Negro is used to their own undoing, they have no one but themselves to blame."

43. Phineas Eastman, "The Southern Negro and One Big Union," *Internationalist Socialist Review,* Vol. XIII, June, 1913, pp. 890–91.

44. Covington Hall, "Labor Struggles in the Deep South," *op. cit.,* p. 149.

45. New Orleans *Times-Democrat,* Feb. 17–20, 1913; *Voice of the People,* Nov. 6, 20, 1913, Jan. 1, 29, March 5, 1914; McCord, *op. cit.,* p. 99; Merle E. Reed, "The I.W.W. and Individual Freedom in Western Louisiana, 1913," *Louisiana History,* Winter, 1913, pp. 61–63.

46. McCord, *op. cit.,* pp. 103–04; *Voice of the People,* Feb. 5, 1914; *Lumberjack,* Feb. 27, 1913; Reed, *op. cit.,* pp. 63–69; Selig Perlman and Philip Taft, *History of Labor in the United States, 1896–1932,* New York, 1935, p. 247.

47. "Our Reason for Being," *The Messenger,* Aug., 1919, pp. 11–12; "Break Up the A.F. of L.," *ibid.,* May–June, 1919, p. 7.

48. Philip Taft, "The Federal Trials of the I.W.W.," *Labor History,* Vol. III, Winter, 1962, pp. 58–91.

Fletcher was the only Negro among the defendants. Early in the trial, he turned to Haywood and remarked: "If it wasn't for me, there'd be no color in this trial at all." Later, when Judge Kenesaw Mountain Landis, who presided at the trial, handed down the severe sentences, he noted ironically: "Judge Landis is using poor English today. His sentences are too long." (Haywood, *op. cit.,* pp. 324–25.)

Fletcher was found guilty of violation of Section 6, 19 and 37 of the Criminal Code of the United States and Section 4 of the "Espionage Act" of June 15, 1917. He was sentenced, the records state, "in the United States Penitentiary at Leavenworth six years on count 1, ten years on counts 2 and 4, and two years on count 3, said sentences to run concurrently and to pay a fine of five thousand dollars on each of counts 1 & 2 and a fine of ten thousand dollars on each of counts 3 & 4 besides the costs in this behalf expended." He was delivered to Leavenworth on September 6, 1918, after having been sentenced on August 21, 1918. On February 21, 1919, Fletcher swore out a writ of appeal of the sentence to a higher court in which it is stated that "because of his poverty he is wholly unable to pay the costs of said writ of error, or to give any security for the same and therefore makes his application for leave to sue out and prosecute the same to a conclusion without being required to prepay any fees or costs or for the printing of the record in said Appellate Court and without being required to give any security therefore." (U.S. versus Wm. Dudley Haywood, Criminal Case No. 6125, Ms. in General Service Administration, Federal Records Office, Chicago, Illinois.) The appeal was turned down by the higher courts.

Interestingly enough, the first conviction for violation of the Espionage Act was also a black labor organizer. On September 14, 1918, Joe Dennis, foreman of a section gang, was arrested for violating the Espionage Act because he had urged a strike on the Texas and Pacific Railroad for better conditions. He was charged with interference with the movement of troops. During his trial, held in New Orleans, Judge Foster charged the jury to bring in a verdict of "guilty if it found the facts bore out the contention of the government attorney, that the defendant has hampered the government in the operation of railroads." After Dennis was found guilty and sentenced to ten years in prison, the New Orleans *Labor Advocate* commented:

"Invoking the Espionage law to convict this Negro appears far-fetched. The intent of that measure, as we understand it, was for a means of handling German spies during the war with Germany. To invoke it to convict a Negro worker because he asked his fellow workers to join him in a demand for living wages not only appears to be wholly inconsistent, but inhuman as well. We believe the judge, whether intentional or not, has taken a step that will stir up considerable more turmoil than he anticipated. To attempt to deny workers the right to strike is a decidely serious matter." (Reprinted in New York *Call,* May 29, 1919.)

49. "Ben Fletcher," *The Messenger,* Aug. 1919, p. 28.

50. Miscellaneous Political Records, Political Prisoners, Department of Justice Files, Dec. 10, 1921, TAF/c2c, National Archives, Washington, D.C.

51. Ben Fletcher, "The Negro and Organized Labor," *The Messenger,* July, 1923, pp. 759–60.

52. *Industrial Solidarity,* Aug. 11, 1931.

Fletcher died in Brooklyn, New York, on July 10, 1949. At his funeral more than 100 men and women, most of them long-time Wobblies, were present. Herbert Mahler of the I.W.W. read the following tribute at the funeral service:

"Rest, rest old fighter, rest.
Scars of battle on your breast
Prove that you have done your best,
Rest, rest old fighter, rest.

"In the hands of eager Youth,
Trust the crimson flag of Truth,
That you carried all the way.
They will guard it till the day,
Of Freedom . . .

"Let no worry mar your sleep.
Though the road be rough and steep,
Fraught with danger, filled with pain,
We will struggle on to gain,
The Victory . . .
While you rest, old fighter, rest.

"Rest, rest old fighter, rest,
Your noble deeds by Memory blest,
Inspire us all in Freedom's quest.
Rest, rest old fighter, rest."

(Industrial Worker, July 22, 1949.)

53. Philip S. Foner, *The Bolshevik Revolution: Its Impact on American Radicals, Liberals, and Labor,* New York, 1967, pp. 13–16, 24–26, 64–66, 100, 254–67, 287–88; John S. Gambs, *The Decline of the I.W.W.,* New York, 1932, pp. 75–125.

Index

235